The New Deal at Home

and Abroad, 1929-1945

SOURCES IN AMERICAN HISTORY

GENERAL EDITOR: *George H. Knoles*

Professor of History and Director of
the Institute of American History,
Stanford University

1. PROVINCIAL AMERICA, 1600-1763
   BRADLEY CHAPIN, *University of Buffalo*

2. THE REVOLUTIONARY GENERATION, 1763-1789

3. THE YOUNG REPUBLIC, 1789-1815
   JOHN C. MILLER, *Stanford University*

4. EXPANSION AND REFORM, 1815-1850
   CHARLES M. WILTSE,
   Chief Historian, United States Army Medical History Unit

5. THE UNION IN CRISIS, 1850-1877
   ROBERT W. JOHANNSEN, *University of Illinois*

6. THE NATIONALIZING OF AMERICAN LIFE, 1877-1900
   RAY GINGER, *Brandeis University*

7. THE RESPONSIBILITIES OF POWER, 1900-1929
   GEORGE H. KNOLES, *Stanford University*

8. THE NEW DEAL AT HOME AND ABROAD, 1929-1945
   CLARKE A. CHAMBERS, *University of Minnesota*

9. THE UNITED STATES IN THE CONTEMPORARY WORLD,
   1945-1962
   RICHARD L. WATSON, JR., *Duke University*

The New Deal at Home and Abroad, 1929-1945

Edited by Clarke A. Chambers

Professor of History
University of Minnesota

The Free Press, New York
Collier-Macmillan Limited, London

Preface

THE FREE PRESS SOURCES IN AMERICAN HISTORY
series reviews the history of the United States from
its beginnings in the seventeenth century to the present. Each of
the nine volumes consists of from 15 to 35 carefully chosen contemporary documents illustrating the major themes—political,
economic, social, and cultural—of American history and civilization. The volume editors, selected for their specialized knowledge of the periods into which the series is divided, have drawn
upon the rich resources of the American past for the materials to
be included in their respective books. They have ranged over the
principal geographical areas of the United States and have exploited a wide variety of genres—governmental and political
party documents, descriptive and analytical accounts, theoretical
writings, and literary products. History is a seamless web and
one learns about himself and his past by exploring the multi-
various experiences of his forbears and their reflections upon
those experiences.

The editors have kept the student in mind while selecting the
items to be reprinted in each volume. They have not only chosen
significant documents, but have respected the intentions of the
original writers to the extent that the materials are offered substantially as the authors produced them with a minimum of cutting and editing. We have, therefore, put together a set of
volumes containing a limited number of major documents re-
produced *in extenso* rather than a series containing hundreds of
snippets which can suggest, at best, only an impressionistic view
of history. To promote thoughtful reading and discussion of
these materials we have introduced each selection with head-
notes containing biographical and bibliographical data. Moreover, we have included in each headnote four or five suggestions
indicating what students should look for in reading the documents; these do not tell the reader what is in the material, but

they are very useful in directing his attention to the salient points covered. Finally, the editors have added to each note two or three titles of books that might be consulted for further study of the author of the document or of the problem or episode dealt with in the selection.

Each volume contains an extended introductory essay, an interpretive narrative written by the volume editor, which treats the period as a whole and relates the documents to the history under consideration. These essays incorporate both factual and conceptual information obtained from recent historical research; they reflect the new findings of contemporary scholarship.

Professor Clarke A. Chambers, in *The New Deal at Home and Abroad, 1929-1945*, has given us a fresh look at the New Deal. As the years pass we see events in clearer perspective than when close to them in time. Major shifts that once seemed largely political in nature are seen to reflect more fundamental economic and social and, perhaps, ideological changes that occurred below the surface of our collective life.

Owing to the greater accumulation of primary materials in the form of collections of diaries, letters, journals, and biographies, and owing to the work of scholars who have in their monographic studies shed new light on the New Deal period, historians today are giving us a more accurate and objective judgment of men and events of the 1930s and 1940s. As a result, we are now more fully aware than formerly that the New Deal years witnessed a process in which social forms were brought into closer correspondence with social realities than during the first 30 years of the twentieth century.

These developments did not, of course, take place free of shocks and strains. The period opened with the panic of 1929, which initiated one of the country's severest depressions; it closed with the greatest and costliest war in history. Meanwhile, proponents and opponents of the New Deal's leadership carried on an extensive, and often bitter, debate over the constitutionality, the wisdom, and the desirability of measures proposed and adopted.

Professor Chambers has managed with a limited number of

selections to bring to us the spirit of the times—the frustration and fear prevailing during the depression years, the sense of urgency in dealing with depression- and war-bred problems, the feeling of hope that perhaps man could manage to redirect his destiny into more satisfying channels. The student will find this volume, its documents, and its introductory essay a very valuable aid in helping to understand the New Deal years, years that in many ways have provided the conditions and the opportunities of our life today.

Stanford University   GEORGE HARMON KNOLES

Contents

**The New Deal at Home
and Abroad, 1929-1945**

Introduction

THE ERA THAT OPENED WITH THE JOYOUS HYSTERIA of the Armistice that concluded World War I (November 11, 1918) ended with a bang in October, 1929, when the panic on the stock exchange signaled the collapse of hectic prosperity. It had been a good decade, filled with excitement and marked by many constructive achievements; it had been a time of "wonderful nonsense," too, and an era of many failures.

True, the nation had turned its back upon collective security and upon such procedures of international law and order as the League of Nations and the World Court modestly provided, but conflict had been avoided in Asia, progressive disarmament seemed to be the role for the future, and in 1928 the civilized nations of the world, still suffering a postwar hangover, came around and took the Kellogg-Briand pledge never again to resort to force as a means of national policy.

After recovery from a brief postwar depression the economy, save for certain "sick" industries—coal, textiles, and agriculture—advanced steadily toward higher levels of technical efficiency, real wages, and profits. The breakaway expansion of the automotive and home-appliance industries contributed a continuing stimulus to economic progress and a higher standard of living for most Americans. The American way of life now included Charlie Chaplin at the movies on Saturday night; electric vacuum cleaners supplemented mechanical carpet sweepers, refrigerators supplanted ice boxes; the convenience of all-but-universal indoor plumbing rendered obsolete the scatological humor of Chic Sales; and the official dream promised a car in every garage and a chicken in every pot.

Rarely had the arts exhibited more imagination than they did in the 1920s. Hemingway, Fitzgerald, Faulkner, Dos Passos, Lewis, Frost, Eliot, and Pound won the attention and the acclaim of the world. Robert Flaherty's experiments in the documentary film matched the comic genius of Chaplin and Keaton. The brilliant canvases of Marsden Hartley, Arthur Dove, Georgia O'Keefe, and John Sloan set new standards of excellence in the visual arts; in architecture the American skyscraper set an example for the world to emulate. Eugene O'Neill became a legitimate heroic figure in the theater, while on another level but with equal verve the American musical comedy dominated the Broadway stage. Lippmann, Krutch, Mumford, Mencken, Sapir, and Parrington provided proof of the exhilarating vitality of social criticism and scholarship. The solo flight of "Lucky Lindy" across the Atlantic captured the imagination and devotion of a world hungry for heroes.

Other names are attached to that remarkable decade—Sacco and Vanzetti, Willian Jennings Bryan, John T. Scopes, Clarence Darrow; William J. Simmons, Imperial Wizard of the Ku Klux Klan; Scarface Al Capone; Samuel Insull; Babe Ruth, Jack Dempsey, Bobby Jones, and Big Bill Tilden. Each of them symbolized, for better or worse, the dynamic thrust that operated in every arena of American life. The attempt to enforce sobriety under the Prohibition Amendment had clearly backfired; syndicates of crime and vice had become big business; corruption and fraud had come to characterize many facets of business and government; the pursuit of the almighty dollar had warped a civilization; religious and political intolerance had put civil liberties in jeopardy; attempts to unionize labor had been broken by apathy or hostility; the nation had rejected Federal action to protect child laborers. In short, the decade was one of glorious success as well as of dismal and often preposterous failure, and no one could say that these had not been exciting times.

But the day of reckoning was bound to come. Good times could gloss over but could not forever conceal the economic and social imbalance that became endemic. Farmers never shared in the general advance of the economy; neither did coal miners and textile workers who labored in marginal industries marked by inefficiency, speculative prices, and uncertain profits. Real wages, while advancing, lagged behind profits, dividends, and productivity. The increasing concentration of wealth and the growing maldistribution of national income meant, in time, that the power to consume could not keep pace with the power to produce; the ever-proliferating products of ever more efficient enterprises could not be taken off the market and consumed. As capital growth leveled off in the midyears of the decade, investment funds were turned to speculative ventures; prices on the stock exchange began their spectacular, soaring flight. What went up had to come down.

F. Scott Fitzgerald, a bull on the literary market of the twenties and critic of the Jazz Age, whose personal "crack-up" coincided with the nation's, recorded the impact of the earthquake that revealed the gross faults in the economy and brought down the flimsy structure of prosperity. That age, he wrote, "as if reluctant to die outmoded in its bed, leaped to a spectacular death in October, 1929."

Not everyone knew what had happened; few indeed could divine the future. Those workers—whether blue-shirted or white-collared—who hung onto their jobs enjoyed a certain if delusive gain, for prices at first tended to fall faster than wages; but as unemployment climbed from two million to four, to ten to twelve or fourteen, fear of an unknown future replaced complacency. The worker lived in weekly dread of the pink slip in his pay envelope that would notify him not to report for work the following Monday. Somehow the families of the unemployed got by, as a study by the National Federation of Settlements under the direction of Helen Hall made clear. Wives and mothers frequently found part-time employment when husbands and fathers were thrown on the streets; families drew on savings or borrowed on insurance policies and homes; they accepted credit from the landlord and grocer; they moved into smaller quarters and pared their expenses. A new dress or suit could wait another month when times were sure to pick up; beans and macaroni appeared more often on the table. A gift basket at Thanksgiving, a temporary job during the Christmas rush might help tide things over, but the consequences of long-term unem-

ployment could not be blocked. Its costs included crowded housing, malnutrition, children kept from school for want of warm
clothing, susceptibility to nerve-sapping ill health; listlessness
and loss of skill; in time, friction and squabbling within the
family, nagging wives, despondent husbands, children bitter because their father could neither hold a job nor bring home a
paycheck. When finally forced to accept a charitable handout or
apply for relief, the family lost all semblance of self-respect.
Most families, concluded Helen Hall, "never reconcile themselves
to accepting help from strangers—it means a serious break in
family pride and self-confidence, a self-confidence which seldom
blossoms again with the same sturdiness." Time and again the
unemployed reported to the settlement investigators: "It's not
the going without we mind—it's the insecurity." That was the
rub—insecurity, uncertainty, anxiety, fear itself.

Farmers did not do much better, although many of them had
become accustomed to tightening their belts well before 1929.
However low prices fell—by 1933 they had often fallen substantially below the point where it paid to invest the additional
labor and capital for the harvest—the farmers at least had a roof
over their heads, a garden to supply potatoes and vegetables,
and perhaps a calf or a pig to slaughter. There was the nagging
worry over the mortgage payments, and beyond that the fear of
foreclosure; with one's farm sold out from under, with farm
prices riding an apparently irreversible toboggan slide, where
next could one seek a home and security? When, in the years of
drought, the topsoil began to blow away, the burdens were all
but unbearable, at least for farmers in the Dust Bowl that
stretched from the Dakotas and Montana southward to the plains
of Oklahoma and Texas. In the South, cotton farmers both Negro
and white suffered not only from domestic overproduction and
world glut, but from sterility of soil rendered thin and infertile
by years of single-cropping, from an outmoded credit system,
from lack of capital, from ignorance, illiteracy, and endemic ill
health. By 1932 and 1933 thousands of farmers were out on
strike, protesting foreclosures, eviction, and a market system
that denied them a decent livelihood.

Small businessmen, retailers and merchants, manufacturers,

and even professional men and women fared little better. Where there was no purchasing power, customers were hard to find; where consumption lagged, advertisers and salesmen were forced to compete fiercely for shrinking revenue. Engineers became clerks or laborers; country doctors were more often paid in kind than in cash; teachers were dismissed or paid partial salaries (sometimes in depreciated scrip). Businesses operated in the red or closed shop; municipal and state governments retrenched in the face of tax delinquency and a shrinking tax base.

Worst of all was the uncertainty and the gnawing anxiety. For a long while people hoped for a revival of activity; the nation had survived other panics, recovery had followed other depressions. Were not the resources present to turn retreat into advance? No nation was ever more blessed with rich soil, favorable climate, mineral resources, natural waterways, vast deposits of coal and oil than the United States. The manpower was there, and the technological and mangerial know-how. Was not the long tradition of the republic proof that the course of history —in the New World at least—described an upward-soaring spiral? Now something was wrong. Some few Americans had responded, a generation or so earlier, to the prophecy of Henry George that poverty was concomitant with progress; but the central commitment of Americans had ever been to optimism, to material progress, to a resolution of social problems through widening affluence. Now all that was challenged. Here was want in the midst of potential plenty—here were the army of the unemployed pounding the streets in search of jobs that did not exist, here was hunger in the face of mounting agricultural surpluses, here men shivered while garment workers sat at home and despaired. Americans were accustomed to straightforward, uncomplicated situations—not to the tensions of social paradox. What were they to make of this paradox bordering on the preposterous that a hard-working people could find no work, that a rich nation could not afford to feed, house, clothe, and educate its citizens?

Some scholars, politicians, artists, leaders of agriculture and labor launched a far-ranging search for social solutions. Some novelists turned to protest, some to tragedy. John Steinbeck distilled a people's bitterness in his now classic novels *In Dubious Battle* and *The Grapes of Wrath*. Of short-story writers none better caught the poignancy of the depression years than Albert Maltz, whose prize-winning, ironic "The Happiest Man on Earth" stood out above the great mass of dreary proletarian literature.

The wonder was that social criticism so rarely turned sour, that dissatisfaction did not lead to rejection, that protest was not transformed into rebellion. Many observers bore testimony to the remarkable tenacity of older customs and the durability of folk wisdom so deeply rooted that the trials of a single decade could not disturb it. Through all the storms of hard times, middle-class America persisted in its belief in honest labor, self-reliance, individualism, and progress, (and a balanced budget). These years—as all generations—were marked by persisting continuities as by traditions broken and recast.

Politics responded sluggishly to hard times. Professional politicians, responsible to constituents trained to one set of issues, were understandably reluctant to seize upon untried expedients. As for the Chief Executive, few men had ever assumed that exalted office seemingly better prepared than Herbert Hoover. A remarkably successful businessman in a business civilization, a widely experienced engineer in a society being constantly remade by science and technology, a canny investor in an age of finance capitalism, a committed humanitarian in a nation that prized good works voluntarily done, the Iowa-born Quaker was the appropriate choice for 1928. A man of intelligence and integrity, Hoover eventually revealed a lack of that flexibility required of national leadership in a time of domestic crisis. Privately fearful that the nation had a longer and harder period of adjustment ahead than most of his contemporaries guessed, the President relied heavily at first upon public expressions of confidence that recovery would come if only the fundamentals of American ways were preserved. Tinkering with methods tried and true was bound, in his view, to compound confusion and retard the return of good times. The responsibility of private charitable institutions and local government for relieving the plight of needy citizens was crucial to the survival of self-reliance and self-respect. Massive government interference in the natural ordering of the market meant social degeneration and tyranny. The scheme of Senator George Norris for the multiple-purpose development of the Tennessee Valley he characterized as socialistic in a ringing veto of a Congressional bill that embodied such a project. If the tariff needed modification, times of international economic anarchy were not appropriate for constructive reform. First and ultimately Hoover clung to the inviolability of the gold standard and the maintenance of a balanced budget, for if the national government did not keep its word and its own house in order then surely there was no hope for the republic.

In holding to these hallowed traditions, the President spoke for what was undoubtedly the common sense of the matter for most Americans. The leadership of the Democratic party in Congress had little better to offer a bewildered nation; indeed when the party of Jefferson and Jackson proposed a national sales tax as a means to balance the budget, it took the extravagant opposition of the irrepressible Republican maverick from New York, Fiorello La Guardia, to block its passage. When government shifted to dead center after the 1930 Congressional elections, the jockeying for position in 1932 took precedence over a serious pursuit of the national welfare. Leaders of the business community, of organized labor, of farm associations, of professional groups possessed no clearer understanding than political leaders of what the times required. Affairs drifted—from bad to worse.

It is more apparent now than it was then, however, that a new consensus in American politics was being shaped. Many old Progressives had kept hot under the collar during the years of normalcy when the nation preferred to keep cool with Coolidge. Frustrated they surely had been, but many of them had not ceased striving for a larger measure of justice in American life. Some had busied themselves crusading for the right of children to be freed from exploitation, whether in field or factory, and when the proposed child-labor amendment failed to win ratification they turned to other measures designed to promote the well-being of youth through education, health, and recreation programs. The mothers' pension movement, for example, rooted in the prewar progressive era of reform, was substantially expanded in the 1920s and the precedents were thereby established upon which the aid-to-dependent-children program of the 1930s would rest. Other reformers explored the consequences of substandard housing, of dependent old age, of employment insecurity, of the denial of the right of labor to organize and bargain collectively through agents of its own choosing; still others campaigned for a policy of judicial restraint which would loosen the legalistic dead hand of the past upon new programs to meet new problems. Some economists toyed with the idea of using public works as a means to take up the slack and to provide jobs (and income) for unemployed; others wondered if taxation could not be used to achieve a more equitable distribution of national income and thereby promote a larger degree of economic balance. Professional social workers, who had long worked with the needy, came to recognize that social insurance could be a means to stabilize purchasing power in times of slump without that sacrifice of self-respect that throwing oneself on the dole implied; they came to see that work relief was better than a handout and that where the resources of local and state government would not suffice, the nation had the obligation of providing relief whether through direct subsidy or (as was preferred) a works program designed to utilize the skills of the unemployed whatever they might be. In varied voluntary associations, and within the Departments of Agriculture and Interior, men began to consider the need for coordinated programs of conservation in which the Federal government would take the initiative in promoting the wise utilization of water and soil, timber and grass.

A handful of Congressmen—progressive Republicans and liberal Democrats—put forward proposals incorporating these ideas, but rarely could they muster a majority. In the meantime some measures were accomplished. Use of the labor injunction was finally curtailed; public works were inaugurated (but never in substantial enough number or size to compensate for their wholesale neglect by hard-pressed local units of government); government corporations purchased agricultural surpluses and removed them from the market (but without production controls surpluses continued to accumulate and prices to sag beneath their weight); through the Reconstruction Finance Corporation the Federal government saved financial institutions—banks, insurance companies, savings and loan associations—from total collapse and thereby held a last line of defense (but if rout became orderly retreat, a counteroffensive was not launched).

The time had come for a new deal. Just how the cards were to be dealt and what the rules of the new game were to be were not exactly clear—not even to the Governor of New York, who had already proved himself something of a shark. That a new shuffle was in order could hardly be denied. The election of 1932 was really no contest; its only surprises were the strong vote the Republicans were able to pull and the failure of the radical Left to draw more than a million votes. The successful candidate had done little to clarify the specific issues during the campaign; to some cynics it seemed that the only direct relief the Democrats proposed was the repeal of the Prohibition Amendment. But it was the tone that mattered—Franklin Roosevelt's personal buoyancy promised assurance that something would be done, that mastery would once more be asserted over aimless drift. Before that moment arrived the nation passed through its most difficult winter. By March a third of the labor force was idle, niggardly relief appropriations had long been exhausted, local government stood on the edge of bankruptcy, and the banks of the nation had been closed either by runs of depositors or by government decree.

Having assured the nation that it had nothing to fear but fear itself, the new President proceeded to the business at hand—to restore flagging morale, to get the wheels of industry turning again, to stimulate prices and wages and profits. The devices were many (and some of them worked at cross-purposes). To business was granted authority for self-discipline—trade association codes set standards of production, wages, and methods of competition that had the force of law. To labor was granted the right to organize and bargain collectively—a verbal assurance that sparked a militant revival of unionization after more than a decade of slump. The farmers of the nation won a drastic program of price support and production control. To Harold Ickes, the blunt and irascible Secretary of the Interior, was assigned direction of a giant public works program, designed to stimulate heavy construction; to Harry Hopkins, a professional social worker who learned quickly to enjoy the rough-and-tumble of politics, was given the task of providing direct Federal relief to the unemployed. With Roosevelt's enthusiastic support, Senator Norris won the authorization to initiate the multipurpose Tennessee Valley Authority—flood control, river-navigation improvement, soil and timber conservation, the manufacture and sale of electric power, promotion of the "economic and social well-being" of the entire region. Through the Civilian Conservation Corps the New Deal took thousands of unemployed young men off the streets and out of rural slums and put them to work in reforestation and flood and fire control. The Farm Credit Act extended government credit for the refinancing of farm mortgages, the Home Owners Loan Corporation for home mortgages. Through the Federal Deposit Insurance Corporation, the government provided security for small savings deposits. The Reconstruction Finance Corporation, created in 1932, was now authorized to lend money to industry and business and to purchase the capital stock of financial institutions. The banks were closed and reopened on a sounder base; the nation was taken off the gold standard and the dollar devalued.

The emergency was equal to the crisis of war, said FDR; and the precedents established for the mobilization of the total resources of the nation, in 1917-1918, were utilized to battle hard times. The President summarized his program under the headings of the three R's—Relief, Recovery, and Reform—but there was no doubt about the assignment of priorities: the main objective in 1933 was simply to keep the ship of state afloat. Massive relief programs represented a humanitarian response to the plight of people in need through no particular fault of their own, but they poured out a sum of purchasing power that helped to stimulate recovery as well. Planned scarcity to raise prices was the strategy of both the National Recovery Administration and the Agricultural Adjustment Act. Under the blanket codes of the NRA, floors were set under wages, ceilings on hours, and the labor of children in interstate commerce was prohibited. The point was to reverse the downward slide of the economy and by the use of whatever expedients to prevent catastrophe.

Measured by such crude objectives, the New Deal programs of 1933-1934 achieved partial success. Some semblance of industrial stability was imposed; prices took a faltering upward course; some millions of men went back to work (whether in private employment or on public projects), and if millions more still pounded the pavements at least they could hope that happier days were on the way. The American people caught some of the cheerful confidence of their President and when, during the campaign of 1934, he asked the citizens if they were better off than they had been last year, they responded by electing more Democrats to Congress than in 1932, a reversal of the usual pattern of off-year elections.

From other perspectives, the results seemed less spectacular. The benefits of the agricultural program flowed generously to the larger commercial farmers, only slightly to tenants and marginal operators and not at all to farm workers. The recovery of prices, production, and employment was partial at best. If the NRA did not quite constitute "fascist tyranny" as some of its critics began to charge, it had granted extravagant powers to large corporations, its labor provisions had often been evaded by the creation of company unions, and many of its administrative procedures had proved to be awkward and confining. To many businessmen, the policies of Hugh Johnson, an old cavalry officer, seemed needlessly arbitrary and autocratic; by 1934, the desperate crisis having passed, the very leaders of industry and finance who had pleaded for coordination and control in 1932 and 1933 were determined to overthrow the monster they had helped to create. When the Supreme Court in May, 1935, killed off the NRA there were not many mourners.

In the meantime, partial recovery unleashed the social criticism and political militance that had been latent during the months and years of drift and despair. Now that something had been accomplished, a public clamor arose for much more to be done. From every side arose complaints that the New Deal had gone too slowly, that it had been too modest in its demands and too intent upon salvaging outmoded ways and interests. On the prairies and plains, agrarian radicals demanded more sweeping reforms that would truly restore the family farmer and the oppressed worker. In California an avowed socialist running on the Democratic ticket, the muckraking novelist Upton Sinclair, almost captured the governorship with a program of production for use. Father Charles E. Coughlin, a political activist Roman Catholic priest, won a wide response to his radio harangues for social justice—a living wage, the nationalization of banks and natural resources, and the regulation of private property for the public good. In Louisiana the dispossessed middle classes and farmers of the South found a champion in Huey Long, who called for government limitations on personal fortunes, government guaranties of minimum family income, free education from kindergarten through college, pensions for the aged. Dr. Francis Townsend—with his slogan "Youth for work, age for leisure"—aroused millions of citizens to political action to achieve a national pension of $200 a month for every citizen past the age of sixty. Associations of independent liberals veered sharply leftward and proposed everything from democratic socialism to progressive taxation, slum clearance and public housing, maximum hours and minimum wages, social insurance against unemployment and old age. Labor, too, was on the march again, organizing the unorganized, demanding more forthright reforms. In 1935 John L. Lewis and his supporters withdrew from the American Federation of Labor and dedicated themselves to organization along industrial rather than craft lines, and to aggressive action in the political arena to win by legislation what could not be wrested from employers by contest at the bargaining table.

The President, a born political animal, surrounded by other politicians who knew their craft well, was acutely aware of the rising popular demand for more drastic action. Furthermore, the paralyzing emergency had been overcome and Roosevelt welcomed the opportunity to pursue policy lines that had been shaping in his own mind for several years. While governor of New York, he had studied the problem of insecurity, which was associated not alone with depression but with the very industrial system itself, and had been the first national political figure of note publicly to embrace a comprehensive system of social insurance. From his experience in the Wilson Administration he had learned the viability of orderly collective bargaining and the desirability of industrial standards imposed by government. From his New York associates he had learned the debilitating social consequences of crowded and squalid housing. Through the influence of Frances Perkins and Harry Hopkins and other welfare workers he had early in his career been led to prefer constructive programs of work relief to the direct dole. The use of taxation and fiscal policies to promote a more equitable distribution of national income he had picked up from various members of his Brain Trust. Even before the Supreme Court knocked out the NRA, Roosevelt had prepared a new program of action, different in emphasis from the first one hundred days of 1933. Partial recovery enabled him to turn to reform; popular agitation made it politically expedient; his own inherent disposition and inclination made it a joyful enterprise. He faced, moreover, a Congress far more deeply committed to social experimentation than the one elected with him back in 1932.

The years 1935 and 1936 brought forth bold new programs. In the Wagner Labor Relations Act the unions finally won truly effective guaranties of the right to organize and a great burst of activity followed. The Social Security Act provided insurance against unemployment and for old age; it also established comprehensive programs of assistance for the handicapped and for dependent children, and grants-in-aid for health and welfare projects. The passage of sharply graduated taxes on incomes and estates aimed at basic reform in income distribution. The National Youth Administration provided part-time jobs, particularly for high school and college students that they might be able to finish their education (and keep out of the glutted labor market). The Works Projects Administration provided jobs for the unemployed suited to their skill and experience—unemployed artists painted murals in public buildings, unemployed actors wrote and produced plays, unemployed librarians compiled bibliographies and catalogues, unemployed musicians gave band and symphony concerts. A Public Utility Holding Company Act took aim and fired at the uneconomic pyramiding of corporate control. When the first AAA was found unconstitutional, a broadened program of subsidy and control (along lines legally more palatable) was enacted at once.

With these reforms accomplished, with national morale restored, and with economic recovery steadily advancing, the Democrats' campaign platform of 1936 promised more of the same. The New Deal won a thumping mandate such as no party had claimed in modern times—over 60 percent of the popular vote and the electoral votes of all the states save Maine and Vermont. Three-quarters of the Senate and four-fifths of the new House were counted as Democrats; thirty-nine states elected Democratic governors and three more named independent reform candidates. From precinct to nation the New Deal had triumphed. Surely now the breakaway forces of reconstruction could realize their goals.

The results were surprisingly meager—slum clearance and public housing, but at levels more modest than Roosevelt asked and substantially more restrictive than obvious need dictated; the creation of a Farm Security Administration to coordinate agricultural credit assistance; a renewed and expanded soil conservation and farm subsidy program; the Fair Labor Standards Act of 1938—this much, but not much more. The proposal to strike at the concentration of wealth and power fizzled out in a series of dramatic but ineffectual reports. Of the suggestion to apply the TVA idea to other river valleys much was heard but little was done. Blueprints for a bold reorganization of the executive and judicial departments never got off the drafting boards, although they created a verbal furor even at that.

The sources of frustration were several. Ironically, the Administration suffered from excessive legislative majorities; with so many Democrats in Congress the incentive to party loyalty weakened and party discipline relaxed. More serious was the reaction of many moderate citizens (and politicians) to the violence that characterized labor-capital strife in these years; wherever the fault could properly be assessed, strikes in these years often broke into violent contests; labor's resort to the "sit-down" tactic aroused middle-class anxiety for the security of property. Until the Supreme Court upheld the validity of the Wagner Act, its terms were often more honored in the breach than in the observance, and it was not until after 1938 that some degree of orderly procedures became the rule. Perhaps labor was becoming too strong, perhaps the Administration was coming too much under the influence of labor leaders—so it seemed to many moderates who forthwith began to drift back toward the center.

The recession, which struck in the fall of 1937, constituted an acute embarrassment to the Administration which had taken credit for the upswing that began in March, 1933. The roots of the 1937 setback were complex but undoubtedly the cutback in Federal spending earlier that year was a major contributing factor. By the spring of 1938, FDR finally made the painful decision explicitly to resort to deficit financing not as a temporary expedient but as a sound means of stimulating prices and investment. However personally distasteful an unbalanced budget was, its economic virtues were reluctantly set forth, but not without a rousing and angry debate. The recession itself had been bad enough; to embrace economic unorthodoxy was a sign, to many, of the utter folly of the New Deal. Roosevelt was damned if he did spend, and damned if he didn't. In any case, the blush was off the rose.

Far more serious in breaking the New Deal majority was the embittered wrangle over judicial reorganization. The courts, by and large, had not been friendly to planks in the New Deal platform considered to be crucial by their proponents. The NRA, measured by any reasonable constitutional criteria, was undoubtedly invalid; other measures that had been struck down, often by a rather evenly divided court, were not that clearly unconstitutional beyond all reasonable doubt. A minority of the Supreme Court—usually numbering Stone, Cardozo, and Brandeis—acted upon the doctrine of judicial self-restraint which held that state and Federal legislative action was to be given the benefit of the doubt unless obviously unconstitutional. The majority, however, were more willing to exercise what was essentially a judicial veto resting more upon considerations of the wisdom of a particular measure rather than its judicial validity.

As Roosevelt prepared to implement the mandate of 1936, he had legitimate grounds to fear for the fate of social security, labor relations, farm controls, and industrial standards. However soundly based his anxieties, his tactics were awkward. Without prior consultation, save with a mere handful of initimate advisers, he publicly proposed to enlarge the Court, adducing with something less than full candor the superannuation of the justices. Charges that Roosevelt sought to pack the court with pliant puppets were made before the day was up and for the next six months there was little chance for a rational discussion of this issue, or any other for that matter. The Republicans, to a man, seized the occasion to cry tyranny and dictatorship, but they were clever enough to follow Senator Vandenberg's lead of letting dissident Democrats take the initiative in opposing the President's will. Lost to FDR's camp were not only many conservative Southern Democrats, who had been waiting for an excuse to bolt, but many moderate and even liberal Democrats upon whose support he had counted. The New Deal coalition was broken. The bill was sent back to committee by a vote of 70 to 20. More serious was the vote in party caucus on the selection of a new President *pro tem* of the Senate in the summer of 1937; the President's candidate, Alben Barkley of Kentucky, squeaked by against a conservative Southerner by the margin of a single vote. The Democrats were split right down the middle and the coalition of Northern Republicans and Southern Democrats that was to dominate Congressional politics for the next generation had been formed.

The Court, in the meantime, had changed its mind—whether because of the mandate of 1936, or in response to Presidential harassment, or because the laws under review were truly more valid than earlier and similar enactments. Social Security, the Wagner Act, and the regulatory powers of state governments were all upheld. FDR was soon able to appoint new justices to the Court (seven in all by 1941) and a constitutional revolution was wrought. Judicial self-restraint became the rule, the commerce power of Federal government and the police powers of state government were greatly enlarged.

By 1941 political deadlock had set in. By that time foreign crises were beginning to divert the attention of the nation and its Chief Executive. Nazi Germany was on the march; England and France were in an appeasing mood; Italy had attacked Ethiopia with impunity; Franco's Fascist forces had destroyed the Spanish Republic; in Asia, Japan had moved first against Manchuria and then China itself. The nation now faced dangers potentially much more fierce than curtailed family budgets and price deflation.

The New Deal played itself out in 1937 and 1938. If it had not offered any ultimate solutions to domestic problems, it had come closer to finding valid, if always partial, answers to very real and pressing issues than any Administration since Wilson's. Full recovery awaited the stimulation of rearmament and war, but great strides toward enlarged opportunity and security in American life had been won. Under the pressure of domestic crisis, directed by leaders who did not fear innovation, the New Deal won reforms long overdue with only minor modification of essentials. For all the talk of regimentation and "creeping socialism," capitalism emerged more stable and more dynamic than ever it had been. As Roosevelt said, identifying himself as a "true conservative," his policies sought to defend and extend a system of "private property and free enterprise by correcting such injustices and inequalities as arise from it." Social security and parity pricing assuredly offered no panaceas but they provided built-in economic stabilizers that helped to promote more orderly economic advance.

The whole body of Roosevelt's public addresses, press conferences, and private papers must be consulted to fathom the fundamental objectives that underlay the twists and turns of specific policy. However, one can find in the Second Inaugural Address (January 20, 1937) a fine summary of ultimate principles and particular plans that were at the heart of the New Deal at the peak of its reform impulse and in the "Economic Bill of Rights" address (January 11, 1944) a projection of these

goals in the midst of the crisis of war. Roosevelt was no ideo-
logue, to be sure; his genius expressed itself more in the realm
of practical politics than in abstract theory. Time and again he
articulated his beliefs that the people of the United States had
a responsibility, working through the instrumentalities of Federal government, constructively to promote the general welfare;
that security and liberty were not antagonistic but mutually
supportive concepts and conditions; that democracy could not
survive in the nation or in the world without a larger measure
of social justice and individual opportunity. Opportunist though
he was, his pragmatism rested upon a foundation of old-fashioned principles—neighborliness, moral humanitarianism, religious faith, the conservation of natural and human resources,
the need for social balance and for individual security if liberty
and opportunity were to be preserved and extended.

The New Deal consensus presented no logically consistent,
coherent, formal system of social thought. Its mixture of pragmatism and moralism was reflected not only in the Chief himself
but in his colleagues who surrounded him and served him—
Henry Wallace, Harold Ickes, Henry Morgenthau, Harry Hopkins and the good, grey Secretary of Labor, Frances Perkins.
Before her fellow social workers, on the eve of the great war,
the matter-of-fact Miss Perkins set forth with disarming naiveté
her concept of the good life. David Lilienthal's account of his
experience was slightly more sophisticated, but finally it came
down to the same fundamentals. In the TVA, for the first time
in American history, the resources of an entire region—natural
and human—were developed as a unified, organic whole. The
Federal government offered overall direction, the advice of technical experts, and good hard cash but the initiative and the implementation were provided at the grass roots by voluntary
associations (cooperatives, community clubs, farmer organizations) and by units of local government. Decisions were ultimately rendered not by distant bureaucrats but by men in the
field. And the proof, finally, was hard and practical—reforested
hillsides, clear blue lakes, river channels busy with barges, flood
waters impounded, rural electrification, and a boom of light

industry. The TVA, to Lilienthal, was the outward sign that the spirit and fact of democracy were on the march.

If the arts demonstrated a rare creative surge during the 1920s, social analysis and criticism excelled in the years of depression. Social work, which had striven toward professional status in the postwar years, came into its own during the 1930s when the only expanding market was for men and women trained in the arts of helping people in need. The contributions made by professional social workers to the formulation of the New Deal consensus, and to its implementation, were evidenced not only in the careers of Frances Perkins and Harry Hopkins but in the unrecorded labors of little-known practitioners who helped to staff the WPA, the Farm Security Administration, the TVA, the NLRA and myriad other public agencies while outside of government service the profession as a whole offered criticism, agitation, and the pioneering of new programs of service and action. The jest that the New Deal created not a welfare state but a social workers' state was meant to be taken in earnest. No better summary of the profound influence of social work upon broad public policy can be found than the presidential address of one of its leaders, the indomitable Grace Coyle, before the National Conference of Social Work in 1940.

The 1930s were a decade of social ferment; from every side came hard analyses of what was wrong and what could be done to restore or to reconstruct American society. The radical left, splintered into many warring factions, proposed various forms of democratic socialism and working-class control; the fanatical right offered as many panaceas as it had demagogic leaders. In the broad center of American politics the debate was more responsible and more consistent with the main stream of development in American life. John Dewey—educator, philosopher, publicist, and grand old man of every reform cause in the twentieth century—kept up a steady pressure upon the New Deal from the liberal left. A vigorous proponent of national relief, public works, and social insurance before these expedients were seized by the Administration, Dewey had by that time moved on to espouse comprehensive national planning, social engineering, democratic socialism. The New Deal had failed, Dewey believed, because it clung to an outmoded system of private profit, it offered a tamed and reformed capitalism when far more thorough problems of readjustment were required. In a series of lectures entitled *Liberalism and Social Action,* Dewey set forth his conviction that pragmatic instrumentalism, the application of creative social intelligence to the problems of economic disorganization and social maladjustment, alone provided the path to order and progress without a sacrifice of the American liberal tradition of free inquiry and civil liberties. John Dewey was but one of many leftward-tending liberal critics; his name graced the letterhead of many reform and radical associations during these years; the power of his intellect was something to reckon.

From the right of center came attacks upon the New Deal for having subverted the basic fundamentals of American life—self-reliance, the free market, fiscal responsibility (a balanced budget), the voluntary exercise of the individual and private institutional will uncoerced by government meddling. Some historians have insisted that it was Herbert Hoover and not Franklin Roosevelt who inaugurated the New Deal. In the sense that the Republican Administration broke sharply from earlier precedents of governmental passivity during times of economic emergency, the conclusion is valid enough. But the New Deal was far more and far other than merely doing something modestly to alleviate the consequences of hard times, as Hoover himself well knew. Throughout the decade he remained a vital, if often lonely figure, flinging jeremiads at "that man" in the White House who would divert American history from its established and true ways. To Hoover, the modern trend was nothing less than a challenge to liberty, a threat to all that was right in the American experience, and he spoke for a substantial and still-influential minority in American life. His criticism, shrill at times, was unrelenting and whereas it was never able to muster a majority it represented a significant segment of protest and made lively the running debate upon both the fundamentals and the details of public policy in that controversy-ridden decade.

A more exotic point of view, one that came in time to have a profound impact upon social philosophy, theology, and public policy, was provided by Reinhold Niebuhr. Influenced by Marxism, by European "crisis theology," and by his own experience as a pastor in a Detroit congregation during the 1920s (before he went to teach at Union Theological Seminary), Niebuhr bore witness to the injustices inherent in contemporary society—the tyranny of factory discipline, the gross insecurity of employment, the fragmentation of the family, the loss of community cohesion at every level of society. For a time, in the depths of the Depression, he felt that only a socialist structure held the promise of a moral society, but by decade's end his political theory and his theology alike were of tougher stuff. Attacking the social gospel for its sentimental utopianism, Niebuhr combined political radicalism (more Christian than doctrinally Marxist) with conservative theology. The Kingdom of God was not to be won on earth, but only in the dimension of time beyond history. He came to assert that human evil emerged less out of a deficient environment than out of man's inclination to assert his radical freedom for selfish ends, and out of the tendency of self-interest to corrupt even the highest ideals. Social disharmony and international violence suggested to Niebuhr that "history does not move forward without catastrophe, happiness is not guaranteed by the multiplication of physical comforts, social harmony is not easily created by more intelligence, and human nature is not as good or as harmless as had been supposed." A vigorous proponent of reforms more drastic than the New Deal provided, Niebuhr was one of the most articulate Protestant spokesman alerting the nation to the dangers of the demonic quality of Nazism and imperialism. In *The Children of Light and the Children of Darkness* he summarized the relevance of Christianity to both the domestic and the world scene.

The breakdown of collective security precipitated a great debate in America regarding the nation's responsibility in world affairs. The prolonged severity of the Depression had led to a concentration on purely domestic issues, not only in the United States but in the Western world generally. As long as desperate poverty and human want persisted, it was difficult for any people to become aroused over what was happening in other and (as it so often seemed) remote parts of the world. In the United States in the mid-1930s, moreover, not many citizens dissented from the popular belief that the nation's entrance into the first world war had been a terrible mistake. Far from making the world safe for democracy, far from ending war, the holocaust had led to an unjust peace, international anarchy, imperialism, communism, the rise of dictatorships, and the elevation of violence as a normal means of governance at home and national policy abroad. Had not the United States, moreover, been tricked into that war by the wily machinations of British propagandists, international bankers, and munitions makers? At least so it seemed to millions of Americans. Was not American policy —and humanity—best served by strict isolationism, by putting the world on notice that next time, if there were a next time, the United States would sit it out as a strict neutral? That was the sense of the Neutrality Acts of 1935 and 1937 which forbade the export of American arms and the extension of American credit to belligerent powers without discriminating between the aggressor and his victim. A feeling of geographical separation and military invulnerability, a sense of disillusionment with the way in which the Great War had turned out, the belief that a realization of America's unique mission in history (to set an example of republican government and human liberty for all to emulate) depended upon absolute freedom of national action; pacifist abhorrence of militarism, and the fear that participation in modern war brings about a totalitarian regime and the end of democracy—all these conspired to turn the nation away from responsible participation in international affairs. A hemispheric good neighbor policy, initiated in the Hoover years and carried through by FDR, brought the nations of North and South America closer together economically and made of the Monroe Doctrine a multilateral obligation; a system of reciprocal trade agreements relaxed the intense protectionism of the previous decade; in other regards, however, the nation's policy pursued neutrality and economic nationalism, or relied upon verbal remonstrances to achieve moral ends, as in the Kellogg-Briand

Peace Pact, and the Stimson Doctrine which chastised Japan for her attack upon Manchuria.

Roosevelt, reluctantly, went along with neutralist sentiment until in October, 1937, in the face of renewed Japanese advance in China, he proposed a quarantine of the aggressor nations. Although the appeal was ambiguous it aroused such extravagant opposition that the President pursued the expedient course of relative silence for a while longer. When Germany, however, having secured her Eastern Front by a nonaggression pact with the Soviet Union, attacked Poland, thus precipitating a second world war, the President and the nation could no longer evade the great issue.

And so the great debate was joined. Some insisted that America could and should go it alone, withdraw into a hemispheric fortress, and keep alive the hope of human liberty. They argued that this war, like all wars, was the product of national imperial rivalries; one might prefer one side to the other, but national self-interest dictated a course of noninvolvement. Colonel Lindbergh, the untarnished "lone eagle" of transatlantic flight, so proclaimed from lecture platforms up and down the nation. His wife, Anne Morrow Lindbergh, put the sentiments in a poignant essay, more poetry than prose, in which she admonished the American people to stay true to their traditions and try to ride out the totalitarian "wave of the future." The sacrifices would be terrible, but the alternative was the destruction not only of self-interest but of the very truths of existence.

Other leaders—rooted in the New Nationalist tradition of an aroused, armed, and righteous people—advocated a vigorous foreign policy which was willing to risk war in order to make possible the survival of Western values and the extended sway of American influence. Henry R. Luce, China-born son of American missionaries, imperious chief of the *Time-Life-Fortune* empire, prophesied an "American century" if only the nation would "accept wholeheartedly our duty and our opportunity as the most powerful and vital nation in the world and in consequence to exert upon the world the full impact of our influence, for such purposes as we see fit and by such means as we see fit."

Franklin Roosevelt, indirectly and vaguely at first (for he had first the electoral challenge of 1940 to overcome and the nation was still in no mood for any policies that even remotely ran the risk of intervention) and then more explicitly and candidly after the November mandate—his third victory at the polls— articulated still another view, one that was in time to prevail. Nazi Germany and imperial Japan threatened the security of the nation and the welfare of free peoples everywhere. Peace was indivisible. He would seek the national interest by granting aid to the Allies short of war; and when the survival of Britain and China was in immediate and great doubt, he would step toward the brink of intervention, but never so briskly as to lose the popular support of an effective majority in the nation. The President's plea that America become the great "arsenal of democracy" was as reluctantly accepted as his request for authorization to lend and lease material to other nations whose survival was deemed essential to American security. The passage of lend-lease in March, 1941, led to an acceleration of aid to Britain and China, and after the Nazi attack upon Russia in June to the Soviet Union as well. When German submarines began to take an unconscionable toll of arms and supplies, the commander in chief established first a naval patrol and then a convoy system half-way across the waters of the North Atlantic. By the fall of 1941 the United States was engaged in a shooting, if undeclared, naval war.

Far across the Pacific, in the meantime, Japan, having joined the Axis Alliance in 1940, was busily expanding her imperial influence until it should comprehend the undefined but vast sphere of greater East Asia. In line of attack were the Philippine Islands and Sino-American friendship dating from the turn of the century. American policy faced a dilemma. To challenge Japan in Asia was to run the risk of conflict in the Pacific at a time when Britain's survival was still in doubt. The United States did not have the power in hand to take on a one-theater war, to say nothing of a two-ocean global engagement. To withdraw from the Western Pacific was to leave China stranded, and perhaps to invite Japanese advance into areas of strategic obligation.

The Administration sought daily to postpone ultimate decisions and prayed for the breaks. In July, 1941, it froze Japanese assets and thus cut off the American source of petroleum products and other supplies. This act forced Japan to choose either to cease her imperial policy and eventually withdraw from the mainland, or to attack in Southeast Asia and the islands of the East Indies in order to secure a new source of supply for strategic commodities. Because the former course did not really constitute a live option, Japan chose the latter, and on the hunch that it meant war with the United States in any case decided to neutralize American naval power by simultaneous attacks on the Philippines, Guam, and Hawaii. With the U. S. Navy knocked out at Pearl Harbor, Japan reasoned she could withdraw and consolidate her position in the West and South Pacific and build there an island defense impregnable to American assault. Japanese-American negotiations in the fall of 1941 were doomed to failure, for neither side was willing to compromise positions and interests deemed to be of ultimate national significance.

And so, on December 7, the war came. The government had predicted that war was imminent and warnings had gone out to theater commanders of a possible strike, probably in the Philippines, but no one had guessed that Pearl Harbor would also be a target. When Germany declared war on the United States a few days later, the nation found itself once more in a world war, a truly global conflict this time. History had come full cycle.

Once again the nation mobilized its resources—economic, human, moral—for what Roosevelt was to call "unconditional surrender" of the enemy. Long months of peril and anxiety followed. The Navy and the Merchant Marine bore the brunt of the battle at first, turning back the Japanese in the central Pacific, fighting a war of attrition with the submarine in the Atlantic and against the Nazi Luftwaffe on the frigid run to Murmansk in Russia. American troops were marched off to prison camps in the Philippines, while General MacArthur, with the combined forces of the Army, Navy, and Marines, began his long journey back to liberation. In North Africa, Sicily, and Italy, American soldiers learned their deadly craft. For all the technological sophistication of modern warfare, service demanded miles of foot-slogging maneuver, it involved filth and fatigue as well as agony. It called forth fear and even panic and from somewhere the courage to get the day's nasty job done. For millions the price was the less-exacting "hurry-up-and-wait." Bill Mauldin caught the grimly comic aspects of the G.I.'s existence in cartoon. Ernie Pyle, the common "dogface's" reporter, put it in words.

Farm production, artificially held back during the 1930s, shot sharply upward, stimulated by good prices and new techniques. Industry tooled up and converted to defense faster than anyone had imagined possible. The miracle of production furnished the food and fiber, the guns, tanks, planes, jeeps, and landing craft to carry the battle to the enemy. The armies of the (hitherto) unemployed marched off to service or into defense plants. Women were recruited into jobs which custom had reserved to men. Another reservoir of labor was tapped in Negroes who moved from the rural South into the steel mills of Pittsburgh, the airplane factories of Detroit, and the shipyards of Portland.

Early in the war Roosevelt dismissed Dr. New Deal and called in Dr. Win-the-War. The energies of the American people were to be devoted to winning the war. Victory, survival, was the war aim. If World War II was not fought with quite the spiritual intensity that was so characteristic of the first crusade, much of its moral idealism did persist. Roosevelt, after all, had served an eight years' apprenticeship in Washington during the Wilson years, and even while aiming at unconditional surrender he planned for reconstruction at home and pursued collective security abroad through the United Nations. The United States was to play a positive role in world affairs, radically unlike its defection from responsibility in 1919.

By 1944 the time had arrived for the kill. Allied bombers were sapping the enemy's strength and morale. On the Eastern Front the Red Army, which had suffered all but catastrophic losses in the early years of the war, was rolling back the Germans in a counteroffensive that did not stop until Berlin was occupied. The Western allies opened up a second front on the

Normandy beaches, broke through the German lines, crossed the Rhine and carried the battle home to the Germans. In the Pacific the strategy of island-hopping, pursued by the classically impossible tactics of amphibious assault, brought American troops to the Marianas and to Okinawa, from whence devastating long-distance bomber raids began the destruction of Japan's home cities.

The Germans folded in May of 1945, a few weeks following the death of Franklin D. Roosevelt; the Japanese, driven from the seas, slowly starved by naval and air blockade, suffering utter destruction from explosion and fire, began to consider a way out with honor. It was not to be found, for the new President, Harry S. Truman, the man from Independence, had already made the decision to employ a secret new weapon unless the Asian enemy surrendered without conditions. The President and his advisers reasoned that the shock of the new bomb would force the Japanese to capitulate; its use, they agreed, would save millions of lives, both American and Japanese, that would otherwise be squandered in a now-needless invasion of the home islands; its immediate use might happily forestall Soviet entry into the Asian War—an event that had seemed so appealing when the arrangements were made at Yalta, but less palatable now that alternative means were at hand. The suggestion that a trial demonstration be held was rejected on the grounds that it might prove to be a dud, and that if the experiment worked the shock value of the bomb would be lost. The plea that explorations with the Japanese government be opened to see if surrender would not be acceptable if the nation were permitted to keep its Emperor was refused. And so the bomb was dropped, first on Hiroshima and then at Nagasaki. The participants ended the war shortly after the big bomb was dropped.

Not only an era but a millennium was ended; for the pillar of fire, blasted flesh, and atomized debris that rose over Hiroshima marked not alone the conclusion of a single war, but a long preatomic age. This was an end and a beginning. Science had closed and opened the doors. Vannevar Bush, who had secretly labored with his colleagues that the United States might be the first to possess this strange new power, had a larger sense of its significance than most of his contemporaries. Nor was he unaware of the impact of science and scholarship upon every aspect of life and history. The task was to mobilize science for human ends.

The task was also to resolve that great dilemma in American life which arose out of the denial of equal justice and liberty to Americans of colored skin. To Gunnar Myrdal, Swedish sociologist, and his American associates it was clear that, in the midst of global conflict, the nation's domestic race problem had taken on worldwide importance. The rising demand of American Negroes to participate fully in American life, to win that self-determination which was the mark of a truly democratic society, was matched by the desire of colored people everywhere in the world to secure self-government. Just as science did not recognize national boundaries, the longing for national independence and human acceptance was not bound by race and color.

This was the age of the great depression, the age of the New Deal, the age of global conflict. Contemporary historians named it for that remarkable man who rode out the storms and, for better or worse, helped shape its contours—the age of Roosevelt. Future historians doubtless will see it in better perspective.

1

The Roaring Twenties in Retrospect
F. Scott Fitzgerald's "Echoes of the Jazz Age"

F. Scott Fitzgerald, the darling of those Americans who relished being members of the "lost generation," demonstrated in story, novel, and essay a remarkable insight into the values and mores of a society which set him apart from many of his contemporaries. Catapulted into notoriety and rather substantial wealth by his early novels, he earned critical acclaim and a permanent niche in letters with his brilliantly ironic criticism of American life in *The Great Gatsby*. An expatriate during several years of the 1920s, Fitzgerald never ceased from longing for the land which he rejected and embraced. His chronicle of the 1920s and its "crack-up" in 1929 remains one of the most poetic, hyperbolic, yet accurate studies in contemporary literature. Although a severely subjective and impressionistic essay, "Echoes of the Jazz Age" touches many aspects of objective reality. For a critical appraisal of Fitzgerald, consult Arthur M. Mizener, *The Far Side of Paradise: A Biography of F. Scott Fitzgerald* (Boston: Houghton Mifflin, 1951). Frederick J. Hoffman's *The Twenties: American Writing in the Postwar Decade* (New York: The Viking Press, 1955) is an excellent literary history of the period. In reading the following selection note (1) what events the author used to date the Jazz Age; (2) the shift in social mores that occurred in the late 'teens and 1920s; (3) the impact of the younger generation on the older; (4) those aspects of the social mores which first experienced liberation; (5) what tensions within American life Fitzgerald exposed; (6) what the author thought was responsible for bringing the Jazz Age into being; and (7) what unresolved tragic issues of American life lay below the surface of superficial gaiety during the Jazz Age.

November, 1931]

IT IS TOO SOON TO WRITE ABOUT THE JAZZ AGE WITH perspective, and without being suspected of premature arteriosclerosis. Many people still succumb to violent

F. Scott Fitzgerald, "Echoes of the Jazz Age," in *The Crack-Up* (New York: New Directions, 1945), pp. 13-22. Originally published in *Scribner's Magazine*, XC:5 (November 1931). Reprinted through the courtesy of Charles Scribner's Sons.

retching when they happen upon any of its characteristic words
—words which have since yielded in vividness to the coinages of
the underworld. It is as dead as were the Yellow Nineties in
1902. Yet the present writer already looks back to it with nostalgia. It bore him up, flattered him and gave him more money
than he had dreamed of, simply for telling people that he felt
as they did, that something had to be done with all the nervous
energy stored up and unexpended in the War.

The ten-year period that, as if reluctant to die outmoded in
its bed, leaped to a spectacular death in October, 1929, began
about the time of the May Day riots in 1919. When the police
rode down the demobilized country boys gaping at the orators
in Madison Square, it was the sort of measure bound to alienate
the more intelligent young men from the prevailing order. We
didn't remember anything about the Bill of Rights until Mencken
began plugging it, but we did know that such tyranny be-
longed in the jittery little countries of South Europe. If goose-
livered business men had this effect on the government, then
maybe we had gone to war for J. P. Morgan's loans after all.
But, because we were tired of Great Causes, there was no more
than a short outbreak of moral indignation, typified by Dos
Passos' *Three Soldiers.* Presently we began to have slices of the
national cake and our idealism only flared up when the newspapers made melodrama out of such stories as Harding and the
Ohio Gang or Sacco and Vanzetti. The events of 1919 left us
cynical rather than revolutionary, in spite of the fact that now
we are all rummaging around in our trunks wondering where
in hell we left the liberty cap—"I know I *had* it"—and the mou-
jik blouse. It was characteristic of the Jazz Age that it had no
interest in politics at all.

It was an age of miracles, it was an age of art, it was an age
of excess, and it was an age of satire. A Stuffed Shirt, squirming
to blackmail in a lifelike way, sat upon the throne of the United
States; a stylish young man hurried over to represent to us the
throne of England. A world of girls yearned for the young
Englishman; the old American groaned in his sleep as he waited
to be poisoned by his wife, upon the advice of the female Ras-

putin who then made the ultimate decision in our national affairs. But such matters apart, we had things our way at last. With Americans ordering suits by the gross in London, the Bond Street tailors perforce agreed to moderate their cut to the American long-waisted figure and loose-fitting taste, something subtle passed to America, the style of man. During the Renaissance, Francis the First looked to Florence to trim his leg. Seventeenth-century England aped the court of France, and fifty years ago the German Guards officer bought his civilian clothes in London. Gentlemen's clothes—symbol of "the power that man must hold and that passes from race to race."

We were the most powerful nation. Who could tell us any longer what was fashionable and what was fun? Isolated during the European War, we had begun combing the unknown South and West for folkways and pastimes, and there were more ready to hand.

The first social revelation created a sensation out of all proportion to its novelty. As far back as 1915 the unchaperoned young people of the smaller cities had discovered the mobile privacy of that automobile given to young Bill at sixteen to make him "self-reliant." At first petting was a desperate adventure even under such favorable conditions, but presently confidences were exchanged and the old commandment broke down. As early as 1917 there were references to such sweet and casual dalliance in any number of the *Yale Record* or the *Princeton Tiger*.

But petting in its more audacious manifestations was confined to the wealthier classes—among other young people the old standard prevailed until after the War, and a kiss meant that a proposal was expected, as young officers in strange cities sometimes discovered to their dismay. Only in 1920 did the veil finally fall—the Jazz Age was in flower.

Scarcely had the staider citizens of the republic caught their breaths when the wildest of all generations, the generation which had been adolescent during the confusion of the War, brusquely shouldered my contemporaries out of the way and danced into the limelight. This was the generation whose girls dramatized themselves as flappers, the generation that corrupted its elders and eventually overreached itself less through lack of morals than through lack of taste. May one offer in exhibit the year 1922! That was the peak of the younger generation, for though the Jazz Age continued, it became less and less an affair of youth.

The sequel was like a children's party taken over by the elders, leaving the children puzzled and rather neglected and rather taken aback. By 1923 their elders, tired of watching the carnival with ill-concealed envy, had discovered that young liquor will take the place of young blood, and with a whoop the orgy began. The younger generation was starred no longer.

A whole race going hedonistic, deciding on pleasure. The precocious intimacies of the younger generation would have come about with or without prohibition—they were implicit in the attempt to adapt English customs to American conditions. (Our South, for example, is tropical and early maturing—it has never been part of the wisdom of France and Spain to let young girls go unchaperoned at sixteen and seventeen.) But the general decision to be amused that began with the cocktail parties of 1921 had more complicated origins.

The word jazz in its progress toward respectability has meant first sex, then dancing, then music. It is associated with a state of nervous stimulation, not unlike that of big cities behind the lines of a war. To many English the War still goes on because all the forces that menace them are still active—Wherefore eat, drink and be merry, for to-morrow we die. But different causes had now brought about a corresponding state in America—though there were entire classes (people over fifty, for example) who spent a whole decade denying its existence even when its puckish face peered into the family circle. Never did they dream that they had contributed to it. The honest citizens of every class, who believed in a strict public morality and were powerful enough to enforce the necessary legislation, did not know that they would necessarily be served by criminals and quacks, and do not really believe it to-day. Rich righteousness had always been able to buy honest and intelligent servants to free the slaves or the Cubans, so when this attempt collapsed our elders stood firm with all the stubbornness of people involved in a weak case, preserving their righteousness and losing their children. Silver-haired women and men with fine old faces, people who never did a consciously dishonest thing in their lives, still assure each other in the apartment hotels of New York and Boston and Washington that "there's a whole generation growing up that will never know the taste of liquor." Meanwhile their granddaughters pass the well-thumbed copy of *Lady Chatterley's Lover* around the boarding-school and, if they get about at all, know the taste of gin or corn at sixteen. But the generation who reached maturity between 1875 and 1895 continue to believe what they want to believe.

Even the intervening generations were incredulous. In 1920 Heywood Broun announced that all this hubbub was nonsense, that young men didn't kiss but told anyhow. But very shortly people over twenty-five came in for an intensive education. Let me trace some of the revelations vouchsafed them by reference to a dozen works written for various types of mentality during the decade. We begin with the suggestion that Don Juan leads an interesting life (*Jurgen*, 1919); then we learn that there's a lot of sex around if we only knew it (*Winesburg, Ohio*, 1920), that adolescents lead very amorous lives (*This Side of Paradise*, 1920), that there are a lot of neglected Anglo-Saxon words (*Ulysses*, 1921), that older people don't always resist sudden temptations (*Cytherea*, 1922), that girls are sometimes seduced without being ruined (*Flaming Youth*, 1922), that even rape often turns out well (*The Sheik*, 1922), that glamorous English ladies are often promsicuous (*The Green Hat*, 1924), that in fact they devote most of their time to it (*The Vortex*, 1926), that it's a damn good thing too (*Lady Chatterley's Lover*, 1928), and finally that there are abnormal variations (*The Well of Loneliness*, 1928, and *Sodom and Gomorrah*, 1929).

In my opinion the erotic element in these works, even *The Sheik*, written for children in the key of *Peter Rabbit*, did not one particle of harm. Everything they described, and much more, was familiar in our contemporary life. The majority of the theses were honest and elucidating—their effect was to restore some dignity to the male as opposed to the he-man in American life. ("And what is a 'He-man'?" demanded Gertrude Stein one day. "Isn't it a large enough order to fill out to the dimensions of all that 'a man' has meant in the past? A '*He*-man'!") The married woman can now discover whether she is being cheated, or whether sex is just something to be endured, and her compensation should be to establish a tyranny of the spirit, as her mother may have hinted. Perhaps many women found that love was meant to be fun. Anyhow the objectives lost their tawdry little case, which is one reason why our literature is now the most living in the world.

Contrary to popular opinion, the movies of the Jazz Age had no effect upon its morals. The social attitude of the producers was timid, behind the times and banal—for example, no picture mirrored even faintly the younger generation until 1923, when magazines had already been started to celebrate it and it had long ceased to be news. There were a few feeble splutters and then Clara Bow in *Flaming Youth;* promptly the Hollywood hacks ran the theme into its cinematographic grave. Throughout the Jazz Age the movies got no farther than Mrs. Jiggs, keeping up with its most blatant superficialities. This was no doubt due to the censorship as well as to innate conditions in the industry. In any case, the Jazz Age now raced along under its own power, served by great filling stations full of money.

The people over thirty, the people all the way up to fifty, had joined the dance. We graybeards (to tread down F.P.A.) remember the uproar when in 1912 grandmothers of forty tossed away their crutches and took lessons in the Tango and the Castle-Walk. A dozen years later a woman might pack the Green Hat with her other affairs as she set off for Europe or New York, but Savonarola was too busy flogging dead horses in Augean stables of his own creation to notice. Society, even in small cities, now dined in separate chambers, and the sober table learned about the gay table only from hearsay. There were very few people left at the sober table. One of its former glories, the less sought-after girls who had become resigned to sublimating a probable celibacy, came across Freud and Jung in seeking their intellectual recompense and came tearing back into the fray.

By 1926 the universal preoccupation with sex had become a nuisance. (I remember a perfectly mated, contented young mother asking my wife's advice about "having an affair right away," though she had no one especially in mind, "because don't you think it's sort of undignified when you get much over thirty?") For a while bootleg Negro records with their phallic euphemisms made everything suggestive, and simultaneously came a wave of erotic plays—young girls from finishing-schools packed the galleries to hear about the romance of being a Lesbian and George Jean Nathan protested. Then one young producer lost his head entirely, drank a beauty's alcoholic bathwater and went to the penitentiary. Somehow his pathetic attempt at romance belongs to the Jazz Age, while his contemporary in prison, Ruth Snyder, had to be hoisted into it by the tabloids—she was, as *The Daily News* hinted deliciously to gourmets, about "to cook, *and sizzle*, AND FRY!" in the electric chair.

The gay elements of society had divided into two main streams, one flowing toward Palm Beach and Deauville, and the other, much smaller, toward the summer Riviera. One could get away with more on the summer Riviera, and whatever happened seemed to have something to do with art. From 1926 to 1929, the great years of the Cap d'Antibes, this corner of France was dominated by a group quite distinct from that American society which is dominated by Europeans. Pretty much of anything went at Antibes—by 1929, at the most gorgeous paradise for swimmers on the Mediterranean no one swam any more, save for a short hang-over dip at noon. There was a picturesque graduation of steep rocks over the sea and somebody's valet and an occasional English girl used to dive from them, but the Americans were content to discuss each other in the bar. This was indicative of something that was taking place in the homeland—Americans were getting soft. There were signs everywhere: we still won the Olympic games but with champions whose names had few vowels in them—teams composed, like the fighting Irish combination of Notre Dame, of fresh overseas blood. Once the French became really interested, the Davis Cup gravitated automatically to their intensity in competition. The vacant lots of the Middle-Western cities were built up now—except for a short period in school, we were not turning out to be an athletic people like the British, after all. The hare and the tortoise. Of

course if we wanted to we could be in a minute; we still had
all those reserves of ancestral vitality, but one day in 1926 we
looked down and found we had flabby arms and a fat pot and
couldn't say boop-boop-a-doop to a Sicilian. Shades of Van
Bibber!—no utopian ideal, God knows. Even golf, once considered an effeminate game, had seemed very strenuous of late—
an emasculated form appeared and proved just right.

By 1927 a wide-spread neurosis began to be evident, faintly
signalled, like a nervous beating of the feet, by the popularity
of cross-word puzzles. I remember a fellow expatriate opening
a letter from a mutual friend of ours, urging him to come home
and be revitalized by the hardy, bracing qualities of the native
soil. It was a strong letter and it affected us both deeply, until
we noticed that it was headed from a nerve sanitarium in Pennsylvania.

By this time contemporaries of mine had begun to disappear
into the dark maw of violence. A classmate killed his wife and
himself on Long Island, another tumbled "accidently" from a
skyscraper in Philadelphia, another purposely from a skyscraper
in New York. One was killed in a speak-easy in Chicago; another was beaten to death in a speak-easy in New York and
crawled home to the Princeton Club to die; still another had
his skull crushed by a maniac's axe in an insane asylum where
he was confined. These are not catastrophes that I went out of
my way to look for—these were my friends; moreover, these
things happened not during the depression but during the boom.

In the spring of '27, something bright and alien flashed across
the sky. A young Minnesotan who seemed to have had nothing
to do with his generation did a heroic thing, and for a moment
people set down their glasses in country clubs and speakeasies
and thought of their old best dreams. Maybe there was a way
out by flying, maybe our restless blood could find frontiers in the
illimitable air. But by that time we were all pretty well committed; and the Jazz Age continued; we would all have one more.

Nevertheless, Americans were wandering ever more widely—
friends seemed eternally bound for Russia, Persia, Abyssinia
and Central Africa. And by 1928 Paris had grown suffocating.
With each new shipment of Americans spewed up by the boom

the quality fell off, until toward the end there was something sinister about the crazy boatloads. They were no longer the simple pa and ma and son and daughter, infinitely superior in their qualities of kindness and curiosity to the corresponding class in Europe, but fantastic neanderthals who believed something, something vague, that you remembered from a very cheap novel. I remember an Italian on a steamer who promenaded the deck in an American Reserve Officer's uniform picking quarrels in broken English with Americans who criticised their own institutions in the bar. I remember a fat Jewess, inlaid with diamonds, who sat behind us at the Russian ballet and said as the curtain rose, "Thad's luffly, dey ought to baint a bicture of it." This was low comedy, but it was evident that money and power were falling into the hands of people in comparison with whom the leader of a village Soviet would be a gold-mine of judgment and culture. There were citizens travelling in luxury in 1928 and 1929 who, in the distortion of their new condition, had the human value of Pekinese, bivalves, cretins, goats. I remember the Judge from some New York district who had taken his daughter to see the Bayeux Tapestries and made a scene in the papers advocating their segregation because one scene was immoral. But in those days life was like the race in *Alice in Wonderland*, there was a prize for every one.

The Jazz Age had had a wild youth and a heady middle age. There was the phase of the necking parties, the Leopold-Loeb murder (I remember the time my wife was arrested on Queensborough Bridge on the suspicion of being the "Bob-haired Bandit") and the John Held Clothes. In the second phase such phenomena as sex and murder became more mature, if much more conventional. Middle age must be served and pajamas came to the beach to save fat thighs and flabby calves from competition with the one-piece bathing-suit. Finally skirts came down and everything was concealed. Everybody was at scratch now. Let's go—

But it was not to be. Somebody had blundered and the most expensive orgy in history was over.

It ended two years ago [1929], because the utter confidence which was its essential prop received an enormous jolt, and it didn't take long for the flimsy structure to settle earthward. And after two years the Jazz Age seems as far away as the days before the War. It was borrowed time anyhow—the whole upper tenth of a nation living with the insouciance of grand ducs and the casualness of chorus girls. But moralizing is easy now and it was pleasant to be in one's twenties in such a certain and unworried time. Even when you were broke you didn't worry about money, because it was in such profusion around you. Toward the end one had a struggle to pay one's share; it was almost a favor to accept hospitality that required any travelling. Charm, notoriety, mere good manners, weighed more than money as a social asset. This was rather splendid, but things were getting thinner and thinner as the eternal necessary human values tried to spread over all that expansion. Writers were geniuses on the strength of one respectable book or play; just as during the War officers of four months' experience commanded hundreds of men, so there were now many little fish lording it over great big bowls. In the theatrical world extravagant productions were carried by a few second-rate stars, and so on up the scale into politics, where it was difficult to interest good men in positions of the highest importance and responsibility, importance and responsibility far exceeding that of business executives but which paid only five or six thousand a year.

Now once more the belt is tight and we summon the proper expression of horror as we look back at our wasted youth. Sometimes, though, there is a ghostly rumble among the drums, an asthmatic whisper in the trombones that swings me back into the early twenties when we drank wood alcohol and every day in every way grew better and better, and there was a first abortive shortening of the skirts, and girls all looked alike in sweater dresses, and people you didn't want to know said "Yes, we have no bananas," and it seemed only a question of a few years before the older people would step aside and let the world be run by those who saw things as they were—and it all seems rosy and romantic to us who were young then, because we will never feel quite so intensely about our surroundings any more.

2

Sociology of the Settlement House
Helen Hall's "Introducing Our Neighbors"

Helen Hall, in 1964 still active in the settlement movement and a crusader for social reforms in the areas of juvenile delinquency and slum clearance, was a social worker whose professional career led her into influential positions first in Philadelphia, then in New York (where she succeeded Lillian Wald as director of the Henry Street Settlement on the Lower East Side), and then in the nation. Combining an idealistic concern for human welfare with a pragmatic sense of harsh realities, Miss Hall was chosen in 1928 by the National Federation of Settlements to direct a study of the origins and social consequences of employment insecurity. Although her research was accomplished before the panic of 1929 had broken the prosperity that generally prevailed during the golden years of American capitalism, her analysis was not completed and published until the early years of the Great Depression. Her preface to the case studies summarized the expedients to which the unemployed resorted before they reluctantly, and then only as a last resort, threw themselves on charity. Without explicitly endorsing social insurance, her study nevertheless presented an implicit rationale for the necessity of programs of comprehensive social insurance; and Miss Hall herself became an influential member of the advisory committee that helped to draw up the social security bill enacted in 1935.

The significance of Miss Hall's study and the impact generally of professional social workers upon social policy is the central theme of Clarke A. Chambers, *Seedtime of Reform; American Social Service and Social Action, 1918-1933* (Minneapolis: University of Minnesota Press, 1963). Irving Bernstein's *The Lean Years: A History of the American Worker, 1920-1933* (Boston: Houghton Mifflin, 1960) provides a stimulating descriptive analysis of the plight of the unemployed during the early years of the depression. In studying the following

Helen Hall, "Introducing Our Neighbors," in Marion Elderton (ed.), *Case Studies of Unemployment* (Philadelphia: University of Pennsylvania Press, 1931), pp. xxii-1. Reprinted through the courtesy of the University of Pennsylvania Press.

39]

selection, note (1) how the author portrays the human demoralization
attendant upon unemployment; (2) the expedients to which the unemployed resorted before asking for charity; (3) the suggestions for
alleviation of the social consequences of prolonged unemployment;
and (4) the anticipation of public policies which would come to be
widely accepted after 1933.

I]

THERE IS NOTHING ABSTRACT OR INTANGIBLE ABOUT
our next-door neighbor; when he is out of a job, the
settlement knows it. We see him go out in the early morning,
looking for work, and come home at noon. We can tell by the
set of his shoulders whether he has found it. We share the
throes of the corner grocer when, to save himself, he has to
stop credit to old customers who cannot pay. We help grandmothers scurry around for cleaning jobs when the younger
generation is not bringing enough in. And there is always the
man in the hall, twisting his hat as he tells his story, who has
come to us for help in his search for work.

It was these neighbors of ours, then, who started the unemployment study of the National Federation of Settlements in
which over a hundred neighborhood houses collaborated. . . .
Experience has taught us to recognize broken work not merely
as a symptom of financial crises, but as a recurring fault of
modern production. We are confronted by unemployment, not
as a single episode in the history of a household, but as something that may come again and again, impeding and stopping
the normal development of the family. . . .

II]

To focus our study on the effects of unemployment, we
divided our schedules into four parts and asked that entries be
made in each case on the pages set aside for economic, physical,
psychological effects, and the cumulative results of all these on
the future of the family. The headings were not rigid categories.

They naturally overlapped. There were no neat box-like compartments leading up to tabulation, for our families were, after all, but samples. We were not after sociological analyses or studies in case treatment. But the schedule as a whole, and the freely written summary with which many of them closed, gave a realistic picture of the family as a going concern, or rather as an interrupted one. . . .

Economic and Physical Effects]

As the cases came in, we were struck by certain sequences. Mrs. Nelson's first analysis brought out a reiterated experience: first, broken work; then a steady degradation of the kind of work, until the casual labor level was reached. We found mechanics, cabinet-makers, shoe-makers and the rest dropping down to the ranks of dock workers, truck drivers, janitors, watchmen, street cleaners, and snow shovelers. Their former skills only made them misfits at manual labor. We soon read of further deterioration caused by accidents, overstrain, and exposure undergone in their new work.

The immediate economic effect at every stage in this sequence is reduced earnings. Its eventual effect is diminished earning power. . . . The butcher, the baker, the business and professional groups of their communities were affected by this drain which undermined the household structure of the families themselves.

In the economic makeshifts resorted to, we found families following much the same lines. First, cash savings are used up; insurance policies lapse; jewelry and furniture are pawned; furniture is sold. Meanwhile, come bills at the grocer's, moves to poorer quarters, and what means most in discouragement to the family, the loss of a house partly paid for. All along this line of march the mother is generally working or looking for work, and the family often living on a semi-starvation diet.

There is also much similarity in the sequence of physical effects. Pared-down food and scant clothing, unheated and sunless rooms at home, exposure in the search for jobs and other untoward circumstances wear away the family's resistance. In a fourth of the cases the effects of malnutrition were obvious enough to be noted by a layman. In those frequent instances where the mother went out to work, the wage-earning burden, combined with worry and undernourishment, overtaxed her physical strength and nervous energy. Underweight, stunted growth, anemia, and rickets recur again and again among the entries. There is the sequence of colds, pneumonia, tuberculosis. Repeatedly is it noted that the families go without needed medical treatment, that teeth are neglected and necessary operations postponed. Babies are born only to die because of insufficient food and the exhaustion of the mother. . . .

Effects on the Spirit]

It is when we turn to the psychological effects that we appreciate the drag of these things on the family as a potentially resourceful and joyous group. Here we see most clearly results that are irremediable. It is here also that we find the greatest divergence, for it is here that the human equation shows itself most variable. Only the most sturdy of our families have come through with nothing more than their economic situation impaired. Their course throws light on the process by which the unemployed men of today become unemployable tomorrow. If you have been hungry, you may build up when you get food. But your whole outlook on life changes when you have been discouraged too often or too long. Chance remarks register this disintegration. "It ain't any good starting saving again." "We've got in so deep I guess we'll never try to get out."

Insanity, suicide and desertion are some of the more startling consequences of the emotional upsets which follow in the wake of discharge. Read the story of Tiorsi, the hand laster of Boston, who had seen his pay envelope flatten from week to week. When finally he brought home only three dollars he tried to hang himself. And read that of Harry Towne, the Chicago truck driver, looking for work, worried because his sisters had to support him, refusing to eat—and then sent to a hospital where he stayed for months receiving treatment for a mental breakdown.

I cannot forget Susie Lock, whom I came to know in my canvass of unemployment in Detroit in 1930. She was in the relief line because her husband had left her and her two small children. "You must be lazy or you'd have gotten a job," she had said to him, and he had gone right out, joined "a guy who's got an old Ford and him and three others have gone off in it. But it's an open car and it's so cold and that was Tuesday and I ain't heard. And I wish I hadn't said it," she finished.

We do not find such a dramatic climax in most stories. They drag on and on, but the effects on the human spirit seem equally devastating.

Take one of our nearest neighbors. Two years ago he was a friendly, bustling man of thirty. He had worked for the Victor Company for ten years without missing one day and he was proud of his record. After his lay-off he was unable to find steady work and took on odd painting jobs, which were few and far between. Gradually his whole disposition changed; he began to complain constantly of headaches. His feelings were always hurt and he became irritable with his children. Finally we were able to persuade him to have a thorough examination. The hospital reported that there was nothing wrong with him physically, but that he must have steady work and no worry because he was in danger of a mental breakdown. If he does break, it will mean that a wife and six children under thirteen will need support.

Take Rocco, the name under which is told the story of a young factory hand of twenty-nine, neighbor to the College Settlement, across town from us in Philadelphia. He is consumed with a desire to "do right by his family." No matter how worried he is, he always beams when he mentions his babies. "I've got a wonderful kid, five years old," he tells you. "I don't want him to go through what I've had. I know what hard sledding is. My father died when I was nine, and I went to work at eleven in a glass factory to help support my mother and little brother. At thirteen I was working on the railroad, and at sixteen did a man's work. I want to make something of my kid, but I can't even give him enough to eat now."

Losing faith and confidence in some one you have leaned upon and trusted is about the worst thing that can come to a human being. When unemployment comes, the husband and wife most often face the situation together. But this unity changes as the wife is harried by debt collectors, the rent man, the insurance man. She sees the children half fed and getting thin, often sick, and needing clothes she can't buy; and then, too, she may be working herself and adding fatigue to worry. In the first days of her husband's job-hunt she is sympathetic and fights to keep his courage up and defends him in the neighborhood. The poignancy of his struggle has not been lost in her own discouragement. I remember when Mrs. White came round to tell of her husband's first pay envelope after nearly a winter's search. "You know," she said, "the look in his face when he give it to me was like a child with a Christmas present." But that was his first winter out. Now, facing the third one, the Whites no longer present a united front. She doesn't believe he tries and is bitter against him, and he no longer cares very much, for he has the gang and is "in on the bottle as it is handed around," and only comes home late to sleep. The strain and disappointment vent themselves in wrangles. As Mrs. White puts it, "There were no ugly words in our house when he was workin', but I'm so tired now I don't know what I'm saying." And to come home from anything as disheartening as "makin' the rounds" only to be accused of not really trying doesn't make for harmony. The blame the husband sometimes gets only bespeaks a nervous strain on the part of the wife, but often she has read in the papers of prosperous times and that adds to her distrust of her husband's earnestness in his job-hunt. "If other men get jobs, as the papers say, why can't he?"

The children cannot pass through all this untouched. The psychologist and psychiatrist help us to understand what a background of strain and bad feeling can do to the growing child. Like adults, children react differently to family tension. In some the spirit is not strong enough to throw it off, but most children unconsciously elude as best they can the pressure of trouble in their home. . . .

The parents' failure, which is driven home harder with each unsuccessful day, not only robs the children of a sense of security, but often of one source of leadership. Mrs. White's bitterness toward her husband is aggravated by the fact that she is no longer able to control her ten- and twelve-year-old boys and they have lost respect for their father so that he can't help her. Then, too, she has had to take her oldest boy out of school.

We do not often relate today's unemployment to the next generation. But as you come to know the families of the unemployed, it sometimes seems that they feel a deeper resentment against their inability to make plans for the future than they do against their immediate sufferings.

Along with the children's education, the unemployed must cut out those things which make for interesting and creative living. Back of this generalization are an infinite number of incidents set down in the case records, some of them seemingly inconsequential in themselves, but often of a sort which put their stamp on life. . . . The oldest child in the Amay family had to stop her violin lessons. Mrs. DeMacio hadn't had money for her newspaper for two years nor "had she gone to a movie" and, she added, in telling of it, "You know how we both like good music!" . . .

To the physical misery and strain is added the broken morale, the wreckage of human relations and hopes for boys and girls. We are perhaps not so quick to feel badly about people's being worried as about their being hungry. But to the families concerned, the effects on the spirit may be more devastating. They tell us so many times, "It's not the going without we mind: it's the insecurity." The man who, with the loss of his job, has lost his sense of belonging, and with it his place in the scheme of his own household, is on new and unsteady footing. Under the emotional upset of fathers and mothers is the sense of trying to build on quicksand. Most of us like to feel that in living we are building and the glimpses we catch of this trait reassure us of the reserves in human nature. The older people have a patience that puts us to shame; but they lack the tools and materials to build anew. The younger married men and women who lose their start have youth on their side, but are goaded by youth's impatience at futility.

What, above all, unemployment does to people is to take the spring out of them.

III]

Out of their own experience, our settlement neighbors tell us what unemployment does to men, women and children. But the telling will have been useless if we stop at this point and are not impelled to do something about it. What significance do we find embedded in these cases which suggests lines of action? However else they differ, these are year-round families who lack year-round incomes. How, then, can we safeguard them at the points where their livelihood breaks down? We must make work steadier and more secure. We must make re-employment swifter when men and women are laid off. And we must insure against want the households of breadwinners who seek work and cannot find it.

Steadier Work]

That first need for stabilizing employment runs through all the cases. There is a finality in those instances where the job itself is gone—where a factory closes down, a coal mine is closed, a commodity drops off the market, or some technological change does away with the worker's function. But there is hope in the seasonal trades, for we know that the builders can, to some extent, if they will, outflank climate and overcome custom by the new methods which are slowly bringing in all-year construction in temperate latitudes. There is hope in industries where wage-earners are taken on and off merely because management has not yet been aroused to the importance of regular production. Each industry, if not each plant, has its own difficulties to overcome, but progressive employers in a great variety of lines have demonstrated that much can be done to iron out the curves. . . .

Closely related to industrial stabilization is the need for long-time planning for public works. The principle has long won acceptance that road building and other construction should be budgeted so that public enterprises can be pushed when private business falls off. But the practical working out of the principle by city, county, state and national governments remains to be done.

The second line for action is to modernize our public employment services, to lift the standards of private agencies, and to weed out the abuses and inefficiencies of our present haphazard methods of labor placement. One of the boys in the neighborhood of University House read an advertisement saying ten men were wanted by a gasoline distributing company. He arrived early, but found two hundred men ahead of him and the fire department playing a hose on them to disperse the crowd. The jobs had been filled before the advertisement had had time to appear. A comprehensive system of labor exchanges should obviate such common wastes as this. In the absence of adequate public help, the displaced workman must look to his own feet as his employment service. Even shoe-leather may go back on him and we find Mrs. Raymond putting pasteboard in her husband's shoes, cotton in their heels, and a brace-back on his knee as an aid in the tramp for work.

After following Jerry on his morning rounds or walking the streets all day with Mr. Zepone, after reading the testimony of Harry Silverman, twelve years in one place, who searches for five months for another, it is not easy to go on cherishing the idea that every man who really wants a job can find one.

As my neighbor, Mrs. Dever, said of her husband: "He ain't one to pick his job nor don't lay his own self off. He'd take anything. He worked seven years in the mill as a dyer before it closed down, and that was last October, seven months ago, and he ain't had a job since. And it ain't for not looking, for the feet's walked off him. He comes home nights and just sits and soaks his feet. Sometimes this winter it's been so bad I thought it was better not to take the wear off his shoes, but he goes just the same. He says there's always the chance he might get something."

Over and over again the cases give us examples of the new unemployment which has come in with advances in applied science and which swells the ranks of footloose men. Jervis, a mixer of colored inks for a Philadelphia publisher, is displaced by a machine; Morrow, the Boston driver, loses his winter's work through the introduction of artificial ice; and then he and his horses are thrown out of delivery work in the summer by the coming of motor trucks. Rafael, the Chicago painter, is crowded out by the spray lacquer system which requires fewer men; Tiorsi, the Boston shoe-maker, sees his hands displaced by knives and punches.

The bitter antagonism the workers often express toward labor-saving devices is easily explained by our inadequate facilities for helping them make adjustments when the changes come. It is no wonder that the man out of a job does not speculate, as do the economists and engineers, on the ultimate effect of technological progress. There are those who assure us that in the long run it creates more work than it supplants. But the man done out of a job only knows that a machine is taking his place. . . .

We may not share their sense of grievance against a management that takes advantage of new machines or motive powers. But why should our business organizers have been so backward in matching these upsetting inventions with a modern employment service, federal, state and local, that will make use of abilities now allowed to go to waste for lack of any adequate system to distribute them?

Insurance]

There remains the underlying need for safeguarding the households of breadwinners who seek work and cannot find it. The control of the business cycle, if we ever achieve it, will help cut down their numbers. So will industrial stabilization and long-time planning of public works. An efficient placement system will also help. Yet no one who scans the ups and downs of American business enterprise, our changes in techniques and styles and markets, the shiftings of industry from one region to another, can but see that there will still be need for protection of some sort against unprevented or unpreventable unemployment over which the worker himself has no control.

It is obvious that the regularization of industry cannot be carried out by the man whom it most directly affects. We put that up to management. But we seem to assume that by some miracle he and his family can underwrite the irregularities of industry. And we have been slow to extend to this hazard of broken work the principle we have applied so successfully to industrial accidents by workmen's compensation laws which spread a share of that risk over our costs of production.

Here are 150 homes in a prosperous country and in a prosperous epoch. Here are 150 families dislodged from their means of subsistence for reasons outside of themselves. Here are 150 breadwinners eager to shoulder the burden of livelihood if they are given the chance. Let us run over the sequence of makeshifts these families resorted to and ask ourselves whether any or all of them seem satisfactory provisions for safeguarding such homes.

Savings]

Savings are the first cushion, cash savings first of all. Many of our families had small savings, but there is nothing in their experience to show that high wages are general enough or continuous enough to enable savings to give any general security. The economists tell us that for three-quarters of the population of the United States the margin between income and necessary outgo is so close as to allow little or no leeway for emergencies. In one out of five of our cases it is recorded that the families had used up whatever savings they had. When it has taken fifteen years to save $700, as it had the DiPesas of Boston, and you wipe it out in one winter of unemployment, you have lost something more than the $700. You do not start again with the same spirit. In one out of ten of the cases, especially those where the work had been seasonal or where there were a larger number of children or there had been previous sickness, the families had not been able to lay by for a "rainy day." Or, as one neighbor put it, it "rained too soon."

Those of us who have followed them in their long line of retrenchments know that not one step is taken without a struggle. After the cash savings are gone, insurance policies lapse. We might well stop at this point, for no family gives up its insurance without a fight. They are small policies, most of them, enough to see them through a decent burial, but they mean something almost symbolic to the poor. The fear of not being able to bury their own dead haunts even the least independent.

There is scarcely a family whose ideal is not to own their own home. A house is savings if you own it or are buying it bit by bit on instalments. This instinct for home ownership survives in spite of discouraging fluctuations in real estate values in our industrial neighborhoods. Many of our immigrant peoples come from countries where their families have lived for generations on the same little plot of ground. With them the instinct to own is deep-seated, and they are willing to put up a fierce struggle to have it satisfied. That struggle must be watched close at hand to understand its full significance. A dozen of our families had engaged in it, only to find the home they had worked for, which had stood for security to them, become a back-breaking load once their earning power was cut. They were in arrears in their payments, behind in their interest on mortgages, and some of them faced foreclosure. . . .

Furniture is savings: and we find furniture sold or, more often, lost to the instalment collector. That was the way with the piano which the Morans in Boston had almost paid for. Then their parlor furniture went. The instalment house stripped the rooms of the DeMacios of Pittsburgh and left only mattresses, broken chairs and a hot plate. It meant more than the actual loss when the young Greens had saved $1500 over five years to buy their furnishings and were forced to sell them for $200. These material things stand for steps along the line of respectability and progress. They mean not only parlor furniture, but the place you take in your community, your being able to have your friends in, your daughter's meeting her boy friend in her own home instead of on the corner. . . .

As we turn the pages of these stories we appreciate the slenderness of savings as a buffer to misfortune, and we cannot feel that they are a convincing answer to the need for security against industrial changes.

Borrowings]

What is the next line of defense these families fall back upon? They borrow. Families without houses, furniture or articles which can be sold or pawned are thrust quickly on the mercy of the landlord and the grocer. To the members of a household who have paid their rent promptly and hold their heads high in the neighborhood, this running into debt is a humiliating business and the daily facing of creditors adds to the strain which is put upon family relationships. Hilda and Herman Reuter had been able to save on $18 a week and their upstanding part in the community had been a great source of satisfaction to them. It is especially noted in their case that when Herman's earnings stopped and they got behind, he it was who saw the creditors. But it is the wife generally who faces them or tries to elude them. You come upon the front door and find it locked; the curtains are down. No one's at home. But if your rap is known, you may find the mother in the kitchen waiting for a chance to steal out and avoid the collector. One out of five of our families ran up bills for groceries, coal, milk and other necessities. "I can tell you what unemployment has done for us," said Mr. Conway of Louisville. "It has got us so deeply in debt that we can never pull out."

And whether it is the wage-earner's family that thus eats up his future earnings, or the small shopkeeper who carries them and runs into banktuptcy all the faster if he has a heart, we cannot think it is good public policy thus to let things drift from bad to worse.

Charity]

Society does not, of course, leave such families altogether to their own devices. When other resources have been exhausted, and in most instances only then, the family asks for charity. Before they were through, a third of our families had done so— but often only after a long struggle. Some few became pauperized, but many could never reconcile themselves to accepting help from strangers.

Often charitable relief is difficult to obtain for a family where there is an able-bodied man. John Schneider of New Orleans wanted to kill himself because he felt that his family would get help if it were not for him. Young Mr. Miller in Pittsburgh refused for a long time to ask for aid because he was a young man, able and willing to work, and was ashamed to receive it from any agency. Mrs. Amay says: "We never asked help from no one. We couldn't bear to let no one, even our own people and they couldn't help us anyway, know of our trouble, but when the children needed food we had to tell some one. The nurse came in and found me crying, so I told her." Mr. Estrada developed a bitter attitude toward life, feeling that a man willing to work should be able to find it. He so resented charity that he refused to eat food that came from outside. Mr. Blanton was keeping a record of the money loaned him by the welfare society and hoped some day to repay. He admitted, however, that he was losing his self-respect and felt that he would lose his mind unless he could find work.

When unemployment insurance is mentioned in this country the cry of "We don't want the dole here" is often raised by people who do not realize that in our relief methods for the unemployed we are using a dole which is much more demoralizing than any plan of insurance would be. Social work has made advances in the deftness with which it helps adjust family troubles, but social work can scarcely underwrite the load of unemployment in its great cyclical manifestations. There is not the money to do the job. Emergency funds are makeshifts, and emergency relief crowds out the constructive work of the social agencies. In good times or bad, to the families of the unemployed, relief from such sources comes more often than not as an added misfortune. They lose something, as they see it, when they take help, even if the cause for asking for it lies outside their own control. It means a serious break in family pride and self-confidence, a self-confidence which seldom blossoms again with the same sturdiness. Even if it covered the ground, charitable relief would not be a convincing answer, either, to industrial dislocation in a democracy.

Other Makeshifts]

Our families turn to other makeshifts they have worked out themselves. They move to cheaper quarters; they break up the home; they cut down on conveniences, on clothing, on food. But are these the workings of a providence that fits our modern world? A bread line stands out like a silhouette of misery in our memories. The relief lines that I came upon at the municipal stations in Detroit last winter, and the employment lines at the plants, etched themselves deeply. But there is another slow-moving procession of which we catch only fragmentary glimpses, but which, if it could be run before us like a film, would leave us with still less peace of mind. That is the search for cheaper quarters on the part of the families of men out of work. Here, in a very tangible way, they beat a retreat, into fewer and fewer rooms, into apartments with less and less comfort, into basements and into fire traps on which no rent is collected. . . .

In the course of it all they sacrifice those conveniences which we associate with the American standard of living. The apartment to which the Mullinses moved, for example, had no bath and only an outside toilet. The two-room shack that the Handels found was little better than a woodshed with its lack of heat and light and water. But even if the family stays on in the same house, what we call the necessities of life may drop out. Our neighbor, Mrs. White, kept her household sitting in the dark, evenings. "Our gas is a twenty-five-cent meter and we didn't have it unless we had the quarter." Repeatedly we hear of lodgers and boarders being "taken in" and between the lines this may mean overcrowding beyond the limits of decency. As many of our families took in boarders as moved; it was an expedient to stave off moving. A line of escape lies in breaking up the home altogether. Among young couples, the man goes back to his people, the wife to hers, and if there are children, she takes them with her. In some instances the children are "put away" in some charitable institution; and in our city of Philadelphia we have had the anomaly these years that while neither the city nor the private philanthropies have had money enough for families out of work, there were always the orphanages and other children's institutions. We could break up a family, but we could not hold it together.

It is hard to think that these disruptions of family life and standards are desirable ways to meet the difficulties such households confront. We can see the helplessness of individuals who thus try to adjust themselves to the changes of industry, with the grocery bill rolling up, back rent accumulating, and the house growing cold in the face of unsteady employment. There is nothing seasonal in the need for food and shelter, and the working man faces a steady demand for his pay envelope in the face of a fluctuating need for his work. "You just can't do with odd jobs and a family. You've got to have that pay envelope every week, or the children don't eat," says Mrs. Raymond.

Cutting Down on Food]

And as the assault on everyday living presses more and more inexorably, the families dig themselves in deeper. As Mrs. Cardani in New York put it to Mrs. Nelson, "You know what we do? If we pay the rent and there isn't enough left, you know what we do. If we're going to live honest, you know what we do." "We eat little—that's what we do," broke in her little girl, thinking her mother had not made herself clear. The Tiorsis of Boston "pulled in their belts." The Giaimos of Madison fed their children all the time on potatoes and bread, with beans for meat. The Monterey children in New Orleans picked up scraps of meat and vegetables cast aside in the market. One winter the Bertleys of Atlanta with their four children managed on less than $5 a week for groceries. This meant that the family ate only two meals a day consisting of corn bread, salt meat and dried beans. When Mrs. Bertley had several fainting spells, they finally got her to a doctor who said that she was not getting enough to eat. . . .

Cutting down on food, then, is one thing the family does for itself. In every third of our neighborhood cases, the families had done it so radically as to prompt the investigator to remark upon it. The unmistakable evidences of malnutrition noted in case after case, and the prevalence among them of sickness that have roots in a weakened resistance, would not lead us to think lightly of this as something society should encourage as a recourse against unemployment.

The Mother Goes to Work]

There is still another reserve that the family finds within itself. The mother goes out to work—for she can often get a job when the man cannot. . . . When the bankers and industrialists, the engineers and managers have not, in their organizations of industry, enough work for the men, enter Mrs. Jenkins, Mrs. Levy, Mrs. Carbino, and the rest.

The stories abound in the results of the double load on their

shoulders. Mrs. Moran was taken ill from lifting too heavy pails
of water in her cleaning job. After two months on her back she
returned to work. Mrs. Walther, who had been doing part-time
work, undertook a full-time position. She went on twelve-hour
night duty at a hospital. In this way she was able to keep her
home and take care of her son during the day. Several months
of this was followed by a nervous breakdown and she spent
months herself as a patient in a hospital. Mrs. Cardani stays up
until one, two, or three o'clock every night trying to keep the
house clean and the children's clothes fit to wear to school. "Maybe
next summer if he gets a job I'll get a chance to rest up," she
says. A near neighbor of ours in Philadelphia cleaned offices in
the daytime and again at night. Her children were asked where
she slept. "Oh, she puts her head down on the table after supper,
and sleeps until she goes out at ten."

As is well known to us who watch the women of our unemployed
coming to the rescue, the courage and the devotion of
these women are not exceptional. But even if they rise to it, that
cannot satisfy those of us who look on.

Still less can we be content that in one out of three of such
families there are children who can be and are taken from school
and put to work. Surely that is not the recourse we are looking
for.

Security]

If these stories, as we believe, are fair cross-sections of experience,
then unemployment strikes in two ways at the security
of wage-earning families.

First, the workman cannot be sure of holding his job. Through
all the cases runs the evidence that perserverance, skill, education,
health, long and excellent work records—that none of these
stands "the breadwinner in certain stead when the bad word is
handed down."

Second, the workman's family has no surety in tiding over the
time he is out of work. Our analyses of the lines on which these
hundred and fifty families fell back in their trouble showed that
neither savings in cash, nor in homes, furniture, or personal keepsakes,
neither charity nor getting into debt to butcher and baker,
neither moving to cheaper quarters nor scrimping on food, nor

the enforced labor of mothers and children gave adequate assurance of livelihood when broken work or no work at all drove these families back on their own resources. All combined, these makeshifts did not offer a reasonable solution of their predicament nor one which we should tolerate as part of our going life. . . .

The ills that flesh is heir to will always swell the stream of unemployment. Sickness, bad habits, insanity, irresponsibility, incapacity, accidents, old age and death put families on the rocks. But these are problems of health and psychiatry, or of relief or other spheres or social treatment. Our settlement study sought to disentangle the unemployed from the unemployable by dealing only with families whose predicament was due to industrial causes outside their control.

Under any scheme of protection which would make industry and the consuming public co-partners in insuring against such risks of broken work, the benefits would cover only a comparatively small share of the loss from broken earnings. The greater share would continue to be borne by the families and the dislodged wage-earners themselves. If these case-stories show anything they show that most families can be counted upon to shoulder that share with fortitude. The benefits would create a minimum social provision against the more extreme forms of distress; and their receipt would come not as an affront to the instinct for self-dependence but as part of the bargain of livelihood for those whose fortunes are bound up in the operation of American industry.

No one who reads any number of these case-records can feel happy in his mind that we should leave it to people so disadvantaged to combat, single-handed, the industrial changes and dislocations which tear at the structure of their homes.

3

The Terror of Unemployment
Albert Maltz's "The Happiest Man on Earth"

Given the impact of hard times on every aspect of American life in the 1930s, it is understandable that artists and authors, particularly those young men and women who came of age in the years of the Great Depression, should have sought to record and interpret the human agony and demoralization that attended social catastrophe they witnessed everywhere about them. The temptation to turn paintings into political posters and to make the pen serve the ends of social protest was not easily resisted. It was natural that many creative persons became propagandists for social reconstruction in an age when even the cleverest of politicians proved unable fully to restore production and employment. Albert Maltz, whose association with various left-of-center causes in the 1930s indicated his political sympathies, was capable of high-level polemicism; but he could also rise above the level of harangue as he did in his prize-winning "The Happiest Man on Earth," first published in *Harper's Magazine* in 1938. Here, by understatement, the horrifying poignancy of prolonged unemployment is portrayed with true artistic integrity. Leo Gurko's *The Angry Decade* (New York: Dodd, Mead, 1947) is a lively account of social discontent during the 1930s. In Daniel Aaron's *Writers on the Left* (New York: Harcourt, Brace & World, Inc., 1961) the reader can find a serious analysis and critical evaluation of proletarian literature in the Depression years. In reading this short story, note (1) what means the author used to portray the desperation of the protagonist, Jesse Fulton; (2) what elements are involved in the ambiguous position of Tom Brackett; and (3) what devices the author used to suggest the profundity of pathos at the heart of the simple story.

Albert Maltz, "The Happiest Man on Earth," in Harry Hansen (ed.), *O. Henry Memorial Award Prize Stories of 1938* (New York: Doubleday, Doran and Company, 1938), pp. 3-15. The story was originally published in *Harper's Magazine* for June, 1938. Reprinted through the courtesy of Albert Maltz and Franz J. Horch Associates, Inc.

JESSE FELT READY TO WEEP. HE HAD BEEN SITTING
in the shanty waiting for Tom to appear, grateful
for the chance to rest his injured foot, quietly, joyously, anticipat-
ing the moment when Tom would say, "Why, of course, Jesse,
you can start whenever you're ready!"

For two weeks he had been pushing himself, from Kansas
City, Missouri, to Tulsa, Oklahoma, through nights of rain and a
week of scorching sun, without sleep or a decent meal, sustained
by the vision of that one moment. And then Tom had come into
the office. He had come in quickly, holding a sheaf of papers in
his hand; he had glanced at Jesse only casually, it was true—
but long enough. He had not known him. He had turned away.
. . . And Tom Brackett was his brother-in-law.

Was it his clothes? Jesse knew he looked terrible. He had tried
to spruce up at a drinking fountain in the park, but even that
had gone badly; in his excitement he had cut himself shaving,
an ugly gash down the side of his cheek. And nothing could get
the red gumbo dust out of his suit even though he had slapped
himself till both arms were worn out. . . . Or was it just that he
had changed so much?

True, they hadn't seen each other for five years; but Tom
looked five years older, that was all. He was still Tom. God!
was *he* so different?

Brackett finished his telephone call. He leaned back in his
swivel chair and glanced over at Jesse with small, clear blue eyes
that were suspicious and unfriendly. He was a heavy, paunchy
man of forty-five, auburn-haired, rather dour-looking; his face
was meaty, his features pronounced and forceful, his nose somewhat bulbous and reddish-hued at the tip. He looked like a
solid, decent, capable businessman who was commander of his
local branch of the American Legion—which he was. He surveyed Jesse with cold indifference, manifestly unwilling to spend
time on him. Even the way he chewed his toothpick seemed
contemptuous to Jesse.

"Yes?" Brackett said suddenly. "What do you want?"

His voice was decent enough, Jesse admitted. He had expected it to be worse. He moved up to the wooden counter that partitioned the shanty. He thrust a hand nervously through his tangled hair.

"I guess you don't recognize me, Tom," he said falteringly. "I'm Jesse Fulton."

"Huh?" Brackett said. That was all.

"Yes, I am, and Ella sends you her love."

Brackett rose and walked over to the counter until they were face to face. He surveyed Fulton incredulously, trying to measure the resemblance to his brother-in-law as he remembered him. This man was tall, about thirty. That fitted! He had straight good features and a lank erect body. That was right too. But the face was too gaunt, the body too spiny under the baggy clothes for him to be sure. His brother-in-law had been a solid, strong young man with muscle and beef to him. It was like looking at a faded, badly taken photograph and trying to recognize the subject: the resemblance was there but the difference was tremendous. He searched the eyes. They at least seemed definitely familiar, gray, with a curiously shy but decent look in them. He had liked that about Fulton.

Jesse stood quiet. Inside he was seething. Brackett was like a man examining a piece of broken-down horseflesh; there was a look of pure pity in his eyes. It made Jesse furious. He knew he wasn't as far gone as all that.

"Yes, I believe you are," Brackett said finally, "but you sure have changed."

"By God, it's five years, ain't it?" Jesse said resentfully. "You only saw me a couple of times anyway." Then, to himself, with his lips locked together, in mingled vehemence and shame, What if I have changed? Don't everybody? I ain't no corpse.

"You was solid-looking," Brackett continued softly, in the same tone of incredulous wonder. "You lost weight, I guess?"

Jesse kept silent. He needed Brackett too much to risk antagonizing him. But it was only by deliberate effort that he could keep from boiling over. The pause lengthened, became painful. Brackett flushed. "Jiminy Christmas, excuse me," he burst out in apology. He jerked the counter up. "Come in. Take a seat.

Good God, boy"—he grasped Jesse's hand and shook it—"I *am* glad to see you; don't think anything else! You just looked so peaked."

"It's all right," Jesse murmured. He sat down, thrusting his hand through his curly, tangled hair.

"Why are you limping?"

"I stepped on a stone; it jagged a hole through my shoe." Jesse pulled his feet back under the chair. He was ashamed of his shoes. They had come from the relief originally, and two weeks on the road had about finished them. All morning, with a kind of delicious, foolish solemnity, he had been vowing to himself that before anything else, before even a suit of clothes, he was going to buy himself a brand-new strong pair of shoes.

Brackett kept his eyes off Jesse's feet. He knew what was bothering the boy and it filled his heart with pity. The whole thing was appalling. He had never seen anyone who looked more down and out. His sister had been writing to him every week, but she hadn't told him they were as badly off as this.

"Well now, listen," Brackett began, "tell me things. How's Ella?"

"Oh, she's pretty good," Jesse replied absently. He had a soft, pleasing, rather shy voice that went with his soft gray eyes. He was worrying over how to get started.

"And the kids?"

"Oh, they're fine. . . . Well, you know," Jesse added, becoming more attentive, "the young one has to wear a brace. He can't run around, you know. But he's smart. He draws pictures and he does things, you know."

"Yes," Brackett said. "That's good." He hesitated. There was a moment's silence. Jesse fidgeted in his chair. Now that the time had arrived, he felt awkward. Brackett leaned forward and put his hand on Jesse's knee, "Ella didn't tell me things were so bad for you, Jesse. I might have helped."

"Well, goodness," Jesse returned softly, "you been having your own troubles, ain't you?"

"Yes," Brackett leaned back. His ruddy face became mournful and darkly bitter. "You know I lost my hardware shop?"

"Well, sure, of course," Jesse answered, surprised. "You wrote us. That's what I mean."

"I forgot," Brackett said. "I keep on being surprised over it myself. Not that it was worth much," he added bitterly. "It was running downhill for three years. I guess I just wanted it because it was mine." He laughed pointlessly, without mirth. "Well, tell me about yourself," he asked. "What happened to the job you had?"

Jesse burst out abruptly, with agitation, "Let it wait, Tom, I got something on my mind."

"It ain't you and Ella?" Brackett interrupted anxiously.

"Why no!" Jesse sat back. "Why however did you come to think that? Why Ella and me—" He stopped, laughing. "Why, Tom, I'm just crazy about Ella. Why she's just wonderful. She's just my whole life, Tom."

"Excuse me. Forget it." Brackett chuckled uncomfortably, turned away. The naked intensity of the youth's burst of love had upset him. It made him wish savagely that he could do something for them. They were both too decent to have had it so hard. Ella was like this boy too, shy and a little soft.

"Tom, listen," Jesse said, "I come here on purpose." He thrust his hand through his hair. "I want you to help me."

"Damn it, boy," Brackett groaned. He had been expecting this. "I can't much. I only get thirty-five a week and I'm damn grateful for it."

"Sure, I know," Jesse emphasized excitedly. He was feeling once again the wild, delicious agitation that had possessed him in the early hours of the morning. "I know you can't help us with money! But we met a man who works for you! He was in our city! He said you could give me a job!"

"Who said?"

"Oh, why didn't you tell me?" Jesse burst out reproachfully. "Why as soon as I heard it I started out. For two weeks now I been pushing ahead like crazy."

Brackett groaned aloud. "You come walking from Kansas City in two weeks so I could give you a job?"

"Sure, Tom, of course. What else could I do?"

"God Almighty, there ain't no jobs, Jesse! It's a slack season.
And you don't know this oil business. It's special. I got my
Legion friends here but they couldn't do nothing now. Don't
you think I'd ask for you as soon as there was a chance?"

Jesse felt stunned. The hope of the last two weeks seemed
rolling up into a ball of agony in his stomach. Then, frantically,
he cried, "But listen, this man said *you* could hire! He *told* me!
He drives trucks for you! He said you *always* need men!"

"Oh! . . . You mean *my* department?" Brackett said in a low
voice.

"*Yes*, Tom. That's it!"

"Oh no, you don't want to work in my department," Brackett
told him in the same low voice. "You don't know what it is."

"Yes, I do," Jesse insisted. "He told me all about it, Tom. You're
a dispatcher, ain't you? You send the dynamite trucks out?"

"Who was the man, Jesse?"

"Everett, Everett, I think."

"Egbert? Man about my size?" Brackett asked slowly.

"Yes, Egbert. He wasn't a phony, was he?"

Brackett laughed. For the second time his laughter was curiously without mirth. "No, he wasn't a phony." Then, in a
changed voice: "Jiminy, boy, you should have asked me before
you trekked all the way down here."

"Oh, I didn't want to," Jesse explained with naïve cunning.
"I knew you'd say no. He told me it was risky work, Tom. But
I don't care."

Brackett locked his fingers together. His solid, meaty face
become very hard. "I'm going to say no anyway, Jesse."

Jesse cried out. It had not occurred to him that Brackett would
not agree. It had seemed as though reaching Tulsa were the only
problem he had to face. "Oh no," he begged, "you can't. Ain't
there any jobs, Tom?"

"Sure, there's jobs. There's even Egbert's job if you want it."

"He's quit?"

"He's dead!"

"Oh!"

"On the job, Jesse. Last night if you want to know."

"Oh!" . . . Then, "I don't care!"

"Now you listen to me," Brackett said. "I'll tell you a few things that you should have asked before you started out. It ain't dynamite you drive. They don't use anything as safe as dynamite in drilling oil wells. They wish they could, but they can't. It's nitroglycerin! Soup!"

"But I know," Jesse told him reassuringly. "He advised me, Tom. You don't have to think I don't know."

"Shut up a minute," Brackett ordered angrily. "Listen! You just have to *look* at this soup, see? You just *cough* loud and it blows! You know how they transport it? In a can that's shaped like this, see, like a fan? That's to give room for compartments, because each compartment has to be lined with rubber. That's the only way you can even *think* of handling it."

"Listen, Tom—"

"Now wait a minute, Jesse. For God's sake just put your mind to this. I know you had your heart set on a job, but you've got to understand. This stuff goes only in special trucks! At night! They got to follow a special route! They can't go through any city! If they lay over, it's got to be in a special garage! Don't you see what that means? Don't that tell you how dangerous it is?"

"I'll drive careful," Jesse said. "I know how to handle a truck. I'll drive slow."

Brackett groaned. "Do you think Egbert didn't drive careful or know how to handle a truck?"

"Tom," Jesse said earnestly, "you can't scare me. I got my mind fixed on only one thing: Egbert said he was getting a dollar a mile. He was making five to six hundred dollars a month for half a month's work, he said. Can I get the same?"

"Sure, you can get the same," Brackett told him savagely. "A dollar a mile. It's easy. But why do you think the company has to pay so much? It's easy—until you run over a stone that your headlights didn't pick out, like Egbert did. Or get a blowout! Or get something in your eye, so the wheel twists and you jar the truck! Or any other God damn thing that nobody ever knows! We can't ask Egbert what happened to him. There's no truck to give any evidence. There's no corpse. There's nothing! Maybe tomorrow somebody'll find a piece of twisted steel way

off in a cornfield. But we never find the driver. Not even a fin-
gernail. All we know is that he don't come in on schedule. Then
we wait for the police to call us. You know what happened last
night? Something went wrong on a bridge. Maybe Egbert was
nervous. Maybe he brushed the side with his fender. Only
there's no bridge any more. No truck. No Egbert. Do you understand now? That's what you get for your God damn dollar
a mile!"

There was a moment of silence. Jesse sat twisting his long
thin hands. His mouth was sagging open, his face was agonized.
Then he shut his eyes and spoke softly. "I don't care about that,
Tom. You told me. Now you got to be good to me and give me
the job."

Brackett slapped the palm of his hand down on his desk.
"No!"

"Listen, Tom," Jesse said softly, "you just don't understand."
He opened his eyes. They were filled with tears. They made
Brackett turn away. "Just look at me, Tom. Don't that tell you
enough? What did you think of me when you first saw me? You
thought: 'Why don't that bum go away and stop panhandling?'
Didn't you, Tom? Tom, I just can't live like this any more. I got
to be able to walk down the street with my head up."

"You're crazy," Brackett muttered. "Every year there's one out
of five drivers gets killed. That's the average. What's worth
that?"

"Is my life worth anything now? We're just starving at home,
Tom. They ain't put us back on relief yet."

"Then you should have told me," Brackett exclaimed harshly.
"It's your own damn fault. A man has no right to have false
pride when his family ain't eating. I'll borrow some money and
we'll telegraph it to Ella. Then you go home and get back on
relief."

"And then what?"

"And then wait, God damn it! You're no old man. You got no
right to throw your life away. Sometime you'll get a job."

"No!" Jesse jumped up. "No. I believed that too. But I don't
now," he cried passionately. "I ain't getting a job no more than
you're getting your hardware store back. I lost my skill, Tom.
Linotyping is skilled work. I'm rusty now. I've been six years on

relief. The only work I've had is pick and shovel. When I got
that job this spring I was supposed to be an A-1 man. But I
wasn't. And they got new machines now. As soon as the slack
started they let me out."

"So what? Brackett said harshly. "Ain't there other jobs?"

"How do I know?" Jesse replied. "There ain't been one for
six years. I'd even be afraid to take one now. It's been too hard
waiting so many weeks to get back on relief."

"Well you got to have some courage," Brackett shouted.
"You've got to keep up hope."

"I got all the courage you want," Jesse retorted vehemently,
"but no, I ain't got no hope. The hope has dried up in me in six
years waiting. You're the only hope I got."

"You're crazy," Brackett muttered. "I won't do it. For God's
sake think of Ella for a minute."

"Don't you *know* I'm thinking about her?" Jesse asked softly.
He plucked at Brackett's sleeve. "That's what decided me, Tom."
His voice became muted into a hushed, pained whisper. "The
night Egbert was at our house I looked at Ella like I'd seen her
for the first time. *She ain't pretty any more, Tom!*" Brackett
jerked his head and moved away. Jesse followed him, taking a
deep, sobbing breath. "Don't that tell you, Tom? Ella was like
a little doll or something, you remember. I couldn't walk down
the street without somebody turning to look at her. She ain't
twenty-nine yet, Tom, and she ain't pretty no more."

Brackett sat down with his shoulders hunched up wearily. He
gripped his hands together and sat leaning forward, staring at
the floor.

Jesse stood over him, his gaunt face flushed with emotion,
almost unpleasant in its look of pleading and bitter humility.
"I ain't done right for Ella, Tom. Ella deserved better. This is
the only chance I see in my whole life to do something for her.
I've just been a failure."

"Don't talk nonsense," Brackett commented without rancor.
"You ain't a failure. No more than me. There's millions of men
in the identical situation. It's just the depression, or the recession, or the God damn New Deal, or . . .!" He swore and lapsed
into silence.

"Oh no," Jesse corrected him in a knowing, sorrowful tone,

"those things maybe excuse other men. But not me. It was up to me to do better. This is my own fault!"

"Oh, beans!" Brackett said. "It's more sun spots than it's you!"

Jesse's face turned an unhealthy mottled red. It looked swollen. "Well I don't care," he cried wildly. "I don't care! You got to give me this! I got to lift my head up. I went through one stretch of hell but I can't go through another. You want me to keep looking at my little boy's legs and tell myself if I had a job he wouldn't be like that? Every time he walks he says to me, 'I got soft bones from the rickets and you give it to me because you didn't feed me right.' Jesus Christ, Tom, you think I'm going to sit there and watch him like that another six years?"

Brackett leaped to his feet. "So what if you do?" he shouted. "You say you're thinking about Ella. How's she going to like it when you get killed?"

"Maybe I won't," Jesse pleaded. "I've got to have some luck sometime."

"That's what they all think," Brackett replied scornfully. "When you take this job your luck is a question mark. The only thing certain is that sooner or later you get killed."

"Okay then," Jesse shouted back. "Then I do! But meanwhile I got something, don't I? I can buy a pair of shoes. Look at me! I can buy a suit that don't say 'Relief' by the way it fits. I can smoke cigarettes. I can buy some candy for the kids. I can eat some myself. Yes, by God, I want to eat some candy. I want a glass of beer once a day. I want Ella dressed up. I want her to eat meat three times a week, four times maybe. I want to take my family to the movies."

Brackett sat down. "Oh, shut up," he said wearily.

"No," Jesse told him softly, passionately, "you can't get rid of me. Listen, Tom," he pleaded, "I got it all figured out. On six hundred a month look how much I can save! If I last only three months, look how much it is—a thousand dollars—more! And maybe I'll last longer. Maybe a couple years. I can fix Ella up for life!"

"You said it," Brackett interposed. "I suppose you think she'll enjoy living when you're on a job like that?"

"I got it all figured out," Jesse answered excitedly. "She don't know, see? I tell her I make only forty. You put the rest in a bank account for her, Tom."

"Oh, shut up," Brackett said. "You think you'll be happy? Every minute, waking and sleeping, you'll be wondering if tomorrow you'll be dead. And the worst days will be your days off, when you're not driving. They have to give you every other day free to get your nerve back. And you lay around the house eating your heart out. That's how happy you'll be."

Jesse laughed. "I'll be happy! Don't you worry, I'll be so happy, I'll be singing. Lord God, Tom, I'm going to feel *proud* of myself for the first time in seven years!"

"Oh, shut up, shut up," Brackett said.

The little shanty became silent. After a moment Jesse whispered: "You got to, Tom. You got to. You got to."

Again there was silence. Brackett raised both hands to his head, pressing the palms against his temples.

"Tom, Tom—" Jesse said.

Brackett sighed. "Oh, God damn it," he said finally, "all right, I'll take you on, God help me." His voice was low, hoarse, infinitely weary. "If you're ready to drive tonight, you can drive tonight."

Jesse didn't answer. He couldn't. Brackett looked up. The tears were running down Jesse's face. He was swallowing and trying to speak, but only making an absurd, gasping noise.

"I'll send a wire to Ella," Brackett said in the same hoarse, weary voice. "I'll tell her you got a job, and you'll send her fare in a couple of days. You'll have some money then—that is, if you last the week out, you jackass!"

Jesse only nodded. His heart felt so close to bursting that he pressed both hands against it, as though to hold it locked within his breast.

"Come back here at six o'clock," Brackett said. "Here's some money. Eat a good meal."

"Thanks," Jesse whispered.

"Wait a minute," Brackett said. "Here's my address." He wrote it on a piece of paper. "Take any car going that way. Ask the conductor where to get off. Take a bath and get some sleep."

"Thanks," Jesse said. "Thanks, Tom."

"Oh, get out of here," Brackett said.

"Tom."

"What?"

"I just—" Jesse stopped. Brackett saw his face. The eyes were still glistening with tears, but the gaunt face was shining now with a kind of fierce radiance.

Brackett turned away. "I'm busy," he said.

Jesse went out. The wet film blinded him but the whole world seemed to have turned golden. He limped slowly, with the blood pounding his temples and a wild, incommunicable joy in his heart. "I'm the happiest man in the world," he whispered to himself. "I'm the happiest man on the whole earth."

Brackett sat watching till finally Jesse turned the corner of the alley and disappeared. Then he hunched himself over, with his head in his hands. His heart was beating painfully, like something old and clogged. He listened to it as it beat. He sat in desperate tranquillity, gripping his head in his hands.

4

The Philosophy of the New Deal

Franklin D. Roosevelt's
Second Inaugural Address, January 20, 1937

The thumping mandate that FDR won in November, 1936 had no equal in twentieth-century politics. It was a Democratic party victory from City Hall to the White House; it was also a victory for the New Deal. In his Second Inaugural Address, the President set forth some of the philosophical foundations upon which the New Deal rested. Particularly did he stress the positive role of government in establishing mastery over the drift of history, and in so doing he drew upon that ancient American confidence that men, by taking thought and acting through the instrumentalities of democratic republican government, could shape their own destiny. Progress required, however, not only social engineering but faith in the future as well. Among the extensive literature on Roosevelt and the New Deal, William E. Leuchtenburg's *Franklin D. Roosevelt and the New Deal, 1932-1940* (New York: Harper & Row, 1963) stands out as one of the most comprehensive and balanced summary evaluations. Arthur M. Schlesinger, Jr.'s three-volume *The Age of Roosevelt* (Boston: Houghton Mifflin, 1957-1960) provides a lively, detailed account down to 1937. Note (1) how Roosevelt sought to reconcile the contradictory demands of security and liberty; (2) what elements comprised the President's inventory of unfinished business; and (3) what proposals the President advanced to deal with this bill of particulars.

My FELLOW COUNTRYMEN:

When four years ago we met to inaugurate a President, the Republic, single-minded in anxiety, stood in spirit here. We dedicated ourselves to the fulfillment of a vision—to

Franklin D. Roosevelt, "The Second Inaugural Address, January 20, 1937," in Samuel I. Rosenman (ed.), *The Public Papers and Addresses of Franklin D. Roosevelt,* Vol. 6 (New York: The Macmillan Company, 1941), pp. 1-6. Reprinted through the courtesy of the trustees of the Franklin D. Roosevelt trust and of Samuel I. Rosenman.

speed the time when there would be for all the people that security and peace essential to the pursuit of happiness. We of the Republic pledged ourselves to drive from the temple of our ancient faith those who had profaned it; to end by action, tireless and unafraid, the stagnation and despair of that day. We did those first things first.

Our covenant with ourselves did not stop there. Instinctively we recognized a deeper need—the need to find through government the instrument of our united purpose to solve for the individual the ever-rising problems of a complex civilization. Repeated attempts at their solution without the aid of government had left us baffled and bewildered. For, without that aid, we had been unable to create those moral controls over the services of science which are necessary to make science a useful servant instead of a ruthless master of mankind. To do this we knew that we must find practical controls over blind economic forces and blindly selfish men.

We of the Republic sensed the truth that democratic government has innate capacity to protect its people against disasters once considered inevitable, to solve problems once considered unsolvable. We would not admit that we could not find a way to master economic epidemics just as, after centuries of fatalistic suffering, we had found a way to master epidemics of disease. We refused to leave the problems of our common welfare to be solved by the winds of chance and the hurricanes of disaster.

In this we Americans were discovering no wholly new truth; we were writing a new chapter in our book of self-government.

This year marks the one hundred and fiftieth anniversary of the Constitutional Convention which made us a nation. At that Convention our forefathers found the way out of the chaos which followed the Revolutionary War; they created a strong government with powers of united action sufficient then and now to solve problems utterly beyond individual or local solution. A century and a half ago they established the Federal Government in order to promote the general welfare and secure the blessings of liberty to the American people.

Today we invoke those same powers of government to achieve the same objectives.

Four years of new experience have not belied our historic instinct. They hold out the clear hope that government within communities, government within the separate States, and government of the United States can do the things the times require, without yielding its democracy. Our tasks in the last four years did not force democracy to take a holiday.

Nearly all of us recognize that as intricacies of human relationships increase, so power to govern them also must increase—power to stop evil; power to do good. The essential democracy of our nation and the safety of our people depend not upon the absence of power but upon lodging it with those whom the people can change or continue at stated intervals through an honest and free system of elections. The Constitution of 1787 did not make our democracy impotent.

In fact, in these last four years, we have made the exercise of all power more democratic; for we have begun to bring private autocratic powers into their proper subordination to the public's government. The legend that they were invincible—above and beyond the processes of a democracy—has been shattered. They have been challenged and beaten.

Our progress out of the depression is obvious. But that is not all that you and I mean by the new order of things. Our pledge was not merely to do a patchwork job with second-hand materials. By using the new materials of social justice we have undertaken to erect on the old foundations a more enduring structure for the better use of future generations.

In that purpose we have been helped by achievements of mind and spirit. Old truths have been relearned; untruths have been unlearned. We have always known that heedless self-interest was bad morals; we know now that it is bad economics. Out of the collapse of a prosperity whose builders boasted their practicality has come the conviction that in the long run economic morality pays. We are beginning to wipe out the line that divides the practical from the ideal; and in so doing we are fashioning an instrument of unimagined power for the establishment of a morally better world.

This new understanding undermines the old admiration of worldly success as such. We are beginning to abandon our tolerance of the abuse of power by those who betray for profit the elementary decencies of life.

In this process evil things formerly accepted will not be so easily condoned. Hard-headedness will not so easily excuse hard-heartedness. We are moving toward an era of good feeling. But we realize that there can be no era of good feeling save among men of good will.

For these reasons I am justified in believing that the greatest change we have witnessed has been the change in the moral climate of America.

Among men of good will, science and democracy together offer an ever-richer life and ever-larger satisfaction to the individual. With this change in our moral climate and our rediscovered ability to improve our economic order, we have set our feet upon the road of enduring progress.

Shall we pause now and turn our back upon the road that lies ahead? Shall we call this the promised land? Or, shall we continue on our way? For "each age is a dream that is dying, or one that is coming to birth."

Many voices are heard as we face a great decision. Comfort says, "Tarry a while." Opportunism says, "This is a good spot." Timidity asks, "How difficult is the road ahead?"

True, we have come far from the days of stagnation and despair. Vitality has been preserved. Courage and confidence have been restored. Mental and moral horizons have been extended.

But our present gains were won under the pressure of more than ordinary circumstance. Advance became imperative under the goad of fear and suffering. The times were on the side of progress.

To hold to progress today, however, is more difficult. Dulled conscience, irresponsibility and ruthless self-interest already reappear. Such symptoms of prosperity may become portents of disaster! Prosperity already tests the persistence of our progressive purpose.

Let us ask again: Have we reached the goal of our vision of that fourth day of March 1933? Have we found our happy valley?

I see a great nation, upon a great continent, blessed with a great wealth of natural resources. Its hundred and thirty million people are at peace among themselves; they are making their country a good neighbor among the nations. I see a United States which can demonstrate that, under democratic methods of government, national wealth can be translated into a spreading volume of human comforts hitherto unknown, and the lowest standard of living can be raised far above the level of mere subsistence.

But here is the challenge to our democracy: In this nation I see tens of millions of its citizens—a substantial part of its whole population—who at this very moment are denied the greater part of what the very lowest standards of today call the necessities of life.

I see millions of families trying to live on incomes so meager that the pall of family disaster hangs over them day by day.

I see millions whose daily lives in city and on farm continue under conditions labeled indecent by a so-called polite society half a century ago.

I see millions denied education, recreation and the opportunity to better their lot and the lot of their children.

I see millions lacking the means to buy the products of farm and factory and by their poverty denying work and productiveness to many other millions.

I see one-third of a nation ill-housed, ill-clad, ill-nourished.

It is not in despair that I paint you that picture. I paint it for you in hope—because the nation, seeing and understanding the injustice in it, proposes to paint it out. We are determined to make every American citizen the subject of his country's interest and concern; and we will never regard any faithful law-abiding group within our borders as superfluous. The test of our progress is not whether we add more to the abundance of those who have much; it is whether we provide enough for those who have too little.

If I know aught of the spirit and purpose of our nation, we will not listen to Comfort, Opportunism, and Timidity. We will carry on.

Overwhelmingly, we of the Republic are men and women of good will; men and women who have more than warm hearts of

dedication; men and women who have cool heads and willing
hands of practical purpose as well. They will insist that every
agency of popular government use effective instruments to carry
out their will.

Government is competent when all who compose it work as
trustees for the whole people. It can make constant progress
when it keeps abreast of all the facts. It can obtain justified
support and legitimate criticism when the people receive true
information of all that government does.

If I know aught of the will of our people, they will demand
that these conditions of effective government shall be created
and maintained. They will demand a nation uncorrupted by
cancers of injustice and, therefore, strong among the nations
in its example of the will to peace.

Today we reconsecrate our country to long-cherished ideals
in a suddenly changed civilization. In every land there are
always at work forces that drive men apart and forces that draw
men together. In our personal ambitions we are individualists.
But in our seeking for economic and political progress as a
nation, we all go up, or else we all go down, as one people.

To maintain a democracy of effort requires a vast amount of
patience in dealing with differing methods, a vast amount of
humility. But out of the confusion of many voices rises an understanding of dominant public need. Then political leadership
can voice common ideals, and aid in their realization.

In taking again the oath of office as President of the United
States, I assume the solemn obligation of leading the American
people forward along the road over which they have chosen to
advance.

While this duty rests upon me I shall do my utmost to speak
their purpose and to do their will, seeking Divine guidance to
help us each and every one to give light to them that sit in
darkness and to guide our feet into the way of peace.

5

Credo in a Depression Decade
Frances Perkins'
"What Is Worth Working for in America?"

Of all Franklin Roosevelt's official family, none perhaps had greater influence on the shaping of domestic policies than the spirited and pragmatic Frances Perkins. A social worker by training and experience, she bridged the older generation of pioneer reformers (Jane Addams, Florence Kelley, and Grace Abbott) and the younger generation of professional social servants (Jane Hoey, Helen Hall, and Mary Dewson, for example). She combined the moral intensity and tough, political shrewdness of the one group with the professional competence and humanitarian impulse of the other. As an adviser to Roosevelt when he was Governor of New York, she provided the social analyses and the personal inspiration which led him to endorse the principle of social insurance well before any other prominent political figure dared take such an advanced position. She exercised surpassing influence on the shaping of the great Social Security Act of 1935. In the field of labor, Frances Perkins helped win the right of labor to organize and bargain collectively through agents of its own choosing and the establishment of effective Federal government regulation over the hours, wages, and conditions of industrial employment (including the prohibition of child labor). Somehow she was able to ride out the storms of labor-capital strife in the 1930s and make significant contributions to the mobilization of manpower during World War II. Through all these events, she maintained a simple poise that so often annoyed her political enemies. "What Is Worth Working for in America?"—like so many of her public addresses—demonstrates that peculiar combination of sophistication and simplicity which was her trademark. Her own books—*People at Work* (New York: The John Day Company, 1934) and *The Roosevelt I Knew* (New York: The

Frances Perkins, "What Is Worth Working for in America?" *Proceedings of the National Conference of Social Work, 1941* (New York: Columbia University Press, 1941), pp. 32-40. Reprinted through the courtesy of the National Conference on Social Welfare.

Viking Press, 1946)—make vital contributions to the understanding of the New Deal. Broadus Mitchell's *Depression Decade, 1929-1941* (New York: Rinehart, 1947) remains one of the best surveys of political and economic issues in those years. The reader will wish to note (1) what significance Miss Perkins gave to such words as "good," "moral sense," "common good," and "spiritual sense"; (2) what the Secretary of Labor thought were the ends and the means of modern democracy; (3) what role she saw for voluntary associations as agents in the achievement of social progress; and (4) the ways in which particular measures and programs underlay the political and social theories here set forth.

WE ARE A POWERFUL NATION WHICH WE KNOW AS a democracy. In the United States of America today resides a generation of people who have been formed by the ideals of democracy. They give form and substance and coherence to those conceptions of a political ideal which are necessary for permanent democracy. Democracy means to us government of the people. We are devoted to it. It underlies silently all that we do. We have long conceived that the rule of the people would be a government which had back of it certain moral judgments, certain conceptions of good, certain aspirations which grow out of moral sense; that government by the people would be government of people who had forsworn exclusive gain for themselves and were devoted for the common good.

What is good in America today? "Good" is a very old word, but it implies much and it tears at every heart. People in America know what they mean by right and wrong; and there has developed here what is essential for a free people, a certain common moral pattern which we respect, aspire to, and feel to be basic in our capacity to give a democratic way of life.

We have a bathtub, electric refrigerator and cheap automobile civilization. We have all those things, but that doesn't make a great people. Unless, back of material civilization, there is moral judgment the material civilization is ineffective. Our material civilization carries with it moral sanctions. This is the genius of our fathers and the continuing good in our modern life. A man may have liberty, all alone by himself upon a remote island, circumscribed and limited only by the elements and his own nature, but it is a meaningless liberty unless measured by, and referred to, relationship to other humans. Liberty alone may be mere loneliness; liberty within a society may be chaos; but self-discipline, agreement, and mutual aid all make a pattern of society in which not we alone, but the many are happy, comfortable, and enlightened.

What do we mean when we ask, "What is good in American life?" I am one of those people who often think of America as, "I love thy rocks and rills, I love thy templed hills"; "I love the cornfields"; "I love the great deserts"; "I love thy rock-bound coast and mighty mountains and the great waving fields of wheat." These things are beautiful. These things we all love. But back of that is our love for the quality and reality of human association which we have uniquely in these United States. Love for those genuine relationships, that true fellowship we experience, is what is back of it all and what we mean when we say, "I love America."

When you have been away from this country for a few weeks and land from the steamer, what is that strange enthusiasm that comes over you? It is a spiritual sense of the society of a free democracy. It is the people and the mutual confidence of life in America which warm the heart. It is a society of expression, it is a society of hope, which constantly and simply recognizes the dignity and worth of each individual and acts accordingly, a society which, because of this, knows a kind of corporate life. We sense that no one of us alone can realize these benefits of liberty and democracy, but that we can achieve these things together as a corporate body. This accounts for our early established and now quite natural social action in the interest of all, a reciprocal relation between citizens. As a people we have to a remarkable degree both faith in each other and hope in our common achievement. We have a kind of faith and hope of social salvation that by loving our neighbor as ourselves we can all have a good life.

In these days that is a broad basis of hope. We of the United States of America are questioning and examining ourselves in real humility as to whether or not we truly do extend this feeling of mutuality in social action to all people within the United States. And can we extend it to other peoples? In particular, these days are days of opportunity to bring forth a sense of brotherliness and neighborliness, at least to all people within this continent.

This Conference has accepted the idea that we must sustain and extend our sense of corporate democratic life and social action to embrace all people in the hemisphere. We believe this relationship will be reciprocal, and as we submit our ways of living to the influences of the civilization to the south of us, that we shall receive enrichment and strength from their ways.

Reciprocity has a double nature for those who take part in it. Each group is anxious to produce what is for the good of the other. Each promotes the life of the other. This is real reciprocity. That is what we must try. In the United States we seem to be constantly pointing out the items that are wrong and unjust and emphasizing the things we need to improve. Social maladjustment or injustice is pointed out in order that it may be faced honestly and so that we may make improvements. This is the way we have corrected those injustices and those social maladjustments in the past. This is one of our good points—the ability to make progress after self-examination and self-accusation. That has been the technique of social reform and social work in the United States. That is the way we have discovered and overcome distress.

We respect the progress that has been made by social survey, analysis, recommendation, and correction by social action. "Find the facts first" has become almost a slogan for reform. Isn't it essential for a great people to see, admit, and correct mistakes? American life is not carried on by the Government but by a larger number of free, self-compelled, self-disciplined associations of individuals related to each other in good faith for the express purpose of carrying on a particular part of American life. This is the way America is.

When I took the oath of office and swore that I would defend the Constitution it meant a great deal to me. That was in 1933, on a day fraught with modern disaster. In those few moments I looked out, as it were, on the breadth of American life from wilderness and pioneer to a modern, complicated, machine-made way of living. I realized all that had been done by our fore-fathers, all that might be done by our children, and some of what must be done by this generation to keep and build what is good in American life. One of the things that is significant is that this had been founded with purpose and intention for a free country. Perhaps that is the most important of our many blessings—that, and the fact that it was dedicated to God. . . .

We are well served in this great country by our practice of self-organization for responsible social living. Our capacity responsibly to organize the people into a great number of free associations which conduct American affairs is one of the characteristics well worth working to preserve.

One of the associations is the free trade union movement. Organizations in every field accomplish more than individuals can. It is by the same technique of association in free and needed organizations that working people will eventually take public responsibility as part of a responsible agency. Many people feel that some of our American trade unions have been irresponsible. Some of them have not shown that sense of public and group responsibility that they will ten years hence.

We know that in each human relation something new and unique appears. This is what is important in the trade unions: men are under a moral obligation to each other, and, as the trade union becomes an institution, under a moral obligation to the rest of society. In trade unions we are bound to get the sense of responsibility, the sense of contract, the new sense of social obligation, just as we do in the bar association and the medical society. Trade unions have become capable today. As they become social institutions like these others in America they will assert over-all responsibility. They promote the life of their membership, the life of their community, the life of their country. In the future their social moral sense is going to be of great importance to all communities. Society must more and more guide itself by a social moral code. We have to go by the Salva-

tion Army's saying, "A man may be down but he is never out."
Growth is necessary for social health. Nothing grows unless it
has a starting point.

We are still a growing country. We have not yet come into
our full stature. We are still trying to find a moral basis for
unity. We have come pretty near to finding a social moral code.
Many people think we are in the midst of an "every man for
himself" period, a period of greed and selfishness. I do not think
that is true. We don't practice very well under our social moral
code but we are improving. The Rotary clubs, chambers of commerce, farmers' associations, trade unions, women's clubs, all
touch all of us because they are expressive of this moral code.
Cooperate with others—do as you would be done by—keep hop-
ing—keep trying to make the world a better place—find your
own better life in company with others. Do together the great
and noble things you can't do alone. This is understood in terms
of cooperation, in rural districts; in terms of community chests
and trade unions and municipal playgrounds, in the cities. It is
an American version of the Golden Rule, of the second great
Commandment to love thy neighbor. If you say it to any casual
companion in American life he will understand you. . . .

We have made some wonderful social progress in American
life. The question raised everywhere today is whether it is good
enough. These are days of trial, and it is natural to doubt. To
point out imperfections and call that the American way of life
is to deceive ourselves. Social injustices exist, but many, many
have been corrected by conscious deliberate social action, often
by law. That is an American method too—to use law as an instrument of order and seemliness in a free and rich society. I remember children working long hours in mines, women working
on the night shifts, at a wage under a living wage. I remember
when all that was a part of American life. . . . It has been
proven over and over again that many Americans can always
be found to sponsor a movement aimed at correcting a known
abuse or misfortune.

Social justice is part of the implication of loving thy neighbor.
This spirit of willingness to correct is a part of the good in
American life. We have no right to complain about the bathtub,

electric refrigerator, cheap automobile civilization in the United States. I think it is good. I am glad so many people have bathtubs and electric refrigerators and cheap automobiles. That means improvement in material life, and when that is comfortable it helps spiritual and cultural development to go forward. It develops leadership by giving people leisure and wider social experience. . . .

In what other country do you find so many livable houses in proportion to population? In what other country are there so many people who have really had good food from childhood? In what other country are there so many people who have had such a high standard of living, of education? In what other country are there so many opportunities for an individual to escape an unfavorable environment and, with access to education, make a place for himself based on his capacity? A free people, yes; but more, a people with kindly purpose to help each other and to use social organization as a means to individual expression and development.

One of the best qualities in America is our sense of humor. We go to the heights and to the depths and find we are only human beings. This is profitable. No one of us is permitted to rise so high as to mistake himself for a long-awaited Messiah. We are able to joke about the best and the greatest of us. I have great respect for the humilities which the humor of the American press imposes upon public officialdom. In the precepts of religion we learn that if we don't manage to achieve humility, we are likely to learn it by humiliation. The cynical assault provides a reason for laughing at each other. That is not cynicism. We laugh because we say, "Look, he is just like me. I am not so good, but together we do pretty well." We should always be grateful for our capacity and freedom to laugh at those in high public office. It would be depressing if they could not be laughed at.

There is nothing for which we can give more sincere thanks than for the American home, and there are few items more worth working for. It is good even though as an institution it is harried by divorce. When the American home shows its best characteristics we see the things that are loveliest in our whole

American life. American home life tends to be a reciprocal society. We recognize in that reciprocity, that gay affection and cheerful sacrifice of each for all and all for each, the pattern of the ideal of American society. We would like to be "a family."

People like to be on good terms with each other. This is true in almost every relationship. Each of us sees special groups and knows these, largely, to be on good terms. If you had seen as much as I have of employers and workmen you would realize how much they think of each other. There was a bitter strike in 1935. Employers and workers and conciliators had met and debated, often acrimoniously, and tensely, plans of settlement, and finally there was one tentatively agreed upon. We sent it out to be typed. Then the employers and workmen sat back with their cigarettes and cigars and relaxed over a cup of coffee and waited for the stenographer to finish her dreary task. I was sitting there with them, waiting, when they began to boast about the ships they had built together. A great light dawned on me. They didn't hate each other at all. They were both saying, telling me, "We build the finest ships ever built in the world on the Delaware river. Most ably managed company in the world —finest and most skilled workmen. Can't beat our ships."

Equalitarian manners are among the hopeful features in our life. Effective relationship between the individual and his community needs these equalitarian manners. They are necessary to a businessman, required for effective professional relationships, cultivated in the American home, basic to the solution of the strains and tensions between groups of conflicting interests. What else would make a Washington taxi driver say, "Lady, shall I turn on the radio or shall we talk?" It is both respect and liking for each other. Equalitarian manners—they can be good manners, fine manners even. They grow, they lubricate our lives, and yet they spring from this moral judgment which moderates our life.

Let us put down among our blessings, among the reasons why we love this blessed country, that we have no crystallized class structure. Some rich and some poor, yes. The poor can become rich and the rich, poor, very quickly here. Life goes up and down rapidly. We are all important all the time. Anyone may be a number one man any time. This gives us a good democratic outlook and we can be thankful for it. That outlook and those manners will preserve our democratic practice even under terrible stress.

The agencies of social work have to consider what they as human beings in free association for a social program can do to develop the moral judgment back of this great social conscience which we have in American life, in our hearts, and minds. We must have these moral judgments as a guide to varied and flexible action in the difficult days ahead. How to determine right and wrong in the field of social progress and social relations? That may be the test for these organizations, so technically competent, so clearly appraising the social budget today. In the next ten years there may be many obstacles that will interfere with this progress.

This is our own country. We love it tenderly. We love it for many reasons and because it is our own. We love it with special devotion because it is a human society dedicated to certain principles of liberty, of love of mankind, of hope for human progress, which we all support. We were born into this society as into our families. We have, therefore, duties and obligations to our country as to our brethren of the flesh. "For better, for worse" we have become one with this unit of the human race—God's children. Those who built here before us built with good purpose and left us a vital growing thing, a goodly heritage. What kind of America we pass on, rests with us, under God.

6

Rebuilding the American Dream
Grace L. Coyle's
"Social Work at the Turn of the Decade"

However widespread unemployment may have been during the depressed 1930s, one professional group at least enjoyed full employment of their resources—the guild of social workers. They were kept busy at the task of administering relief, and that aspect of social service alone was enough to keep thousands of them on the job. Their special talents, however, were engaged in many other projects: in social security, slum clearance, agricultural resettlement, care for migratory workers, in recreational and educational projects under governmental auspices, and in constructive tasks of all sorts through traditional private and voluntary agencies.

Grace Coyle (1893-1962), whose presidential address before the National Conference of Social Work in 1940 is here condensed, had a long career as a scholar and a social work practitioner before she became a leading force in social work education. Based on sound experience as a settlement worker in New York City and a group worker in the coal mining regions of Pennsylvania, Miss Coyle's research and teaching (at Western Reserve University from 1934 to her death in 1962) were always deeply rooted in practical reality. Moved by a philosophy of humane pragmatism, she set down in 1940 the contributions of social service workers to the general welfare during the decade of hard times. They sought first the alleviation of human suffering, she said; but beyond that they aimed at the reconstruction of a finer and stronger society. Professional social work also elaborated a new consensus of social theory and policy which became, in time, an integral part of New Deal points of view and programs. In Dixon Wecter's *The Age of the Great Depression, 1929-1941* (New York: Macmillan, 1948) the reader can find a fine summary of social history during these years. Grace Abbott's *From Relief to Social*

Grace L. Coyle, "Social Work at the Turn of the Decade," *Proceedings of the National Conference of Social Work, 1940* (New York: Columbia University Press, 1940), pp. 3-16. Reprinted through the courtesy of the National Conference on Social Welfare.

Security (Chicago: University of Chicago Press, 1941) is still the best account of welfare policies during the depression years. In reading this selection, note (1) the component parts of Miss Coyle's philosophy of democratic, experimental social planning; (2) the ways in which particular programs were aimed at the implementation of social ideals; (3) the interrelationship of relief, recovery, reform, and preventive measures; and (4) the relationship of professional social welfare to the elaboration of public policy.

WE MEET IN THE SHADOW OF A WORLD TRAGEDY. IN the face of the destruction of human life and of the very foundation of the Western World, our concerns, both individual and collective, seem dwarfed into insignificance. We are oppressed not only by the weight of the present, but by the threat of the future. In such a time we are assembled to discuss our concerns as social workers, and in such an hour to find courage in collective effort and in the hope which makes effort possible.

The surrounding terror and hate seem to heighten for us the value of every island of peace, every stream of good will, every evidence that men are capable of generosity, of consideration, of mutual respect, of deliberative and intelligent cooperation. One of the greatest evidences of this capacity is the existence and extent of social work today. It is itself one proof of the gains made by the humane and the intelligent forces among us, and its accomplishments in the protection and enhancement of life are themselves a rampart against the engulfing barbarism which produces and which accompanies war. . . .

The year 1940 may well mark a turning point in our history. . . .

The decade of the thirties began with the great depression and ended with the beginning of a greater war. Between lie the years of mass unemployment and lowered standards of living, with all the human ills accompanying them so familiar to social workers. Such widespread human suffering, such dislocation of family and community relations cannot go on without exacting a toll, not only from the individuals involved, but also from the total society in which they occur. The depth and scope of the depression, like a social earthquake or the erosion and destruction of a great flood, have changed the national landscape.

The impact of this disaster has threatened some of the most cherished possessions of the American people. It has undermined the belief in the opportunity for economic achievement on which America has based its dreams. It has threatened with disillusion and despair the 4,000,000 youth who find all doors closed against them. It has produced a generation of old people without resources or the security necessary for a serene old age. It has uprooted farm families by the thousand and turned them into depression refugees in their own land. In addition to the lack of physical necessities essential to health and decency, this situation shatters profoundly the underlying unity of a people moving forward with hope and determination toward its common good. It raises basic questions about the soundness of our economic system and the capacity of a political democracy for dealing with its ills.

Then, as the decade closed, Europe broke into flames. Not only are human life, property, and the priceless treasures of European culture being destroyed in this conflagration, but there is also in it a deeper conflict. The slowly achieved humane impulses which gave rise to democracy itself, the values of objective truth upon which both science and human justice rest, the attempt to order relations between nations on the slowly emerging foundations of international law—all these hang in the balance. . . .

Social work, if it has insight and determination, is in a position to make a more extensive and more definite contribution to our national life than ever before. In 1930 there were approximately forty thousand social workers. In 1940 there are, according to reliable estimates, double that number. The funds, both public and private, now invested in social work have probably increased in even greater proportion. Inadequate though our resources may be in the face of constantly unmet needs, this enlarged scope of social work gives new weight to our efforts. If we recognize the significance of this, it will perhaps sharpen our sense of social responsibility. Not only are we responsible as practitioners or as laymen to the individual client and to the individual agency, but also we must, whether we will or not, have some part in the dynamic interplay of great social forces in our society. . . .

One of the most encouraging developments is the new sense of social responsibility which has expressed itself in the assumption by the community of the care of the victims of the depression. Until the mass unemployment of this period developed there was a lingering belief born of our pioneer individualism that if people were out of work or were paid low wages, it was a sign of individual shiftlessness or incompetence. That belief was largely washed out in the flood of the depression. True, it still remains here and there. It reappears in WPA jokes and comes openly into the budget hearings on relief appropriations. But the bulk of our citizens, I believe, has accepted the fact that the mass of personal misfortunes arising out of the depression is socially caused. Our first response to this understanding is the recognition that the misfortunes, therefore, must be met by the combined resources of the community. It is the widening acceptance of this conviction so long familiar to social workers which may provide a new impetus for the development of adequate social services.

The extension of government services is the chief answer which we have given to our new sense of social responsibility. We shall not have fully accepted it until we are providing for such services by adequate taxation on a permanent and equitable basis. But the steps taken in the direction of government responsibility, not only for social security and public assistance, but also for such areas as agricultural policy, flood and erosion control, and public housing are not likely to be retraced. They are, of course, not a new development. Such use of government to do for us collectively what we cannot do individually is one of the oldest ways the democratic state has found to express its basic concern for the good of all. Under our eyes during the thirties we have seen this expand with great speed and into new areas of our social life.

Arising also out of the depression experience is a new conviction slowly dawning on the American people. We are beginning to see that disasters which are socially caused must be socially cured. While we must obviously give immediate relief to the victims of a disaster, we are coming to ask whether prevention rather than relief is not a more adequate social policy. During recent years the social origins of many individual misfortunes and inadequacies so long apparent to social workers have become increasingly clear to the general public both through studies of undoubted accuracy and, more powerfully, through the wide-spread experience of the depression. The conviction that undernourished children, unemployed young people, and demoralized adult workers are a social liability is, I believe, slowly growing among us. It is a shortsighted as well as inhuman policy which only picks up the debris of a social flood and does nothing to prevent the disaster by adequate measures upstream.

One result of the appearance of this conviction during the decade can be found in the new attitude toward social planning. American culture is typically unplanned, chaotic, disjointed. This is in part rooted in the characteristics of the pioneer period just past. In part it is the very essence of free enterprise, and our conviction that if each pursues his own interest the invisible hand which guides our destiny as a nation will in some way work the separate strands into a harmonius whole. But within the thirties this faith had a rude jolt. Some of us, no doubt, remember that winter of 1933 when the idea of planning seemed to break over the American public like the crest of a wave. Some of its manifestations were crude and unsound, but the basic strength which it developed and has kept in succeeding years grew out of profound causes. The depression had given us a vivid and forceful lesson in the results of our unplanned economic order. That experience has made us ask how by foresight and planning we can forestall such disasters. Moreover, the extension of government services into various areas of our life is producing the practical necessity for extensive planning. In public housing, in soil conservation, in erosion control, in rural resettlement, in public health, in social security, and in other areas here and there in experimental fashion we are learning how to apply scientific method to human situations. One of the wholesome aspects of this present trend is its limited and concrete character. This is no utopian blanket proposal for a planned economy. This is not the regimentation of a totalitarian dictatorship by which a few plan the lives of the many for their own interest. This is the experimental, slow-moving, cautious, and often fumbling process by which a free people deals with its problems. Out of this experience we are just beginning to see our problems in country-wide and century-long terms and to envisage the preventive measures essential to the intelligent development of both the human and the material resources of this continent.

Born of our recent experience, there may be seen also, I believe, the dawn of another widespread conviction, namely, the belief that every American should have at least the essential minimum for health and decency. The appearance of this idea shows itself in the passage of the Fair Labor Standards Act, the extension of state minimum wage laws, the provisions of the Social Security Act, and the pressure to pull up the levels of public assistance. There is obviously plenty of evidence that such a standard is far from acceptance and that powerful groups and forces stand in the way of such developments. The concept of such provision as a right, not a charity, is still farther from actuality. But it seems fair to say that out of the mass unemployment of the thirties there is beginning to crystallize the belief that every member of the community should have as his right at least the mimimum basis of life.

This belief has been given some realistic underpinning by two related developments. At the very depth of the depression when standards of living were spiraling downward, several groups of economists and engineers, notably the Brookings Institute, announced that the abolition of poverty had become technically a possibility. Our resources and our technological skill are now sufficient to provide an adequate standard of living for all our population. The startling paradox of starvation in the midst of potential plenty was dramatically revealed against the contrasting blackness of the depression.

Almost equally important in its effect on the public mind was the belief which appeared from many sources at about the same time that mass production could be kept at its full capacity only if it were complemented by mass consumption. Wider mass purchasing power was hailed as the clew to stabilizing production. This belief does not have the undisputed support among economists accorded to the fact of potential plenty, but it has accumulated powerful popular influence. These two developments gave sanction and impetus to the demand for a universal minimum standard of living for all as an economic foundation. . . .

The significance of these small and hardly won gains of the great depression rests not in their emergence alone, but in the fact that they are the latest expression of the underlying stream of our democratic life. . . . We can claim to be a democracy, I believe, by virtue, not of a legal framework of representative government, although that is essential, but more by a deeply rooted conviction that is held among us. This is our traditional belief that each individual is of value and should have an opportunity to develop his powers and fulfill himself within the framework of the same need on the part of others and, moreover, that the government and other social institutions exist primarily for the benefit of the citizens. This, in turn, implies a responsibility for and participation in the control of government by all its citizens in the interest of the common good. . . .

Whether our democratic institutions and the traditions from which they spring can survive the economic dislocations of the thirties is the major issue that confronts us. We are not at present threatened as other countries are by the imposition of despotism from without. The "fifth column" which has penetrated within our gates is the malnutrition of our population, the frustration and despair of our unemployed, the racial inequalities and antagonisms heightened by economic tensions, and the inhuman cynicism of those among us who can realize these conditions without attempting to remedy them. European experience should teach us that the despair of the people is the opportunity of the dictator.

The basic issues of the forties arise, therefore, at two points. In the first place, we must preserve and strengthen the underlying attitudes essential to a democracy—attitudes of fraternal consideration for every individual, of respect for the rights of all of us to freedom of thought and speech, and of active responsibility for the public concerns of vital importance to our national life. This, however, will be insufficient unless, in the second place, we look to the economic inadequacies and inequalities which not only weaken the stamina of our people, but which also cynically refute our democratic pretensions. Beyond that we cannot be content until we have provided out of our rich resources not only the minimum essentials for health and decency, but also the opportunities for the higher attainments of a civilized people in education, recreation, and the other arts of life.

Against this social backdrop what part can we play as social workers in the strengthening of democratic attitudes and in the provision of the conditions of life which are the only convincing proof of the value of our democratic institutions?

We have as social workers, three major relationships: to our clientele, to our immediate community, and to the larger social scene. I wish to suggest in concrete terms some of the opportunities in each of these areas by which we may contribute to the extension of democratic relations and to the development of a more adequate basis for human life. . . .

The essence of social work lies in what happens through the contact of social worker and client whether that client be an applicant for public relief, a child in an institution, or a youth in a settlement club. Treatment and education are but aspects of the same process. When health is restored, or the family becomes self-supporting, or the dependent child is placed in the foster home, there still remains the question of whether life can be made rich, interesting, satisfying. This is often dependent on opportunities for further education, companionship, for creative expression during leisure time. Some of us work at one end of the scale, some at the other, but the common purpose is the growth and enhancement of the individual life. What has this, our primary purpose, to do with the preservation and development of a democratic society? . . .

This democratization of social work practice appears in every aspect of the field. In case work it has substituted understanding of each individual for individual reform and high-pressure methods. In the leisure-time agencies it replaces superimposed programs artfully designed by adults for the building of character, especially in the so-called underprivileged, by self-governing groups and programs growing out of the interests of the members. It develops in the field of relief the attempt to avoid the stigma of charity and to replace it by self-respecting work or by the concept of rights established through social insurance. Everywhere the ferment of democracy has been at work among us, and while its effect is still incomplete, the accomplishments to date give us hope that the transformation may continue.

Equally significant for the practice of social work has been the effect upon us of the developing science of personality and of society. There is no doubt that the most significant event of the twenties for social work was the application to case work practice of the growing knowledge gained from psychiatry and psychoanalysis. As powerful in the area of recreation and informal education was the similar impact of the newer educational ideas formulated especially in the progressive education movement. The effect on the two fields of work has been, I believe, similar in many ways. The application of the new psychological knowledge has deepened our understanding of the uniqueness of each individual. It has enhanced our understanding of the emotional factors in experience. It has made clear the unity of personality and the necessity for dealing with the whole person. It has developed a new respect for the need of each person to be a self-determining and, in so far as he can be, creative human being. The extent to which we have been able to apply the new scientific knowledge of personality to our own situation is one measure of our claim to being a profession. Here too our accomplishments are incomplete and are unevenly distributed over the whole field of practice. . . .

We have become increasingly aware of the need to go below the surface of individual behavior, to track symptoms back to their causes, to guide treatment by such deeper understanding. I believe we have still to acquire a similar depth of understanding of the way in which our clients and ourselves are affected by the cultural situation. Within the last few years, for example, our clients have been subjected to such tides of social change as the rise of the C.I.O., the mechanization of agriculture, and the growth of anti-Semitic or anti-alien feeling. Constantly we deal with our native sons and daughters upon whom the full impact

of our peculiar institutions of race relations has left an indelible
and often a ruinous imprint. I do not mean that we have been
unaware of the social factors affecting individuals, but I think
there is considerable evidence that while we have delved deeper
into the inner life of the individual, with increasing value to our
practice, we have been content to allow our knowledge of social
movements and social factors to remain relatively superficial.
This, in a period of severe economic maladjustment, of tremendous social dislocation, and possibly of international turmoil,
seems particularly shortsighted. Profound as our knowledge of
any individual may be, it remains superficial unless it reveals in
what ways he bears upon him the imprint of the great streams
of the cultural heritage and what part he is playing inevitably
in the creation of the society of the future. As the last decade
has deepened our understanding of the emotional and internal
factors, the forties must deepen in a similar way our knowledge
of the part of each of us in the life stream of the community.

In actual fact, we cannot work with either individuals or
groups without some set of social values derived from the larger
setting. Both treatment and education have no meaning except
as we gauge success by some idea of the socially desirable. I
believe, however, that we need to discuss more clearly the objectives and values by which we actually are governed.

Social workers, on the whole, often have been unwilling to
admit that they had values—that they could use the word "good,"
for example. They hesitate to define the norms which necessarily
are guiding treatment. This reticence about values grew, I think,
out of several circumstances. It was a reaction against the excessive and coercive moralism of the Victorian period. It was the
result of the anonymity of city life in which many of us were
ourselves enjoying the pleasures of escape from the restraints
of convention. It was an acceptance of a kind of social relativity
which said one man's judgment is as good as another's. It was
at its best an attempt to put ourselves sensitively in the place of
a client, without imposing extreme judgments of praise and
blame, in order to encourage self-direction and independent
growth. As a result, we have tended to use neutral words that
left entirely implicit our real purposes. We have talked of ad-

justment, of self-expression, of maturity, of social and antisocial behavior, of the socially desirable. This indicated our good intentions but left pleasantly vague exactly what we were driving at.

The situation here is, I believe, changing. For one thing, the clearly defined and ardently propagated values of the new totalitarian way of life have made vivid for us anew the reality of moral values. As we see the individual subordinated to the state, the rise of an elite based on race and power, the unabashed glorification of violence and trickery, we are shocked into the need for defining, in order to defend, the corresponding mores of a democratic society. We are entering, I hope, a new phase of thought in regard to treatment and education—a phase in which we feel the need of clarifying for ourselves what kind of a society we want and therefore what we mean by the social and the antisocial. We need in these days to face our responsibility for a positive—though not a moralistic—position.

And what are such values that might become a guide to practice? That is one of the problems which we must solve if we are to become an effective part of the struggle for increased democracy. I believe one difficulty with such values in the past —and of course we have had them in spite of ourselves—is that they have been concerned almost wholly with the private aspects of people's lives.

In the area of person-to-person relations, we could, I believe, if put to it, define fairly well what we believe to be our objectives. In family life, in the treatment of children, in the face-to-face relations of small groups, we could probably come to some agreement on the "socially desirable" toward which we aim. In terms of the person we have some conception of what it means to grow up as it affects the creative use of one's powers, the capacity for outgoing affection, the ability to carry responsibility and similar achievements.

However, in regard to those public relations which each individual bears to his community, we seem to me to be relatively silent. What is the normal or desirable attitude for an adult toward his participation in local politics, in the growth of organization in his industry, in the racial or nationality relations of his community? How can this youth growing up in an area of bad housing and no jobs relate himself, if at all, to the constructive forces of a changing society? So far, we are content if we can prevent delinquency in such cases. The effective development in our clients and in ourselves of those super-personal relations which reach out beyond family and friends into party, union, nationality, society, and election booth are a neglected and a significant part of our practice. These relations are significant for two reasons. First, the worth and dignity of the individual as he conceives it are, I believe, profoundly affected by these ties to a larger whole. Where such relations develop as they should, they give balance, perspective, and meaning to life. More than that, the very existence of a democratic society depends upon the acceptance by its citizens of a responsible relation to public issues and their ability to handle them effectively.

We deal in our clientele with thousands of individuals. Some of these have been rendered hostile to the organized forces of society by unfortunate environment or individual maladjustments. Many more are inert, unawakened to their own stake in the community life about them, and so of little positive value in the creation of a sound community by democratic means. Obviously, the antisocial must be reclaimed or, at worst, restrained. But for all, is it not essential that whether we deal with treatment or with education, we are dominated by a clear and dynamic conviction of the need for each to participate as he can, not only in his family or his group, but also in the wider life of his community? In short, we need to include among our values the public virtues—the concern for the common good and the habits of effective participation—if we are to contribute toward the creation of a democratic citizenry. . . .

It is, in fact, possible that if we turned on this question of the emotional and intellectual requisites for a citizen in a democracy all that we now know about the individual, we might make an outstanding contribution. From what we know of the emotional maturity essential to successful family life, from our knowledge of how to develop social attitudes through cooperative group experience, and from all our intimate acquaintance with human beings, might be born an understanding of the motivations essential to making democracy work. The dictators have, so far, proved themselves extremely skillful psychologists in their use of the irrational and the destructive impulses in the service of their cause. The democracies leave the development of the attitudes essential for their continuance largely to chance or the rather dull ministrations of high school civics classes. One of the major needs of our time is to discover how to direct the irrational and unconscious motivations of men in ways that will produce the common well-being of all, and how to develop more fully the rational and creative social impulses. In so far as we can contribute to the creation of active and intelligent participation in public issues by all those we touch we will encourage that growth of social responsibility which underlies a healthy community. In a democracy it is not enough to interpret social needs to the privileged or the powerful alone. The only permanent and wholesome basis for a democratic community is an awakened sensitiveness to human values in all parts of our population, a communal sense that the injury of any is the concern of all, and a widespread willingness to assume the necessary responsibility to meet our common needs. . . .

As our cities have grown in size and diversity of population, the ties of common interest and common purpose which unite smaller communities are weakened. Cleavages of economic interest, of nationality, and of racial background create social chasms across which we have built few bridges of community feeling. Human beings need a vivid and constant linkage to a large social whole whose common ideals they share and in whose life their participation is obviously essential. In time of war or disaster we find such meanings, but in time of peace or depression the democracies have been curiously unable to dramatize for us all the potent goals of common enterprise. It is only where there arise from the common life of a democratic people concrete and potent objectives for common enterprise that the bond of the community is strengthened and the individual can be stimulated to active participation in its behalf.

How could social work contribute to such a development? . . . The first step must lie, I believe, in the creation of a taste or, perhaps, an appetite for democratic relations through our methods of administering our own agencies. Obviously this is not likely to spread outward from the social agencies unless it is prevalent within them. It is of little use to set out to democratize the community if we cannot administer our own affairs on that basis. . . .

In the area of the expanding public services a new and, in many ways, more difficult situation is arising. It is not only true that government is vitally affecting more areas of life than ever before, but it is also true that in certain of these areas—notably the provision of work relief and public assistance—it is now responsible for the actual maintenance of millions of its citizens. Simultaneously with this is the fact that as it has become more vitally responsible, it has moved farther away geographically from the control of those it serves. Few of us would wish the return of relief to the meager resources of the local community. There confronts us, however, in the increasing centralization of government a problem which calls urgently for some new kind of community organization if we are to keep fresh and vital the democratic control over services in the interests of those affected and the total community.

With a larger proportion of our people than ever before directly dependent for the means of life itself upon legislative action, the control over such action has become increasingly difficult to exercise. Even in the local community, especially in larger cities, the plight of the relief clients can go unrecognized and actual starvation occur without the realization of it arousing community action. And when the controlling hand is—or can be said to be—in the state capital or the remote halls of Congress, the potency of democracy wears very thin indeed. If the control over such essential services is to remain in part in state and Federal hands, we must invent new instruments by which the actual conditions of local communities can vitally affect such decisions. We have yet to discover an effective instrument by which centralized and remote control can be kept in constant adaptation to the vital needs of those for whom it functions. The more vital the need, the more essential is this development. For those whose chance to work and to eat lies in the hands of our legislators, the forging of such an instrument by which to express their needs is the natural step of a democratic people. So far, citizens' committees of varying degrees of usefulness and the action of pressure groups of the unemployed have been the chief methods used. Occasionally, organized social workers have tried to take a hand without much outstanding success. At best such action is sporadic, without authorization from the community, and often none too welcome to those responsible for the government policies. An acceptable and recognized method for relating local needs to centralized control will have to be developed if we are to escape the evils of bureaucracy or a cynical disillusion with the workings of our democracy. This is a concern in which social workers and their clientele might well join in cooperative endeavor. . . .

So far I have dealt chiefly with the relation of social workers to the extension of democratic habits of mind both in our direct relation to their clientele and in their relation to the local community. This, however, is only part of the issue confronting us. If our society cannot provide the basic satisfactions of life for its citizens, all our democratic traditions and attitudes will not hold against the rising tide of thwarted human life. One of the most serious threats to our institutions lies in our inability to provide the minimum necessities of life for all under conditions of security and self-respect. Social workers by the very nature of their functions have a unique opportunity to understand this and to affect it. . . .

While it is true that many of the difficulties with which we deal are personal in origin, it is also true that many of them are directly related to the social situation. There is no reasonable doubt that poverty itself is responsible for increased illness, that unemployment breeds unemployability, that crowded housing undermines family life, that undernourished children will grow into incompetent workers. These are truisms. But the inertia which allows such conditions to continue brings us a growing pyramid of financial and human costs.

Basic to all these ills is the overshadowing poverty of the American people—and that in a country whose resources and skill make poverty no longer necessary. . . . We know as few in the community do, except those directly involved, what the consequences of unnecessary poverty are to human life. But if we allow our accumulated experience to lie idle, if we become absorbed in individual misfortunes or in our own techniques for dealing with them, or if we become so accustomed to conditions that we too accept them as inevitable, there is lost to the community a driving power which might be used to change men's minds. . . . If we have the insight and the determination we can draw conclusions, see trends, point out consequences. These, if geared to the awakened public understanding, might start the wheels of change.

In fulfilling this responsibility we shall be contributing to the customary way in which we deal with such problems in America. In one area after another during the 150 years of our history we have moved forward gropingly by these methods. The struggle to establish public education, to develop public health, to protect women and children in industry, and, more recently, to provide a limited measure of security from unemployment and old age, all illustrate the same attempt to modify basic social institutions in the interest of better opportunity for human beings. Agains terrific odds, which often seem at the time like the labors of Sisyphus himself, our predecessors have won a slowly expanding measure of life. . . .

We can take heart from some of the legislative achievements of the last decade, from the rising understanding of the necessity for an adequate minimum for all, and from the realization that plenty for all is within the realms of scientific possibility if not yet of social reality. But with all this, we know only too well that such gains as have been won are scattered and inadequate at best.

As the understanding of the need for social prevention spreads, our experience at various points has unique value. Programs of preventive medicine and provisions for medical care need our testimony as to the consequences which flow from our present dearth of such services. Programs for vocational guidance and for work for unemployed youth can be strengthened by our experience of the present result of idleness and frustration. The creation of endurable conditions of life for migratory agricultural workers calls for the contribution which rural social workers might make to public understanding. From such raw material can come the means with which to control our social disasters at their source. Our experience with the human consequences of social conditions contains a rich ore which should be mined by observation and forged into instruments for the creation of an informed public opinion.

Perhaps in times like these it is visionary to suggest that the day may come when unnecessary poverty itself might be abolished. . . . No one can tell whether or when the abolition of unnecessary poverty can become a reality. A world engulfed in war seems to negate this ancient dream of peace and plenty which is the basic hope of democratic peoples. Yet there is a certain toughness to human aspiration which, when it is combined with favorable external factors like technology, has a remarkable power to remove obstacles as a rising tide can lift a stranded ship. If America can escape at least the worst of the avalanche of war, can we not believe that it may be its destiny to achieve in time this ancient hope?

As to the immediate future, it seems clear that we have a significant job before us. Even if, as we hope, we may stay out of war itself, the demands of national defense are likely to transform not only our economy, but our entire national life. But in that transformation we must become more and not less the democratic nation that we claim to be. Such a development must rest upon the ancient foundations of freedom of thought and speech. It must grow from the well-founded hope that willingness and effort will yield fruit in security and achievement. The firmest foundation for the ultimate preservation of our democratic heritage lies in a sound people well-nourished in body, healthy in mind, fully developed each according to his powers. Such a people are the best preparedness for the free cooperative endeavor for common goals, not only of defense—essential as that may be for the time—but also for the permanent achievement of a great culture. Toward this goal we as social workers must bend every vital energy, in every individual contact, in every local community, and in the wider areas where certain established social institutions must be remodeled to allow human life its fullest development.

For this achievement we need a profound insight and an unshaken courage. . . . The rise of science, the achievement of political democracy, the abolition of slavery, the extension of medical care, the free education of the young, and the development of that vast body of social services which we represent—these are but part of that struggle for a civilized life. Our generation is called upon to hold this line and to press forward. This struggle is the great adventure of mankind, faltering, broken, uncertain, but with it all, superb.

7

Voice in the New Deal Wilderness
Herbert Hoover's *The Challenge to Liberty*

No one spoke critically of the New Deal from the right of center with more eloquence and more authority than Herbert Hoover, President of the United States during the desperate years of the early depression when affairs had drifted steadily from bad to worse. Few scholars today accept as objectively valid the notion that President Hoover "caused" the depression, nor that his administration was callous and obtuse—although both views were expressed often enough by his opponents at the time. That his policies were inadequate to reverse the downward plunge, however, and that the national failure to respond quickly and effectively to new challenges were, in substantial part at least, personal responsibilities that every president assumes with that highest office. Although widely and popularly discredited at the time, Hoover spoke for hundreds of thousands of citizens who found the central tendencies of the New Deal subversive of the American way of life. Defeated for reelection in 1932, he was able to articulate the anxieties of many Americans with a vigor and a clarity that he had rarely mustered while holding power. Through times of domestic turmoil and international demoralization, Hoover won many adherents to his point of view, and thus maintained some of the essentials of an old and hallowed tradition. That his philosophy never again represented a majority consensus is not to deny the devotion it continued to earn in many quarters and the significant weight it continued to bear in the modification of national attitudes and policies. Herbert Hoover's *Memoirs*, 3 vols. (New York: Macmillan, 1951-1952) are the very best source for understanding his career and ideology. Harris G. Warren's *Herbert Hoover and the Great Depression* (New York: Oxford University Press, 1959) is as dispassionate an account as one could hope for. Edgar E. Robinson's *The Roosevelt Leadership, 1933-1945* (Philadelphia: J. B. Lippincott Co., 1955) provides a

Herbert Hoover, "National Regimentation," and "We May Sum Up," from *The Challenge to Liberty* (New York: Charles Scribner's Sons, 1934), pp. 76-103, 189-205. Reprinted through the courtesy of Charles Scribner's Sons.

critical evaluation of Roosevelt from premises that are quite parallel to those of Mr. Hoover's. In reading these selections, note (1) what Hoover regarded as the chief danger involved in Roosevelt's exercise of power in the presidential office; (2) his views as to the origins and consequences of coercive measures against liberties and properties; (3) what he thought would be the end result of "national regimentation"; and (4) his program for the restoration of true liberalism and liberty.

National Regimentation]

THE ORIGINS, CHARACTER, AND AFFINITIES OF THE Regimentation theory of economics and government, its impacts upon true American Liberalism, and its departures from it can best be determined by an examination of the actions taken and measures adopted in the United States during recent months. . . .

From this examination we may dismiss measures of relief of distress from depression, and reform of our laws regulating business when such actions conform to the domain of true Liberty, for these are, as I shall indicate, not Regimentation.

The first step of economic Regimentation is a vast centralization of power in the Executive. Without tedious recitation of the acts of the Congress delegating powers over the people to the Executive or his assistants, and omitting relief and regulatory acts, the powers which have been assumed include, directly or indirectly, the following:

To debase the coin and set its value; to inflate the currency; to buy and sell gold and silver; to buy Government bonds, other securities, and foreign exchange; to seize private stocks of gold at a price fixed by the Government; in effect giving to the Executive the power to "manage" the currency;

To levy sales taxes on food, clothing, and upon goods competitive to them (the processing tax) at such times and in such amounts as the Executive may determine;

To expend enormous sums from the appropriations for public works, relief, and agriculture upon projects not announced to the Congress at the time appropriations were made;

To create corporations for a wide variety of business activities, heretofore the exclusive field of private enterprise;

To install services and to manufacture commodities in competition with citizens;

To buy and sell commodities; to fix minimum prices for industries or dealers; to fix handling charges and therefore profits; to eliminate "unfair" trade practices;

To allot the amount of production to individual farms and factories and the character of goods they shall produce; to destroy commodities; to fix stocks of commodities to be on hand;

To estop expansion or development of industries or of specific plant and equipment;

To establish minimum wages; to fix maximum hours and conditions of labor;

To impose collective bargaining;

To organize administrative agencies outside the Civil Service requirements;

To abrogate the effect of the anti-trust acts;

To raise and lower the tariffs and to discriminate between nations in their application;

To abrogate certain governmental contracts without compensation or review by the courts;

To enforce most of these powers where they affect the individual by fine and imprisonment through prosecution in the courts, with a further reserved authority in many trades through license to deprive men of their business and livelihood without any appeal to the courts.

Most of these powers may be delegated by the Executive to any appointee and the appointees are mostly without the usual confirmation by the Senate. The staffs of most of the new organizations are not selected by the merit requirements of the Civil Service. These direct or indirect powers were practically all of them delegated by the Congress to the Executive upon the representation that they were "emergency" authorities, and most of them are limited to a specific time for the purpose of bringing about national recovery from the depression.

At some time or place all of these authorities already have been used. Powers once delegated are bound to be used, for one step drives to another. Moreover, some group somewhere gains benefits or privilege by the use of every power. Once a power is granted, therefore, groups begin to exert the pressure necessary to force its use. Once used, a vested interest is created which thereafter opposes any relaxation and thereby makes for permanence. But beyond this, many steps once taken set economic forces in motion which cannot be retrieved. Already we have witnessed all these processes in action.

The manner of use of these powers and their immediate impacts upon the concepts of true American Liberty may first be examined under the five groups or ideas into which they naturally fall—Regimented Industry and Commerce, Regimented Agriculture, Government in Competitive Business, Managed Currency and Credit, and Managed Foreign Trade.

Regimented Industry and Commerce]

The application of Regimentation to business has made great strides. We now have the important branches of industry and commerce organized into trade groups, each presided over by a committee of part trade and part governmental representatives heading up through an "Administrator" to the Executive. There are a number of advisory boards for various purposes whose personnel is part trade and part bureaucratic. More than 400 separate trades have been so organized, estimated to cover 1,500,000 establishments or about 90 per cent of the business of the country outside of farming.

In this organization of commerce and industry the trades were called upon to propose codes of management for their special callings. Parts of each of these codes are, however, imposed by law, whether the trades propose them or not. The determination as to who represents the trade is reserved to the Executive, and in the absence of a satisfactory proposal he may himself make and promulgate a code. He may force deletion of any proposed provision and may similarly impose provisions and exceptions.

Each of the codes is directly or indirectly binding upon every member of the trade whether he was represented in its making or whether he agreed or not. It has the force of statutory law, enforceable by fine and jail through the courts. Originally the Executive could require every member of a trade to take out a license to do business. In this license he could impose the conditions under which persons may continue to do business. The

Executive could revoke a license without affording any appeal to or a protection of the courts. This licensing power has expired in general industry but still stands as an authority to the Secretary of Agriculture over all producers, processors, and dealers in agricultural products. That is a very considerable part of American business. Except as an example of the extent of violation of freedom this licensing provision is not important, as the other provisions and methods are sufficiently coercive without it.

The codes impose minimum wages and maximum hours and provide, further, for collective agreement with labor as to wages and conditions of work beyond the minimums. By far the major use of the codes is, however, devoted to the elimination of "unfair competitive practices." This expression or its counterpart, "fair competition," has been interpreted not alone to cover "unethical" practices, but to include the forced elimination of much normal functioning of competition through reduced production, the prevention of plant expansion, and a score of devices for fixing of minimum prices and trade margins. From so innocent terms as "fair competition" and its counterpart have been builded this gigantic dictation—itself a profound example of the growth of power when once granted.

In this mobilization there has been constant use of the term "co-operation." However, the law itself makes important parts of the codes compulsory and by their indirect powers can impose any of them. As practical persons observing their working, we may dismiss voluntary impulses as the motivation of this organization. At best it is "coercive co-operation." Free will and consent, the essential elements in co-operation, have not often been present. The spirit of the whole process has been coercive, principally through the overshadowing authority to impose the codes and the terror of effective deprival to any man of his business and his livelihood. The mere fact of charges made by bureaucrats can act to deprive him of his reputation. Where such authority arises among free men is difficult to discern.

Ample evidence of coercion is found in the bludgeoning proceedings of many important code conferences, in the changes forced in some codes, from which there was no appeal or refuge; in the incitement to public boycott; and in the contracts required in all dealings with the government itself. One need but read the vast flood of propaganda, of threat and pressure, the daily statements of the administering officials, and follow the actions of "compliance" boards and other agencies, in every town or village, to confirm the fact of coercion. Men have been fined or ordered to jail for the crime of selling goods or services at lower prices than their competitors. One of the sad results is the arraying of neighbor against neighbor, group against group, all grasping for desperate advantages from the law.

There are "unfair practices" which need reform because of the failure of some States to rise fully to their responsibilities. The codes have served admirably to reduce child labor by about 25 per cent, and they have eliminated sweating in certain trades. They have eliminated some unethical business practices, but they have stimulated many more new ones through "chiseling." This sort of reform is within the powers of the States, and laws to this purpose have been enacted by most of them. If we have determined that we must nationally force these measures on delinquent States and if they be within the constitutional powers of the Federal Government, then they can be carried out by specific law enforced by the judicial arm and do not require the regimentation of the economic system. But in practical working only a small part of the codes are devoted to these ends.

The most effective part of the code operations are devoted to limitation of real competition. It is true that the law provided that there should be no monopolies or monopolistic practices. The major aspiration of those seeking to avoid the anti-trust acts always has been precisely the fixing of minimum prices and restriction of output, and these objectives, so earnestly yearned for in some quarters, now have been imposed by law. The economic results, so far as the trades and consumers are concerned, are about the same as if the anti-trust acts had been abolished. Naturally, if these industrial regiments hold to discipline they are at once constituted as complete guild monopolies as any in the Elizabethan period, from which we derived much of our American antagonism to monopoly.

But an equally regrettable social effect has been that the imposition of larger costs, and the fixing of minimum prices and trade differentials crashes down at once on smaller units of business. If persisted in there can be no destiny of these processes in the long run but a gradual absorption of business by the larger units. All this is in fact the greatest legal mechanism ever devised for squeezing the smaller competitor out of action, easily and by the majesty of the law. Yet the small business is the very fibre of our community life.

Over it all is now the daily dictation by Government in every town and village every day in the week, of how men are to conduct their daily lives—under constant threat of jail, for crimes which have no moral turpitude. All this is the most stupendous invasion of the whole spirit of Liberty that the nation has witnessed since the days of Colonial America.

Regimented Agriculture]

The farmer is the most tragic figure in our present situation. From the collapse of war inflation, from boom, from displacement of work-animals by mechanization, from the breakdown of foreign markets, from the financial debacle of Europe, and from drought, he has suffered almost beyond human endurance.

Instead of temporarily reducing the production of marginal lands by measures of relief pending world recovery, the great majority of farmers were regimented to reduce production from the fertile lands. The idea of a subsidy to a farmer to reduce his production in a particular "staple commodity" was expanded by requiring a contract that he would follow orders from the Secretary of Agriculture in the production of other "staple commodities." Voluntary action was further submerged by threats that if he did not sign up he would have difficulty in obtaining credit.

The whole process has been a profound example both of how bureaucracy, once given powers to invade Liberty, proceeds to fatten and enlarge its activities, and of how departures from practical human nature and economic experience soon find themselves so entangled as to force more and more violent steps.

To escape the embarrassment of the failure to reduce production by these methods, still further steps were taken into coercion and regimentation. Yet more "staples," not authorized by

the Congress to be controlled when the contracts were signed,
were added to the list. A further step was to use the taxing
power on excess production of cotton and to set quotas on
sugar. Directly or indirectly, on many farms these devices
create a privilege and destroy a right. Since only those who
have had the habit of producing cotton and some other commodities may now do so, they are given a monopoly and any
other farmer is precluded from turning his land to that purpose.

And recently still further powers were demanded from the
Congress by which the last details of complete coercion and
dictation might be exerted not alone to farmers but to everyone
who manufactures and distributes farm products. That all this
is marching to full regimentation of thirty millions of our agricultural population is obvious enough.

But we are told that the farmer must, in the future, sacrifice
Liberty to economic comfort. The economic comfort up to date
may be questioned, as likewise the longevity of any comfort, for
the basic premise is not tenable.

The stark fact is that if part of Liberty to a particular farmer
is removed, the program must move quickly into complete dictation, for there are here no intermediate stages. The nature of
agriculture makes it impossible to have regimentation up to a
point and freedom of action beyond that point. Either the farmer
must use his own judgment, must be free to plant and sell as he
wills, or he must take orders from the corporal put above him.

The whole thesis behind this program is the very theory that
man is but the pawn of the state. It is usurpation of the primary
liberties of men by government.

Government in Competitive Business]

The deliberate entry of the government into business in competition with the citizen, or in replacement of private enterprise,
(other than as a minor incident to some major public purpose);
is regimentation of the people directly into a bureaucracy. That,
of course, is Socialism in the connotation of any sociologist or
economist and is confirmed as such today by the acclaim of the
Socialists.

As an instance we may cite the Tennessee Valley Authority,

where the major purpose of the government is the purchase, construction, operation, transmission, and sale of electricity in the Tennessee Valley and neighborhood, together with the manufacture and merchandising of appliances, fertilizers, chemicals, and other commodities. Other instances occur where Public Works money has been allotted to the erection of dams and reservoirs, and to the construction of power plants, the major purpose of which is to undertake the production and sale of electricity in competition with the citizen.

There have long been instances of public works for the real major purpose of flood control, irrigation, or navigation, which produce water-power as a by-product. Here, if the government leases this power under proper protection to the public, the competition with the citizen is avoided. Here is one of the definite boundaries between Liberty and Socialism. Under Liberty, the citizen must have strong regulation of the rates and profits of power companies to protect him from oppression by the operator of a natural monopoly. But where the government deliberately enters into the power business as a major purpose in competition with the citizen—that is Socialism. . . .

These entries into Socialism were not an important emergency call to relieve unemployment. The total expenditures provided will employ but a very small percentage of the unemployed. In fact, the threat to private enterprise will probably stifle employment of more men in the damage to existing enterprises. There is already an ample private capacity to supply any of the commodities they produce, whether electricity, fertilizers, rum, or furniture. Whatever their output is, its production will displace that much private employment somewhere. We have only to examine a fragment of the statements of their sponsors to find that their purposes, although sometimes offered as employment, are in fact further blows pounding in the wedge of Socialism as a part of regimenting the people into a bureaucracy. . . .

Managed Currency and Credit]

The scope of this survey does not include a full examination of the monetary, fiscal, and credit policies. I am here concerned solely with profound departures from Liberty.

Without entering upon the recent technical monetary steps taken, it may be said at once that the intent of the powers given to alter the unit value of currency is, by "managed currency," to enable the government to change from time to time the purchasing power of the currency for all commodities, wages, salaries, and income. One underlying intent of the monetary measures was the transfer of income and property from one individual to another, or from one group to another, upon an enormous scale without judicial processes. Whether the theory under this assumption will produce the effects intended or not, the intent is definitely expressed.

The installation of managed currency required the repudiation of the government contract to meet its obligations in gold. And the repudiation of the gold clause extended much farther than repudiation of government obligations alone, for it changed the value of all contracts between citizens far beyond the present appreciation of the citizen of its possible results—if it shall prove to have the effect which was intended.

One of the major objectives stated was to reduce unbearable debt. It was asserted that the value of the dollar as represented in its purchasing power for goods or services had changed from its value when the original bargains of debt were made. Under this operation the citizens were regimented into two groups, debtors and creditors. An empirical and universal amount of 40 to 50 per cent was set as the degree of shift in the value of all property to the debtor regiment from the creditor regiment.

This act involved the widest responsibility which the government bears to its citizens, and that individuals bear toward each other. For fidelity to contract, unless determined unconscionable by an independent tribunal, is the very integrity of Liberty and of an economic society. Where the debt of certain groups such as part of the farmers and home-owners becomes oppressive, and its social results of the entire nation are of vital importance, such a service is justified, but it should not have been undertaken at the particular cost of those honest creditors whose savings have been thus invested but should have been a special burden upon the whole nation. But the injustice is far wider than this.

These monetary acts extend the assumption of unbearable debt over the whole of the private and public debts of the nation. That this attempt at universal shift of 40 to 50 per cent of the value of all debts was neither necessary nor just can be demonstrated in a few sentences. The theory mistakenly assumed that the distorted prices and values at the depth of a banking panic were permanent. It assumed that the recovery from depression in progress through the world would not extend to the United States. Of even more importance, this theory also assumed that every single debt had become oppressive; that every single creditor had benefited by about one-half since the initial bargain; that every single debtor had lost by this amount; that no debtor could carry out his initial bargain; and that the respective rights of every debtor and every creditor in every kind of property should be shifted from debtor to creditor without any inquiry or process of justice. Debt is an individual thing, not a mass transaction. The circumstances of every debt vary.

Certainly the Government cannot contend that its debt was oppressive. No man has yet stated that the Government could not have paid its obligations in full. It was not insolvent. It was not bankrupt.

In large areas of private debt the borrower was amply able to meet his obligations. In other great areas he had already profited by large dividends or earnings, or otherwise by the use of the savings of lenders which he had deliberately solicited. A huge part of the bond issues of railways, of power companies, of industrial companies, of foreign governments, current commercial debt, the bank deposits, urban mortgages and what not belong to these categories.

The evidence of the volume of debts which require governmental relief as a social necessity does not by any conceivable calculation indicate more than a very minor percentage of the total public and private debt. Extensive provisions for the adjustment between individuals of their debts were made by new facilities under the bankruptcy acts and the further relief measures provided through the use of government credit.

But let us examine the injustice under this managed currency more particularly. In a great category where debt required adjustment there had already been many compromises between debtors and investors, as witness the many reorganizations of urban building loans, and corporate and other obligations, which were the products of inflation. The people's savings invested in these cases are required, by depreciation of the dollar, to submit to a still further loss.

Most lending is ultimately from savings which mean somebody's self-denial of the joy of spending today in order to provide for the future. But the borrower is often enough a person who secured these joys and is now to be relieved of part payment, although a large part of these borrowers are able to pay. The man who borrowed from an insurance company to build himself a more expensive and enjoyable house has secured these joys at the cost of the policyholder, who had hoped by self-denial to escape dependency. This applies equally to the huge debt of industrial and commercial businesses which profited by their borrowings from the policyholder and the depositor in a savings bank.

Those self-denying investors—the thrifty of the nation—who were willing to accept a low rate of interest in order to obtain the maximum security, are under this theory to have the purchasing value of their savings now shrunken in exactly the same ratio as the avaricious who received extortionate rates, or the reckless who took high risks. The holders of hard-won savings —the widow's mite—invested in 3¼ per cent first mortgage industrial bonds are called upon to sacrifice the same proportion as the holders of 7 per cent third mortgages. By the transfer of values from the first mortgage bondholder to the common stockholder the security of these speculative bonds is even increased. At once we see the evidence of this in the marked advance in the prices of these speculative debts. This disregard of prudence and this benefit to recklessness particularly penalizes a very large part of insurance and the great public endowment assets.

Ten billions of endowments in educational, hospitalization, and welfare activities—creditors whose debtors are mostly corporations and governments—are to be depleted in purchasing power. These endowed institutions give the leadership necessary to all our vast complex of public institutions. Yet if this theory eventuate, their activities must diminish by 40 per cent.

Furthermore, if this theory shall succeed, in the great bulk of industrial debt, the empirical reduction of purchasing power of the regiments of bondholders transfers this purchasing power to the regiments of common stockholders. Any inspection of who are the rank and file in these regiments will at once demonstrate the double injustice. The holders of bonds are largely the insurance company, the savings bank depositor, the small investor, and the endowed institution.

If this intent of devaluation shall eventuate, the transfer of property by government fiat from sixty million insurance policyholders to ten million stockholders is not even diffusion of wealth. It is further concentration of wealth. As a matter of fact, any survey of the total results would show (if the theory of these acts works out) that it will benefit the richest members of the community, because their property is, in the main, in equities. The hardship will fall upon the great mass of the people who are indirect holders of obligations through their savings in insurance, in savings bank deposits, as well as those who directly hold bonds and mortgages. That is, in our modern American economy the rich are more largely the holders of equities and those of moderate means more largely the holders of obligations. Thus the rich hereby become richer, the poor poorer.

Monetary shifts in their very nature are mostly irretrievable. There can be little turning back.

In "managed currency"—a power of government fiat over the values of wages, income, and property—we find many by-products from the invasion of Liberty. To some academic theorists the Commodity Dollar may be perfect. But for thousands of years the whole human race has esteemed gold as the final gauge of values. Whether the sign of the index number, which is the kernel of this branch of "planned economics," be theoretically a better gauge or not, the fact remains that gold is a matter of faith. Men will long delay full faith in an abstraction such as the commodity index, with its uncertainties of political manipulation or of Executive determination. This has a pertinent application today. Those people who are employed are heaping up their savings. Yet these potential investors have hitherto hesitated to loan their savings over a long period, not knowing with what they may be paid in years to come nor what their rights may be. The durable goods industries are dependent upon this investment in the form of long-term credits. At the same time the country has an accumulated need for a vast amount of homes and equipment. As these credits are much restricted, vast numbers out of work suffer the injustice of cruel delays in otherwise possible employment.

How far the Regimentation of banking and the government dictation of credit through various government agencies may extend is not yet clear. There are national stresses in which the government must support private financial institutions, but it is unnecessary for it to enter into competitive business to accomplish this. And lest the government step over the line into Socialism this support must be limited to activities where there is no competition, or so organized as ultimately to be absorbed into the hands of private ownership. The original Reconstruction Finance Corporation is an example of the former and the Federal Reserve Banks, the Home Loan Banks, the Federal Land Banks, of the latter. There are, however, some of the new financial agencies and some uses being made of the old agencies which forecast occupation beyond these fields, and threaten dictation as to who may and who may not have credit. The threat to farmers of withholding credit to force them to sign crop contracts with the government is a current example of possibilities.

The reduction of the independence of the Federal Reserve Board and the Farm Loan System to dependency upon the political administration, the provisions for appointment of officials in the banks by government agencies, and certain provisions in the new regulatory acts, all at least give enormous powers of "managed credit."

If the purpose of all these activities is to enable the government to dictate which business or individual shall have credit and which shall not, we will witness a tyranny never before contemplated in our history.

The wounds to Liberty—and to justice upon which Liberty rests—in these monetary actions and policies are thus myriad. It is again a specific demonstration of a social philosophy defensible only on the ground that the citizen is but the pawn of the state —the negation of the whole philosophy of Liberty. Executive power over the coin is one of the oldest components of despotism. . . .

This brief survey of examples of experience up to this time is sufficient to make clear the definition and nature of National Regimentation and its progress in the United States. There are other channels in which our economic and social life is being regimented which could be developed. These instances are certainly sufficient to show that its very spirit is government direction, management, and dictation of social and economic life. It is a vast shift from the American concept of human rights which even the government may not infringe to those social philosophies where men are wholly subjective to the state. It is a vast casualty to Liberty if it shall be continued. . . .

We May Sum Up]

THE ISSUE OF CIVILIZATION TODAY IS WHETHER LIBerty can survive the wounds it has received in these recent years.

After the war Liberalism came into a vast ascendency. The arms of democracy had been victorious over the legions of despotism. Those dismembered nations hastened with high hopes to adopt the forms and endeavored to develop the spirit of individual Liberty. Then came the dreadful aftermaths—the vengeful peace, the continuation of hate, the realization of losses from the gigantic destruction, the rise of bitter nationalism with all its barriers and snatching for advantage, the attempts by inflations to shift and postpone the debt burdens of the day, the vicious speculation and exploitation to which inflation gives opportunity, the dislocations from rapid advances of scientific discovery and labor-saving devices, and the final plunge into the liquidation by the great depression. The human misery that has flowed from it all has discredited the social systems of all nations, no matter how great their concept of liberty, justice, and peace.

Liberalism fell first in its new-born regions, and today it is under attack in the great areas of its origins and development. Indeed, the fate of Liberalism rests today mainly upon three great nations, America, the British Commonwealth, and France. It is within these areas where the fortresses of freedom though much weakened can be held. If they fail the lesser outworks will fall. In America, where Liberty blazed brightest and by its glow shed light to all others, it is today impaired and endangered.

In anxiety and hope, in the yearnings of humanity for betterment, alternative philosophies of society have sprung into life, offering "solutions" for all difficulties. Whatever their names be —Fascism, Socialism, or Communism—they have this common result: wherever these systems have been imposed tyranny has been erected, government by the people abolished. The protection of law has vanished before dictation; no person is secure in justice; even the old right of *habeas corpus* is forgotten; the right of property is wholly removed or its use permitted only upon sufferance by the state; free speech, free press, the right of assembly have been banished; whispers and terrors replace security and freedom of spirit. From these repressive measures comes the banishment of freedom itself.

Be it noted that even "temporary" dictatorships are achieved by the direct and emphatic promise to the people that their liberties eventually will be restored. In Russia, the theory runs that some liberty will be restored when the revolution of the proletariat is "consummated." In Italy, liberties will be restored as the people earn them by faithful obeisance before the throne of Fascism. Under Naziism, liberties will be restored when the "National Consolidation" is secured.

A sobering commentary upon the processes of mass psychology is the idea in all of these countries that Liberty may be achieved and secured only by sacrifice of liberties to the efficiency of tyranny. Certainly, it is not illogical to suggest that if the ultimate purpose of dictatorships is the restoration of Liberty, the first aim of existing liberal governments should be the defense and maintenance of Liberty.

The proponents of these rival programs are often men of burning zeal. In their zeal they are willing to wipe out centuries of achievement, to ignore the bloody road over which the human race has travelled, evolving as it went the very ideals of justice and liberty. They envisage these ideals as their own and sole discovery, they adopt actions and measures which this long road of trial has proved disastrous, and they abandon the gains of freedom so painfully acquired.

From the examples of National Regimentation that we have examined it is obvious that many of its measures represent not reform or relief within the boundaries of Liberty, but that they are emulating parts of some of these other systems with the hope of speeding recovery from the depression.

One may disagree and keep silent as to the justification of some of these measures if they are to be limited to "emergency," for in the march of a great people that is relatively unimportant if that is all of it. Then these dangers and stresses will disappear as an eddy in the stream of national life. The important thing is whether this drift from essential liberties is to be permanent. If not permanent, these emergency measures will have served the purpose of having exhausted the pent-up panaceas of a generation and broken them on the wheel of resistant human behavior and the spirit of a people with a heritage of liberty.

The threat of the continuance of these "emergency" acts is a threat to join the Continental retreat of human progress backward through the long corridor of time. In the demands for continuance there lies a mixture of desperate seeking for justification of their adoption and subtle ambitions of those advocating other philosophies. Whatever the motive, the promise of permanence now stares the American people starkly in the face. It is not the mere evolution of an economic procedure that this Regimentation implies—it steps off the solid highways of true

American Liberty into the dangerous quicksands of governmental dictation.

Thus what I am interested in in this inquiry is something that transcends the transitory actions, as important as they are, something far more pregnant with disaster to all that America has been to its people and to the world. No nation can introduce a new social philosophy or a new culture alien to its growth without moral and spiritual chaos. I am anxious for the future of freedom and liberty of men. That America has stood for; that has created her greatness; that is all the future holds that is worth while.

The unit of American life is the family and the home. Through it vibrates every hope of the future. It is the economic unit as well as the moral and spiritual unit. But it is more than this. It is the beginning of self-government. It is the throne of our highest ideals. It is the center of the spiritual energy of our people.

The purpose of American life is the constant betterment of all these homes. If we sustain that purpose every individual may have the vision of decent and improving life. That vision is the urge of America. It creates the buoyant spirit of our country. The inspiring hope of every real American is for an enlarged opportunity for his children. The obligation of our generation to them is to pass on the heritage of Liberty which was entrusted to us. To secure the blessings of Liberty to ourselves and to our posterity was the purpose in sacrifice of our fathers. We have no right to load upon our children unnecessary debts from our follies or to force them to meet life in regimented forms which limit their self-expression, their opportunities, their achievements. St. Paul said nearly two thousand years ago, "Ye have been called unto liberty."

Our American System and its great purpose are builded upon the positive conception that "men are endowed by their Creator with certain unalienable Rights, that among these are Life, Liberty, and the pursuit of Happiness"; that the purpose and structure of government is to protect these rights; that upon them the government itself shall not encroach. From these liberties has come that unloosing of creative instincts and aspirations which have builded this, the greatest nation of all time.

The Bill of Rights—our forefathers' listing of unalienable liberties and personal securities—was written a century and a half ago. We have had need to work out both practical application of these liberties and the machinery for maintaining them in the changing scene of the years. We have seen some of them fade from memory, such as the protection from quartering of troops. We have had to add some new rights to assure freedom from slavery and to give universal franchise. We have had to keep the balance as between some of them and to see that some—chiefly property rights—are not used to override other rights. We have steadily developed from the spirit of freedom high standards and ideals of human relationship, a great system of advancement of mankind. We have at times failed to live up to our ideals, but that they shall continue to shine brightly is the important thing.

Those are today denounced who, on one hand, dare assert that these liberties and personal securities still live, and, on the other, they are equally denounced who assert that they have been transgressed. It will be denied that any one of them has ever been mentioned in our country for repeal or modification. Nor has it been proposed today that any new rights and securities should be added to those guaranteed by the Constitution. Therein lies the intellectual dishonesty of the attack upon them. If we have discovered that any one of these liberties is not our individual endowment by the Creator, the right thing is to propose a change in the Constitution and allow us to examine it, not to extinguish it by indirection. Such an alteration would not get far, for whether people know them by name or not, the principles of liberty and security are embedded in their daily thought and action. Perhaps not one in a hundred thousand of our people knows the detailed list of liberties our forefathers insisted upon, or the development of them since, but never a day goes by that every man and woman does not instinctively rely upon these liberties.

Yet today forces have come into action from ignorance, panic, or design which, either by subtle encroachment or by the breaking down of their safeguards, do endanger their primary purpose. These liberties are of urgent practical importance. The very employment upon which millions depend for their bread is today delayed because of the disturbance of confidence in their security.

There are those who assert that revolution has swept the United States. That is not true. But there are some who are trying to bring it about. At least they are following the vocal technique which has led elsewhere to the tragedy of Liberty. Their slogans; their promise of Utopia; their denunciation of individual wickednesses as if these were the wards of Liberty; their misrepresentation of deep-seated causes; their will to destruction of confidence and consequent disorganization in order to justify action; their stirring of class feeling and hatred; their will to clip and atrophy the legislative arm; their resentment of criticism; their chatter of boycott, of threat and of force—all are typical enough of the methods of more violent action.

In our blind groping we have stumbled into philosophies which lead to the surrender of freedom. The proposals before our country do not necessarily lead to the European forms of Fascism, of Socialism, or of Communism, but they certainly lead definitely from the path of liberty. The danger lies in the tested human exprience, that a step away from liberty itself impels a second step, a second compels a third. The appetite for power grows with every opportunity to assume it, and power over the rights of men leads not to humility but to arrogance, and arrogance incessantly demands more power. A few steps so dislocate social forces that some form of depotism becomes inevitable and Liberty dies.

No country or no society can be conducted by partly acknowledging the securities of Liberty and partly denying them, nor by recognizing some of them and denying others. That is part democracy and part tyranny. At once there are conflicts and interferences which not only damage the whole economic mechanism but drive unceasingly for more and more dictation.

Even partial regimentation cannot be made to work and still maintain live democratic institutions. Representative government will sooner or later be at conflict with it along the whole front, both in the incidentals of daily working and in the whole field of free choice by the people. If it be continued the Congress must further surrender its checks and balances on administration and its free criticism since these, with intensified duties to its constituents, create interferences that will make efficient administration of this regimented machine impossible.

For any plan of Regimentation to succeed it must have not only powers of rigid discipline but adamant continuity. Does anyone believe that with the interferences of the Congress and the storms of a free press any government can impose discipline and follow a consistent and undeviating course in directing the activities of 125,000,000 highly diversified people? Because such a course is impossible Fascism and Sovietism have suppressed both free speech and representative government.

We are confronted with a maze of problems. The boom and depression brought discouraging increases and disclosures of the abuses of Liberty and the growth of economic oppressions. I have discussed these abuses at length in previous chapters because these betrayals of trust, exploitation, monopoly, and all the rest of them are the battle-grounds of Liberty.

The American System had steadily evolved the protections of Liberty. In the early days of road traffic we secured a respect for liberties of others by standards of decency and courtesy in conduct between neighbors. But with the crowding of highways and streets we have invented Stop and Go signals which apply to everybody alike, in order to maintain the same ordered Liberty. But traffic signals are not a sacrifice of Liberty, they are the preservation of it. Under them each citizens moves more swiftly to his own individual purpose and attainment. That is a far different thing from the corner policeman being given the right to determine whether the citizen's mission warrants his passing and whether he is competent to execute it, and then telling him which way he should go, whether he likes it or not. That is the whole distance between ordered Liberty and Regimentation.

The achievements of our own economic system have brought us new problems in stability in business, in agriculture, and in employment, and greater security of living. But the first constructive step in solution is the preservation of Liberty, for in that sphere alone are the dynamic forces with which to solve our problems successfully.

The whole history of humanity has been a struggle against famine and want. Within less than half a century the American System has achieved a triumph in this age-long struggle by producing a plenty.

The other systems now urged for permanent adoption propose to solve the remaining problem of distribution of a hard-won plenty by restrictions which will abolish the plenty. To adopt this course would be an abject surrender. Worse, it would be a surrender to the complexities of distribution after the major battle, which is production, has been won. It may be repeated that if we undermine the stimulants to individual effort which come alone from the spirit of Liberty, we may well cease to discuss the greater "diffusion of income," "of wealth," "minimum standards," and "economic security," the "abolition of poverty," and its fears. Those are possibilities only in an economy of plenty.

It is not that the proposals or philosophies or tendencies of National Regimentation are new discoveries to humanity, which offer the bright hope of new invention or new genius in human leadership. They have the common characteristic of these other philosophies of society and of those of the Middle Ages—that the liberties of men flow only from the state; that men are subjective to the state; that men shall be regimented, not free men. Herein is the flat conflict with true Liberalism. It is all old, very, very old, the idea that the good of men arises from the direction of centralized executive power, whether it be exercised through bureaucracies, mild dictatorships or despotisms, monarchies or autocracies. For Liberty is the emancipation of men from power and servitude and the substitution of freedom for force of government.

Liberty comes alone and lives alone where the hard-won rights of men are held unalienable, where governments themselves may not infringe, where governments are indeed but the mechanisms to protect and sustain these liberties from encroachment. It was this for which our fathers died, it was this heritage they gave to us. It was not the provisions with regard to interstate commerce or the determination of weights and measures or coinage, for which the Constitution was devised—it was the guaranties that men possessed fundamental liberties apart from the state, that they were not the pawns but the masters of the state. It has not been for the aid and comfort of any form of economic domination that our liberties have been hallowed by sacrifice. It has not been for the comfort of machinery that we have builded and extended these liberties, but for the independence and comfort of homes.

Those who proclaim that in a Machine Age there is created an irreconcilable conflict in which liberty cannot survive should not forget the battles of liberty over the centuries, for let it be remembered that in the end both big business and machinery will vanish before freedom if that be necessary. But it is not necessary. It is not because Liberty is unworkable, but because we have not worked it conscientiously or have forgotten its true meaning that we often get the notion of the irreconcilable conflict with the Machine Age.

We cannot extend the mastery of government over the daily life of a people without somewhere making it master of people's souls and thoughts. That is going on today. It is part of all regimentation.

Even if the government conduct of business could give us the maximum of efficiency instead of least efficiency, it would be purchased at the cost of freedom. It would increase rather than decrease abuse and corruption, stifle initiative and invention, undermine the development of leadership, cripple the mental and spiritual energies of our people, extinguish equality of opportunity, and dry up the spirit of liberty and the forces which make progress.

It is a false Liberalism that interprets itself into government dictation, or operation of commerce, industry and agriculture. Every move in that direction poisons the very springs of true Liberalism. It poisons political equality, free thought, free press, and equality of opportunity. It is the road not to liberty but to less liberty. True Liberalism is found not in striving to spread bureaucracy, but in striving to set bounds to it. Liberalism is a force proceeding from the deep realization that economic freedom cannot be sacrificed if political freedom is to be preserved. True Liberalism seeks all legitimate freedom first in the confident belief that without such freedom the pursuit of other blessings is in vain.

The nation seeks for solution of its many difficulties. These solutions can come alone through the constructive forces from the system built upon Liberty. They cannot be achieved by the destructive forces of Regimentation. The purification of Liberty from abuses, the restoration of confidence in the rights of men, the release of the dynamic forces of initiative and enterprise are alone the methods by which these solutions can be found and the purpose of American life assured.

The structure of human betterment cannot be built upon foundations of materialism or business, but upon the bedrock of individual character in free men and women. It must be builded by those who, holding to ideals of its high purpose, using the molds of justice, lay brick upon brick from the materials of scientific research, the painstaking sifting of truth from collections of facts and experience, the advancing ideals, morals and spiritual inspirations. Any other foundations are sand, any other mold is distorted; and any other bricks are without straw.

I have no fear that the inherent and unconquerable forces of freedom will not triumph. But it is as true today as when first uttered that "the condition upon which God hath given liberty to man is eternal vigilance." We have in our lifetime seen the subjection of Liberty in one nation after another. It has been defeated by the untruth that some form of dictation by government alone can overcome immediate difficulties and can assure entry into economic perfection. America must not and it will not succumb to that lure. That is the issue of our generation, not a partisan issue but the issue of human liberty.

The spark of liberty in the mind and spirit of man cannot be long extinguished; it will break into flames that will destroy every coercion which seeks to limit it.

8

American Protestantism and the New Deal
Reinhold Niebuhr's
The Children of Light and the Children of Darkness

If liberal Protestant theology had often strayed far afield from traditional religious tenets and from social and political reality, American
Protestantism found in the career and scholarship of Reinhold Niebuhr
a new orthodoxy and a radical social realism. As pastor of an urban
congregation in Detroit during the 1920s, Niebuhr had been brought
face to face with the social insecurity, the family disorganization, and
the psychological anxieties which were endemic in the town that Ford
built. Traditional individualism and customary piety he found irrelevant to the human needs and social tensions of contemporary industrial society. In Marxian analyses (whatever their deficiencies) he
found tools for opening up an understanding of property and class
relationships in the modern era. It is clear, however, that the sweeping
reconstruction of religious and political thought that Niebuhr wrought
in an age of unrelenting crises owed more to St. Paul than to Marx.
The political philosophy he elaborated and the programs he embraced
were radically (which is to say thoroughly and fundamentally) Christian. His influence, in turn, bore upon both social acts and upon
theological reformulations. Although other writings had preceded *The
Children of Light and the Children of Darkness*, it was this work that
vaulted Niebuhr to a position of great influence. His criticism of the
fundamentals of "bourgeois democracy" was bound to have profound
impact in an era in which the institutions of Western capitalism were
so severely challenged. Donald B. Meyer's *The Protestant Search for
Political Realism, 1919-1941* (Berkeley: University of California Press,
1960) is a particularly incisive and critical analysis of Niebuhr's social
and theological influence. A well-balanced account of the political
implications of religion is Robert M. Miller's *American Protestantism*

Reinhold Niebuhr, *The Children of Light and the Children of Darkness*
(New York: Charles Scribner's Sons, 1944), pp. 1-41. Reprinted through
the courtesy of Charles Scribner's Sons.

and Social Issues, 1919-1939 (Chapel Hill: University of North Carolina Press, 1958).

In reading this selection, note (1) Niebuhr's social and theological views of human nature; (2) what he thought of the individualism which had marked liberal religion and liberal democracy in the interwar years; (3) what he thought was needed in order for individual liberty to become truly meaningful; (4) what he regarded as the fatal error that modern democratic civilization had committed in estimating human capabilities; and (5) how he balanced his conservative, neoorthodox theological position and his radical political views.

I]

DEMOCRACY, AS EVERY OTHER HISTORIC IDEAL AND institution, contains both ephemeral and more permanently valid elements. Democracy is on the one hand the characteristic fruit of a bourgeois civilization; on the other hand it is a perennially valuable form of social organization in which freedom and order are made to support, and not to contradict, each other.

Democracy is a "bourgeois ideology" in so far as it expresses the typical viewpoints of the middle classes who have risen to power in European civilization in the past three or four centuries. Most of the democratic ideals, as we know them, were weapons of the commercial classes who engaged in stubborn, and ultimately victorious, conflict with the ecclesiastical and aristocratic rulers of the feudal-medieval world. The ideal of equality, unknown in the democratic life of the Greek city states and derived partly from Christian and partly from Stoic sources, gave the bourgeois classes a sense of self-respect in overcoming the aristocratic pretension and condescension of the feudal overlords of medieval society. The middle classes defeated the combination of economic and political power of mercantilism by stressing economic liberty; and, through the principles of political liberty, they added the political power of suffrage to their growing economic power. The implicit assumptions, as well as the explicit ideals, of democratic civilization were also largely the fruit of middle-class existence. The social and historical optimism of democratic life, for instance, represents the typical illusion of an advancing class which mistook its own progress for the progress of the world.

Since bourgeois civilization, which came to birth in the sixteenth to eighteenth centuries and reached its zenith in the nineteenth century, is now obviously in grave peril, if not actually in *rigor mortis* in the twentieth century, it must be obvious that democracy, in so far as it is a middle-class ideology, also faces its doom.

This fate of democracy might be viewed with equanimity, but for the fact that it has a deeper dimension and broader validity than its middle-class character. Ideally democracy is a permanently valid form of social and political organization which does justice to two dimensions of human existence: to man's spiritual stature and his social character; to the uniqueness and variety of life, as well as to the common necessities of all men. Bourgeois democracy frequently exalted the individual at the expense of the community; but its emphasis upon liberty contained a valid element, which transcended its excessive individualism. The community requires liberty as much as does the individual; and the individual requires community more than bourgeois thought comprehended. Democracy can therefore not be equated with freedom. An ideal democratic order seeks unity within the conditions of freedom; and maintains freedom within the framework of order.

Man requires freedom in his social organization because he is "essentially" free, which is to say that he has the capacity for indeterminate transcendence over the processes and limitations of nature. This freedom enables him to make history and to elaborate communal organizations in boundless variety and in endless breadth and extent. But he also requires community because he is by nature social. He cannot fulfill his life within himself but only in responsible and mutual relations with his fellows.

Bourgeois democrats are inclined to believe that freedom is primarily a necessity for the individual, and that community and social order are necessary only because there are many individuals in a small world, so that minimal restrictions are required to prevent confusion. Actually the community requires freedom as much as the individual; and the individual requires order as much as does the community.

Both the individual and the community require freedom so that neither communal nor historical restraints may prematurely arrest the potencies which inhere in man's essential freedom and which express themselves collectively as well as individually. It is true that individuals are usually the initiators of new insights and the proponents of novel methods. Yet there are collective forces at work in society which are not the conscious contrivance of individuals. In any event society is as much the beneficiary of freedom as the individual. In a free society new forces may enter into competition with the old and gradually establish themselves. In a traditional or tyrannical form of social organization new forces are either suppressed, or they establish themselves at the price of social convulsion and upheaval.

The order of a community is, on the other hand, a boon to the individual as well as to the community. The individual cannot be a true self in isolation. Nor can he live within the confines of the community which "nature" establishes in the minimal cohesion of family and herd. His freedom transcends these limits of nature, and therefore makes larger and larger social units both possible and necessary. It is precisely because of the essential freedom of man that he requires a contrived order in his community.

The democratic ideal is thus more valid than the libertarian and individualistic version of it which bourgeois civilization elaborated. Since the bourgeois version has been discredited by the events of contemporary history and since, in any event bourgeois civilization is in process of disintegration, it becomes important to distinguish and save what is permanently valid from what is ephemeral in the democratic order.

If democracy is to survive it must find a more adequate cultural basis than the philosophy which has informed the building of the bourgeois world. The inadequacy of the presuppositions upon which the democratic experiment rests does not consist merely in the excessive individualism and libertarianism of the bourgeois world view; though it must be noted that this excessive individualism prompted a civil war in the whole western world in which the rising proletarian pitted an excessive collectivism against the false individualism of middle-class life. This civil conflict contributed to the weakness of democratic civilization when faced with the threat of barbarism. Neither the individualism nor the collectivism did justice to all the requirements of man's social life, and the conflict between half-truth and half-truth divided the civilized world in such a way that the barbarians were able to claim first one side and then the other in this civil conflict as their provisional allies.

But there is a more fundamental error in the social philosophy of democratic civilization than the individualism of bourgeois democracy and the collectivism of Marxism. It is the confidence of both bourgeois and proletarian idealists in the possibility of achieving an easy resolution of the tension and conflict between self-interest and the general interest. Modern bourgeois civilization is not, as Catholic philosophers and medievalists generally assert, a rebellion against universal law, or a defiance of universal standards of justice, or a war against the historic institutions which sought to achieve and preserve some general social and international harmony. Modern secularism is not, as religious idealists usually aver, merely a rationalization of self-interest, either individual or collective. Bourgeois individualism may be excessive and it may destroy the individual's organic relation to the community; but it was not intended to destroy either the national or the international order. On the contrary the social idealism which informs our democratic civilization had a touching faith in the possibility of achieving a simple harmony between self-interest and the general welfare on every level.

It is not true that Nazism is the final fruit of a moral cynicism which had its rise in the Renaissance and Reformation, as Catholic apologists aver. Nazi barbarism is the final fruit of a moral cynicism which was only a subordinate note in the cultural life of the modern period, and which remained subordinate until very recently. Modern civilization did indeed seek to give the individual a greater freedom in the national community than the traditional feudal order had given him; and it did seek to free the nations of restraints placed upon their freedom by the international church. But it never cynically defied the general interest in the name of self-interest, either individual or collective. It came closer to doing this nationally than individually. Machiavelli's amoral "Prince," who knows no law beyond his own will and power, is made to bear the whole burden of the Catholic polemic against the modern world. It must be admitted that Machiavelli is the first of a long line of moral cynics in the field of international relations. But this moral cynicism only qualifies, and does not efface, the general universalistic overtone of modern liberal idealism. In the field of domestic politics the war of uncontrolled interests may have been the consquence, but it was certainly not the intention, of middle-class individualists. Nor was the conflict between nations in our modern world their intention. They did demand a greater degree of freedom for the nations; but they believed that it was possible to achieve an uncontrolled harmony between them, once the allegedly irrelevant restrictions of the old religio-political order were removed. In this they proved to be mistaken. They did not make the mistake, however, of giving simple moral sanction to self-interest. They depended rather upon controls and restraints which proved to be inadequate.

II]

In illumining this important distinction more fully, we may well designate the moral cynics, who know no law beyond their will and interest, with a scriptural designation of "children of this world" or "children of darkness." Those who believe that self-interest should be brought under the discipline of a higher law could then be termed "the children of light." This is no mere arbitrary device; for evil is always the assertion of some self-interest without regard to the whole, whether the whole be conceived as the immediate community, or the total community of mankind, or the total order of the world. The good is, on the other hand, always the harmony of the whole on various levels. Devotion to a subordinate and premature "whole" such as the nation, may of course become evil, viewed from the perspective of a larger whole, such as the community of mankind. The "children of light" may thus be defined as those who seek to bring self-interest under the discipline of a more universal law and in harmony with a more universal good.

According to the scripture "the children of this world are in their generation wiser than the children of light." This observation fits the modern situation. Our democratic civilization has been built, not by children of darkness but by foolish children of light. It has been under attack by the children of darkness, by the moral cynics, who declare that a strong nation need acknowledge no law beyond its strength. It has come close to complete disaster under this attack, not because it accepted the same creed as the cynics; but because it underestimated the power of self-interest, both individual and collective, in modern society. The children of light have not been as wise as the children of darkness.

The children of darkness are evil because they know no law beyond the self. They are wise, though evil, because they understand the power of self-interest. The children of light are virtuous because they have some conception of a higher law than their own will. They are usually foolish because they do not know the power of self-will. They underestimate the peril of anarchy in both the national and the international community. Modern democratic civilization is, in short, sentimental rather than cynical. It has an easy solution for the problem of anarchy and chaos on both the national and international level of community, because of its fatuous and superficial view of man. It does not know that the same man who is ostensibly devoted to the "common good' may have desires and ambitions, hopes and fears, which set him at variance with his neighbor.

It must be understood that the children of light are foolish not merely because they underestimate the power of self-interest among the children of darkness. They underestimate this power among themselves. The democratic world came so close to disaster not merely because it never believed that Nazism possessed the demonic fury which it avowed. Civilization refused to recognize the power of class interest in its own communities. It also spoke glibly of an international conscience; but the children of darkness meanwhile skilfully set nation against nation. They were thereby enabled to despoil one nation after another, without every civilized nation coming to the defence of each. Moral cynicism had a provisional advantage over moral sentimentality. Its advantage lay not merely in its own lack of moral scruple but also in its shrewd assessment of the power of self-interest, individual and national, among the children of light, despite their moral protestations.

While our modern children of light, the secularized idealists, were particularly foolish and blind, the more "Christian" children of light have been almost equally guilty of this error. Modern liberal Protestantism was probably even more sentimental in its appraisal of the moral realities in our political life than secular idealism, and Catholicism could see nothing but cynical rebellion in the modern secular revolt against Catholic universalism and a Catholic "Christian" civilization. In Catholic thought medieval political universalism is always accepted at face value. Rebellion against medieval culture is therefore invariably regarded as the fruit of moral cynicism. Actually the middle-class revolt against the feudal order was partially prompted by a generous idealism, not unmixed of course with peculiar middle-class interests. The feudal order was not so simply a Christian civilization as Catholic defenders of it aver. It compounded its devotion to a universal order with the special interests of the priestly and aristocratic bearers of effective social power. The rationalization of their unique position in the feudal order may not have been more marked than the subsequent rationalization of bourgeois interests in the liberal world. But it is idle to deny this "ideological taint" in the feudal order and to pretend that rebels against the order were merely rebels against order as such. They were rebels against a particular order which gave an undue advantage to the aristocratic opponents of the middle classes. The blindness of Catholicism to its own ideological taint is typical of the blindness of the children of light.

Our modern civilization, as a middle-class revolt against an aristocratic and clerical order, was irreligious partly because a Catholic civilization had so compounded the eternal sanctities with the contingent and relative justice and injustice of an agrarian-feudal order, that the new and dynamic bourgeois social force was compelled to challenge not only the political-economic arrangements of the order but also the eternal sanctities which hallowed it.

If modern civilization represents a bourgeois revolt against feudalism, modern culture represents the revolt of new thought, informed by modern science, against a culture in which religious authority had fixed premature and too narrow limits for the expansion of science and had sought to restrain the curiosity of the human mind from inquiring into "secondary causes." The culture which venerated science in place of religion, worshipped natural causation in place of God, and which regarded the cool prudence of bourgeois man as morally more normative than Christian love, has proved itself to be less profound than it appeared to be in the seventeenth and eighteenth centuries. But these inadequacies, which must be further examined as typical of the foolishness of modern children of light, do not validate the judgment that these modern rebels were really children of darkness, intent upon defying the truth or destroying universal order.

The modern revolt against the feudal order and the medieval culture was occasioned by the assertion of new vitalities in the social order and the discovery of new dimensions in the cultural enterprise of mankind. It was truly democratic in so far as it challenged the premature and tentative unity of a society and the stabilization of a culture, and in so far as it developed new social and cultural possibilities. The conflict between the middle classes and the aristocrats, between the scientists and the priests, was not a conflict between children of darkness and children of light. It was a conflict between pious and less pious children of light, both of whom were unconscious of the corruption of self-interest in all ideal achievements and pretensions of human culture.

III]

In this conflict the devotees of medieval religion were largely unconscious of the corruption of self-interest in their own position; but it must be admitted that they were not as foolish as their secular successors in their estimate of the force of self-interest in human society. Catholicism did strive for an inner and religious discipline upon inordinate desire; and it had a statesmanlike conception of the necessity of legal and political restraint upon the power of egotism, both individual and collective, in the national and the more universal human community.

Our modern civilization, on the other hand, was ushered in on a wave of boundless social optimism. Modern secularism is divided into many schools. But all the various schools agreed in rejecting the Christian doctrine of original sin. It is not possible to explain the subtleties or to measure the profundity of this doctrine in this connection. But it is necessary to point out that the doctrine makes an important contribution to any adequate social and political theory the lack of which has robbed bourgeois theory of real wisdom; for it emphasizes a fact which every page of human history attests. Through it one may understand that no matter how wide the perspectives which the human mind may reach, how broad the loyalties which the human imagination may conceive, how universal the community which human statecraft may organize or how pure the aspirations of the saintliest idealists may be, there is no level of human moral or social achievement in which there is not some corruption of inordinate self-love.

This sober and true view of the human situation was neatly rejected by modern culture. That is why it conceived so many fatuous and futile plans for resolving the conflict between the self and the community; and between the national and the world community. Whenever modern idealists are confronted with the divisive and corrosive effects of man's self-love, they look for some immediate cause of this perennial tendency, usually in some specific form of social organization. One school holds that men would be good if only political institutions would not corrupt them; another believes that they would be good if the prior evil of a faulty economic organization could be eliminated. Or another school thinks of this evil as no more than ignorance, and therefore waits for a more perfect educational process to redeem man from his partial and particular loyalties. But no school asks how it is that an essentially good man could have produced corrupting and tyrannical political organizations or exploiting economic organizations, or fanatical and superstitious religious organizations.

The result of this persistent blindness to the obvious and tragic facts of man's social history is that democracy has had to maintain itself precariously against the guile and the malice of the children of darkness, while its statesmen and guides conjured up all sorts of abstract and abortive plans for the creation of perfect national and international communities.

The confidence of modern secular idealism in the possibility of an easy resolution of the tension between individual and community, or between classes, races and nations is derived from a too optimistic view of human nature. This too generous estimate of human virtue is intimately related to an erroneous estimate of the dimensions of the human stature. The conception of human nature which underlies the social and political attitudes of a liberal democratic culture is that of an essentially harmless individual. The survival impulse, which man shares with the animals, is regarded as the normative form of his egoistic drive. If this were a true picture of the human situation man might be, or might become, as harmless as seventeenth- and eighteenth-century thought assumed. Unfortunately for the validity of this picture of man, the most significant distinction between the human and the animal world is that the impulses of the former are "spiritualized" in the human world. Human capacities for evil as well as for good are derived from this spiritualization. There is of course always a natural survival impulse at the core of all human ambition. But this survival impulse cannot be neatly disentangled from two forms of its spiritualization. The one form is the desire to fulfill the potentialities of life and not merely to maintain its existence. Man is the kind of animal who cannot merely live. If he lives at all he is bound to seek the realization of his true nature; and to his true nature belongs his fulfillment in the lives of others. The will to live is thus transmuted into the will to self-realization; and self-realization involves self-giving in relations to others. When this desire for self-realization is fully explored it becomes apparent that it is subject to the paradox that the highest form of self-realization is the consequence of self-giving, but that it cannot be the intended consequence without being prematurely limited. Thus the will to live is finally transmuted into its opposite in the sense that only in self-giving can the self be fulfilled, for: "He that findeth his life shall lose it: and he that loseth his life for my sake shall find it."

On the other hand the will-to-live is also spiritually transmuted into the will-to-power or into the desire for "power and glory." Man, being more than a natural creature, is not interested merely in physical survival but in prestige and social approval. Having the intelligence to anticipate the perils in which he stands in nature and history, he invariably seeks to gain security against these perils by enhancing his power, individually and collectively. Possessing a darkly unconscious sense of his insignificance in the total scheme of things, he seeks to compensate for his insignificance by pretensions of pride. The conflicts between men are thus never simple conflicts between competing survival impulses. They are conflicts in which each man or group seeks to guard its power and prestige against the peril of competing expressions of power and pride. Since the very possession of power and prestige always involves some encroachment upon the prestige and power of others, this conflict is by its very nature a more stubborn and difficult one than the mere competition between various survival impulses in nature. It remains to be added that this conflict expresses itself even more cruelly in collective than in individual terms. Human behavior being less individualistic than secular liberalism assumed, the struggle between classes, races and other groups in human society is not as easily resolved by the expedient of dissolving the groups as liberal democratic idealists assumed.

Since the survival impulse in nature is transmuted into two different and contradictory spiritualized forms, which we may briefly designate as the will-to-live-truly and the will-to-power, man is at variance with himself. The power of the second impulse places him more fundamentally in conflict with his fellow-man than democratic liberalism realizes. The fact that he cannot realize himself, except in organic relation with his fellows, makes the community more important than bourgeois individualism understands. The fact that the two impulses, though standing in contradiction to each other, are also mixed and compounded with each other on every level of human life, makes the simple distinctions between good and evil, between selfishness and altruism, with which liberal idealism has tried to estimate moral and political facts, invalid. The fact that the will-to-power inevitably justifies itself in terms of the morally more acceptable will to realize man's true nature means that the egoistic corruption of universal ideals is a much more persistent fact in human conduct than any moralistic creed is inclined to admit.

If we survey any period of history, and not merely the present tragic era of world catastrophe, it becomes quite apparent that human ambitions, lusts and desires, are more inevitably inordinate, that both human creativity and human evil reach greater heights, and that conflicts in the community between varying conceptions of the good and between competing expressions of vitality are of more tragic proportions than was anticipated in the basic philosophy which underlies democratic civilization.

There is a specially ironic element in the effort of the seventeenth century to confine man to the limits of a harmless "nature" or to bring all his actions under the discipline of a cool prudence. For a while democratic social philosophy was elaborating the picture of a harmless individual, moved by no more than a survival impulse, living in a social peace guaranteed by a pre-established harmony of nature, the advancing natural sciences were enabling man to harness the powers of nature, and to give his desires and ambitions a more limitless scope than they previously had. The static inequalities of an agrarian society were transmuted into the dynamic inequalities of an industrial age. The temptation to inordinate expressions of the possessive impulse, created by the new wealth of a technical civilization, stood in curious and ironic contradiction to the picture of esssentially moderate and ordinate desires which underlay the social philosophy of the physiocrats and of Adam Smith. Furthermore a technical society developed new and more intensive forms of social cohesion and a greater centralization of economic process in defiance of the individualistic conception of social relations which informed the liberal philosophy.

The demonic fury of fascist politics in which a collective will expresses boundless ambitions and imperial desires and in which the instruments of a technical civilization are used to arm this will with a destructive power, previously unknown in history, represents a melancholy historical refutation of the eighteenth- and nineteenth-century conceptions of a harmless and essentially individual human life. Human desires are expressed more collectively, are less under the discipline of prudent calculation, and are more the masters of, and less limited by, natural forces than the democratic creed had understood.

While the fury of fascist politics represent a particularly vivid refutation of the democratic view of human nature, the developments within the confines of democratic civilization itself offer almost as telling a refutation. The liberal creed is never an explicit instrument of the children of darkness. But it is surprising to what degree the forces of darkness are able to make covert use of the creed. One must therefore, in analyzing the liberal hope of a simple social and political harmony, be equally aware of the universalistic presuppositions which underlie the hope and of the egoistic corruptions (both individual and collective) which inevitably express themselves in our culture in terms of, and in despite of, the creed. One must understand that it is a creed of children of light; but also that it betrays their blindness to the forces of darkness.

In the social philosophy of Adam Smith there was both a religious guarantee of the preservation of community and a moral demand that the individual consider its claims. The religious guarantee was contained in Smith's secularized version of providence. Smith believed that when a man is guided by self-interest he is also "led by an invisible hand to promote an end which is not his intention." This "invisible hand" is of course the power of a pre-established social harmony, conceived as a harmony of nature, which transmutes conflicts of self-interest into a vast scheme of mutual service.

Despite this determinism Smith does not hesitate to make

moral demands upon men to sacrifice their interests to the wider interest. The universalistic presupposition which underlies Smith's thought is clearly indicated for instance in such an observation as this: "The wise and virtuous man is at all times willing that his own private interests should be sacrificed to the public interest of his own particular order of society—that the interests of this order of society be sacrificed to the greater interest of the state. He should therefore be equally willing that all those inferior interests should be sacrificed to the greater interests of the universe, to the interests of that great society of all sensible and intelligent beings, of which God himself is the immediate administrator and director."

It must be noted that in Smith's conception the "wider interest" does not stop at the boundary of the national state. His was a real universalism in intent. *Laissez faire* was intended to establish a world community as well as a natural harmony of interests within each nation. Smith clearly belongs to the children of light. But the children of darkness were able to make good use of his creed. A dogma which was intended to guarantee the economic freedom of the individual became the "ideology" of vast corporate structures of a later period of capitalism, used by them, and still used, to prevent a proper political control of their power. His vision of international harmony was transmuted into the sorry realities of an international capitalism which recognized neither moral scruples nor political restraints in expanding its power over the world. His vision of a democratic harmony of society, founded upon the free play of economic forces, was refuted by the tragic realities of the class conflicts in western society. Individual and collective egotism usually employed the political philosophy of this creed, but always defied the moral idealism which informed it.

The political theory of liberalism, as distinct from the economic theory, based its confidence in the identity of particular and universal interests, not so much upon the natural limits of egotism as upon either the capacity of reason to transmute egotism into a concern for the general welfare, or upon the ability of government to overcome the potential conflict of wills in society. But even when this confidence lies in reason or in government, the actual character of the egotism which must be restrained is frequently measured in the dimension of the natural impulse of survival only. Thus John Locke, who thinks government necessary in order to overcome the "inconvenience of the state of nature," sees self-interest in conflict with the general interest only on the low level where "self-preservation" stands in contrast to the interests of others. He therefore can express the sense of obligation to others in terms which assume no final conflict between egotism and the wider interest: "Everyone," he writes, "as he is bound to preserve himself and not to quit his station willfully, so by the like reason, when his own preservation comes not into competition, ought as much as he can preserve the rest of mankind." This is obviously no creed of a moral cynic; but neither is it a profound expression of the sense of universal obligation. For most of the gigantic conflicts of will in human history, whether between individuals or groups, take place on a level, where "self-preservation" is not immediately but only indirectly involved. They are conflicts of rival lusts and ambitions.

The general confidence of an identity between self-interest and the commonweal, which underlies liberal democratic political theory, is succinctly expressed in Thomas Paine's simple creed: "Public good is not a term opposed to the good of the individual; on the contrary it is the good of every individual collected. It is the good of all, because it is the good of every one; for as the public body is every individual collected, so the public good is the collected good of those individuals."

While there is a sense in which this identity between a particular and the general interest is ultimately true, it is never absolutely true in an immediate situation; and such identity as could be validly claimed in an immediate situation is not usually recognized by the proponents of particular interest. Human intelligence is never as pure an instrument of the universal perspective as the liberal democratic theory assumes, though neither is it as purely the instrument of the ego, as is assumed by the anti-democratic theory, derived from the pessimism of such men as Thomas Hobbes and Martin Luther.

The most naive form of the democratic faith in an identity

between the individual and the general interest is developed by the utilitarians of the eighteenth and nineteenth centuries. Their theory manages to extract a covertly expressed sense of obligation toward the "greatest good of the greatest number" from a hedonistic analysis of morals which really lacks all logical presuppositions for any idea of obligation, and which cannot logically rise above an egotistic view of life. This utilitarianism therefore expresses the stupidity of the children of light in its most vivid form. Traditional moralists may point to any hedonistic doctrine as the creed of the children of darkness, because it has no real escape from egotism. But since it thinks it has, it illustrates the stupidity of the children of light, rather than the malice of the children of darkness. It must be observed of course that the children of darkness are well able to make use of such a creed. Utilitarianism's conception of the wise egotist, who in his prudence manages to serve interests wider than his own, supported exactly the same kind of political philosophy as Adam Smith's conception of the harmless egotist, who did not even have to be wise, since the providential laws of nature held his egotism in check. So Jeremy Bentham's influence was added to that of Adam Smith in support of a *laissez-faire* political philosophy; and this philosophy encouraged an unrestrained expression of human greed at the precise moment in history when an advancing industrialism required more, rather than less, moral and political restraint upon economic forces.

It must be added that, whenever the democratic idealists were challenged to explain the contrast between the actual behaviour of men and their conception of it, they had recourse to the evolutionary hope; and declared with William Godwin, that human history is moving toward a form of rationality which will finally achieve a perfect identity of self-interest and the public good.

Perhaps the most remarkable proof of the power of this optimistic creed, which underlies democratic thought, is that Marxism, which is ostensibly a revolt against it, manages to express the same optimism in another form. While liberal democrats dreamed of a simple social harmony, to be achieved by a cool prudence and a calculating egotism, the actual facts of social history revealed that the static class struggle of agrarian societies had been fanned into the flame of a dynamic struggle. Marxism was the social creed and the social cry of those classes who knew by their miseries that the creed of the liberal optimists was a snare and a delusion. Marxism insisted that the increasingly overt social conflict in democratic society would have to become even more overt, and would finally be fought to a bitter conclusion. But Marxism was also convinced that after the triumph of the lower classes of society, a new society would emerge in which exactly that kind of harmony between all social forces would be established, which Adam Smith had regarded as a possibility for any kind of society. The similarities between classical *laissez-faire* theory and the vision of an anarchistic millennium in Marxism are significant, whatever may be the superficial differences. Thus the provisionally cynical Lenin, who can trace all the complexities of social conflict in contemporary society with penetrating shrewdness, can also express the utopian hope that the revolution will usher in a period of history which will culminate in the Marxist millennium of anarchism. "All need for force will vanish," declared Lenin, "since people will grow accustomed to observing the elementary conditions of social existence without force and without subjection."

The Roman Catholic polemic against Marxism is no more valid than its strictures against democratic liberalism. The charge that this is a creed of moral cynicism cannot be justified. However strong the dose of provisional cynicism, which the creed may contain, it is a sentimental and not a cynical creed. The Marxists, too, are children of light. Their provisional cynicism does not even save them from the usual stupidity, nor from the fate, of other stupid children of light. That fate is to have their creed become the vehicle and instrument of the children of darkness. A new oligarchy is arising in Russia, the spiritual characteristics of which can hardly be distinguished from those of the American "go-getters" of the latter nineteenth and early twentieth centuries. And in the light of history Stalin will probably have the same relation to the early dreamers of the Marxist dreams which Napoleon has to the liberal dreamers of the eighteenth century.

Democratic theory, whether in its liberal or in its more radical form, is just as stupid in analyzing the relation between the national and the international community as in seeking a too simple harmony between the individual and the national community. Here, too, modern liberal culture exhibits few traces of moral cynicism. The morally autonomous modern national state does indeed arise; and it acknowledges no law beyond its interests. The actual behaviour of the nations is cynical. But the creed of liberal civilization is sentimental. This is true not only of the theorists whose creed was used by the architects of economic imperialism and of the more covert forms of national egotism in the international community, but also of those whose theories were appropriated by the proponents of an explicit national egotism. A straight line runs from Mazzini to Mussolini in the history of Italian nationalism. Yet there was not a touch of moral cynicism in the thought of Mazzini. He was, on the contrary, a pure universalist.

Even the philosophy of German romanticism, which has been accused with some justification of making specific contributions to the creed of German Nazism, reveals the stupidity of the children of light much more than the malice of the children of darkness. There is of course a strong note of moral nihilism in the final fruit of this romantic movement as we have it in Nietzsche; though even Nietzsche was no nationalist. But the earlier romantics usually express the same combination of individualism and universalism which characterizes the theory of the more naturalistic and rationalistic democrats of the western countries. Fichte resolved the conflict between the individual and the community through the instrumentality of the "just law" almost as easily as the utilitarians resolved it by the calculations of the prudent egotist and as easily as Rousseau resolved it by his conception of a "general will," which would fulfill the best purposes of each individual will. This was no creed of a community, making itself the idolatrous end of human existence. The theory was actually truer than the more individualistic and naturalistic forms of the democratic creed; for romanticism understood that the individual requires the community for his fulfillment. Thus even Hegel, who is sometimes regarded as the father of state absolutism in modern culture, thought of the national state as providing "for the reasonable will, insofar as it is in the individual only implicitly the universal will coming to a consciousness and an understanding of itself and being found."

This was not the creed of a collective egotism which negated the right of the individual. Rather it was a theory which, unlike the more purely democratic creed, understood the necessity of social fulfillment for the individual, and which, in common with the more liberal theories, regarded this as a much too simple process.

If the theory was not directed toward the annihilation of the individual, as is the creed of modern religious nationalism, to what degree was it directed against the universal community? Was it an expression of the national community's defiance of any interest or law above and beyond itself? This also is not the case. Herder believed that "fatherlands" might "lie peaceably side by side and aid each other as families. It is the grossest barbarity of human speech to speak of fatherlands in bloody battle with each other." Unfortunately this is something more than a barbarity of speech. Herder was a universalist, who thought a nice harmony between various communities could be achieved if only the right would be granted to each to express itself according to its unique and peculiar genius. He thought the false universalism of imperialism, according to which one community makes itself the standard and the governor of others, was merely the consequence of a false philosophy, whereas it is in fact one of the perennial corruptions of man's collective life.

Fichte, too, was a universalist who was fully conscious of moral obligations which transcend the national community. His difficulty, like that of all the children of light, was that he had a too easy resolution of the conflict between the nation and the community of nations. He thought that philosophy, particularly German philosophy, could achieve a synthesis between national and universal interest. "The patriot," he declared, "wishes the purpose of mankind to be reached first of all in that nation of which he is a member. . . . This purpose is the only possible patriotic goal. . . . Cosmopolitanism is the will that the purpose of life and of man be attained in all mankind. Patriotism is the will that this purpose be attained first of all in that nation of which we are members." It is absurd to regard such doctrine as the dogma of national egotism, though Fichte could not express it without insinuating a certain degree of national pride into it. The pride took the form of the complacent assumption that German philosophy enabled the German nation to achieve a more perfect relation to the community of mankind than any other nation. He was, in other words, one of the many stupid children of light, who failed to understand the difficulty of the problem which he was considering; and his blindness included failure to see the significance of the implicit denial of an ideal in the thought and action of the very idealist who propounds it.

Hegel, too, belongs to the children of light. To be sure he saw little possibility of constructing a legal structure of universal proportions which might guard the interests of the universal community and place a check upon the will of nations. He declared "states find themselves in a natural, more than a legal, relation to each other. Therefore there is a continuous struggle between them. . . . They maintain and procure their rights through their own power and must as a matter of necessity plunge into war." It may be observed in passing that this is a more accurate description of the actual realities of international relations than that of any of the theorists thus far considered. But the question is whether Hegel regarded this actual situation as morally normative. Hegel's thought upon this matter was ambiguous. On the one hand he tended to regard the demands of the state as final because he saw no way of achieving a legal or political implementation of the inchoate community which lies beyond the state. But on the other hand he believed that a more ultimate law stood over the nation, that it "had its real content in *Weltgeschichte,* the realm of the world mind which holds the supreme absolute truth." This mind, he believed, "constitutes itself the obsolute judge over states." The nation is thus politically, but not morally, autonomous. This is no doctrine of moral cynicism. Rather it is a sentimental doctrine. Hegel imagined that the nation, free of political but not of moral inhibitions, could nevertheless, by thinking "in *Weltgeschichte*" (that is, by becoming fully conscious of its relation to mankind), thereby "lay hold of its concrete universality." The error is very similar to that of Fichte and of all the universalists, whether naturalistic or idealistic, positivist or romantic. It is the error of a too great reliance upon the human capacity for transcendence over self-interest. There is indeed such a capacity. If there were not, any form of social harmony among men would be impossible; and certainly a democratic version of such harmony would be quite unthinkable. But the same man who displays this capacity also reveals varying degrees of the power of self-interest and of the subservience of the mind to these interests. Sometimes this egotism stands in frank contradiction to the professed ideal or sense of obligation to higher and wider values, and sometimes it uses the ideal as its instrument.

It is this fact which a few pessimists in our modern culture have realized, only to draw undemocratic and sometimes completely cynical conclusions from it. The democratic idealists of practically all schools of thought have managed to remain remarkably oblivious to the obvious facts. Democratic theory therefore has not squared with the facts of history. This grave defect in democratic theory was comparatively innocuous in the heyday of the bourgeois period, when the youth and the power of democratic civilization surmounted all errors of judgment and confusions of mind. But in this latter day, when it has become important to save what is valuable in democratic life from the destruction of what is false in bourgeois civilization, it has also become necessary to distinguish what is false in democratic theory from what is true in democratic life.

The preservation of a democratic civilization requires the wisdom of the serpent and the harmlessness of the dove. The children of light must be armed with the wisdom of the children of darkness but remain free from their malice. They must know the power of self-interest in human society without giving it moral justification. They must have this wisdom in order that they may beguile, deflect, harness and restrain self-interest, individual and collective, for the sake of the community.

9

The Individual in a World of Strife
Anne Morrow Lindbergh's
The Wave of the Future—A Confession of Faith

Anne Morrow Lindbergh—daughter of a distinguished financier and diplomat, Dwight W. Morrow, and wife of the lonely and heroic aviator, Charles A. Lindbergh, Jr.—is a woman of stature in her own right. She shared with her husband daring flights to many parts of the globe; she suffered with him the awful grief that followed the kidnapping and murder of their beloved infant son, and bore with him the glare of sensational publicity during the trial of the perpetrator of the crime. With her husband she fled abroad in a futile search for privacy and security—in a world and in an era that would tolerate neither the rights of the individual nor the peace of mankind. There, in Europe, she witnessed the emergence of organized terror and tight police control as the chief instruments of governance. An essayist and poet, a woman of immense sensitivity and sensibility, she engaged her mind and her heart in the pursuit of a policy that might offer some chance, however slim, for the survival of all she held dear—the inviolability of the human personality, the procedures of an open, democratic society. As the forces of totalitarianism (red, brown, and black), and the forces of militarism everywhere gained ascendancy in the decade of the 1930s, Anne Morrow Lindbergh poured out her proposals for survival against the feared and despised "wave of the future." If her husband was driven to polemicism and to direct political action, through the auspices of the America First Committee, against the Roosevelt foreign policy, she felt under no such compulsion herself to offer concrete programs for national action. What she offered, rather, was a subjective and impassioned confession of faith in an age of total crisis, a confession which was appropriately more poetry than prose. Her point of view reflected a deep longing of millions of Americans to hold aloof and to ,maintain some semblance of

Anne Morrow Lindbergh, *The Wave of the Future—A Confession of Faith* (New York: Harcourt, Brace and Company, 1940), pp. 3-41. Reprinted through the courtesy of Harcourt, Brace & World, Inc.

sanity in a world gone mad; the force of her style, in turn, helped to define a national mood which was not finally transformed until the bombs fell that fateful day at Pearl Harbor. Her essay remains as a poignant documentation of the intense human longing for stability, love, and peace in a world of turmoil, hate, and strife. It may also stand for the pragmatic insufficiency of good intentions however soundly rooted in experience. Wayne Cole's *America First: the Battle against Intervention, 1940-1941* (Madison: University of Wisconsin Press, 1953) is a fine study of the forces of isolation. It can be read in company with Donald F. Drummond's *The Passing of American Neutrality, 1937-41* (Ann Arbor: University of Michigan Press, 1955) for a balanced view of these events. In reading this "confession of faith," note (1) the author's attitude toward the successes and failures of the West; (2) what the author thought the United States should do in the international crisis of the late 1930s; (3) what reasons she advanced to support such advice; and (4) what hope she displayed for the future of the United States.

CENTURIES AGO, IN AN AGE NOT UNLIKE OUR OWN, when the established world was cracking, a long period of peace was coming to an end, and a dream of civilized order and unity was dying, Boethius, a Roman philosopher and scholar, sat at his desk and contemplated his changing world with a troubled and uneasy mind. He wrote a poem, full of the questions that were besieging him. How can this truth be reconciled to the truth? this right to that right? How can all these conflicting facts be adjusted in one man's thoughts? Near the end of the poem, as a desperate acknowledgment of the dilemma, though not a solution, come these lines:

> "And therefore whoso seeks the truth
> Shall find in no wise peace of heart."

When I first read those words, a few months ago, I had that supreme thrill, across the centuries, of feeling in sympathy with the mind of another human being, far from me in time, language, race. For an instant the gulfs were swept away; I knew what that man felt.

I have myself been the victim of corroding uneasiness, doubt, and fear these past years. What thinking person has not been? What thinking person can survey the world tragedies today without crying out in torture of mind, "But *why* has this come? And what should one do about it?" . . .

I do not write to urge my point of view upon you; nor do I offer any concrete solution. There are enough people in the world already offering solutions. Some of these people are high-minded idealists; some are politicians, sincere or otherwise; some are eager promoters; some are skillful propagandists. But, however much they may differ, they are all pleading a case; they have the answer. They are convinced of their answer and they urge it upon us with the zeal of an early missionary.

I do not think the problems of the world today can be solved as simply as most of these enthusiasts claim, or that the issues are as crystal clear as they would have us believe, or that those who write and talk have the ultimate revelation or divine judgment as to the best plan of action. . . .

The intellectual is constantly betrayed by his own vanity. God-like, he blandly assumes that he can express everything in words; whereas the things one loves, lives, and dies for are not, in the last analysis, completely expressible in words. To write or to speak is almost inevitably to lie a little. It is an attempt to clothe an intangible in a tangible form; to compress an immeasurable into a mold. And in the act of compression, how Truth is mangled and torn! . . .

I offer, then not a solution but a record of my attempt to reconcile the many conflicting points of view which have assailed me in travels abroad and at home during the last troubled years. Perhaps it would be better called a confession of faith. A faith—though it may spring from long periods of thought and analysis —is not seen, but felt; not proved, but believed; not a program, but a dream.

In recent years, my generation has seen the beliefs, the formulas, and the creeds, that we were brought up to trust implicitly, one by one thrown in danger, if not actually discarded: the sacredness of property, the infallibility of the democratic way of life, the efficiency of the capitalistic system—to mention only a few of the better known household gods which seem to be threatened or dislodged from their sacrosanct niches. Even such fundamental concepts as the goodness of God, the quality of man, and the Christian ethical code are rudely swept away in many parts of the world today.

Looking at the facts alone, as reported to us day by day, we can see that innocent people are being punished, and peaceful nations overrun by force and aggression, which we were taught to believe were outmoded forms of action in our stage of civilization. What are we to stand on? What are we to teach our children—the same things we were taught? . . .

It is quite clear, answer my Ally and Pro-Ally friends (for along with other discarded ideals has also vanished the tolerant world of my father, in which one could discuss two sides of a question without being fiercely labeled Pro or Anti before any discussion began); you have seen it yourself. The world in which we were brought up—the good, the Christian, the democratic, the capitalistic world—is in danger of toppling, and we are fighting to save it. It is, as you must see, purely and simply a case of a crusade against evil. The Forces of Good are fighting the Forces of Evil, and we are on the side of the Forces of Good.

What answer is there to these sincere and fine people? . . . What answer can one give to these friends, except that they are right, and therefore we should be in the war against evil? (What *moral* answer, irrespective of any material answer, vital as it may be, of unpreparedness.) . . .

Are persecution, aggression, war, and theft sins, or are they not?

They *are* sins; there is no doubt about it, and I stand against them. But there are other sins, such as blindness, selfishness, irresponsibility, smugness, lethargy, and resistance to change—sins which we "Democracies," all of us, are guilty of. There are sins of omission as well as sins of commission; and in this world we suffer for our sins, regardless of what category they are in. . . . And there is no sin punished more implacably by nature than the sin of resistance to change. For change is the very essence of living matter. To resist change is to sin against life itself.

The moral case of the "Democracies" (in which I include

America) seems to me to find its equivalent in the Bible story of the rich young man. You remember he was an attractive, fine young man. He followed the rules and the ethics of the Old Testament. And we are told that Christ loved him. He was no sinner; he was a good man—as we "Democracies" are good nations. He claimed as much in his talk with Christ.

To the questions of Christ on his way of life, he replied that he had followed the Commandments: Thou shalt not kill; thou shalt not steal; thou shalt not commit adultery; honor thy father and thy mother.

You remember Christ's answer. He said there was only one thing lacking: "Sell whatsoever thou hast, and give to the poor."

And the young man "went away grieved: for he had great possessions."

I am not here speaking literally, although a very good case can be, and has been, built up for the "Have-not Nations" deserving more share in the possessions of the world, largely in the hands of the "Have Nations." And, in fact, many of the most intelligent minds in the United States, England, and France, years before the war, argued this case courageously and well. Perhaps had they been listened to earlier, had postwar Republican Germany been given more support and aid by the "Democracies," had reasonable territorial and economic concessions been made to a moderate government, there would have been no Naziism and no war.

I do not believe that this case, right as it may be, excuses the methods of aggression and war; but it does, to some degree, explain them. Frustration and privation *explain* theft; they do not *excuse* it. . . .

I am trying to answer my own question and the question in so many minds today which I stated earlier: "*Why* has this come?" And I am trying to find a deeper and truer answer than the superficial and facile one, given so freely and accepted so unquestioningly today: "It has come because the German people are innately evil, and are led by evil leaders. It has come simply because of the accidental occurrence, in a good world, of a few individuals who happen to be a scourge of mankind." But evil does not seem to me to spring without reason in a pure and blameless world; nor scourges rise without some cause. It is this cause I want to fathom. . . .

What was pushing behind Communism? What behind Fascism in Italy? What behind Naziism? Is it nothing but a "return to barbarism," to be crushed at all costs by a "crusade"? Or is some new, and perhaps even ultimately good, conception of humanity trying to come to birth, often through evil and horrible forms and abortive attempts?

What will the historian, looking back on us from the distant future, think of these movements? How will he explain and group them? Will he not class them all together, possibly, as expressions of a common movement in the history of mankind—a movement perhaps, in some measure, caused by our great material advance at the expense of our moral and spiritual one; by our faulty attempts to digest, absorb, and use for the benefit of more of mankind than hitherto, our scientific accumulations and discoveries? From this ultimate point of view, the war might be only an expression of one of those great mutations in the history of the world—and only one of many expressions, numbers of which we do not yet recognize as such.

Whitehead has given the best definition of this type of change when he said, "Human life is driven forward by its dim apprehension of notions too general for its existing language." Something, one feels, is pushing up through the crust of custom. One does not know what—some new conception of humanity and its place on the earth. I believe that it is, in its essence, good; but because we are blind we cannot see it, and because we are slow to change, it must force its way through the heavy crust violently—in eruptions. Some of these eruptions take terrible forms, unrecognizable and evil forms. "Great ideas enter into reality with evil associates and with disgusting alliances. But the greatness remains, nerving the race in its slow ascent."

No, I cannot see the war as a "crusade." If I could label it at all, I would label it part of a vast revolution. I am not here defending the forms this revolution has taken: aggression, terror, class or race persecution. I oppose these as deeply as any American. But I do feel that had the world been able, by peaceful revolution, to foresee and forestall the changes, to correct the abuses that pushed behind the Communist and Fascist revolutions, we would not now have to come to them by such terrible means. The world has been forced to its knees. Unhappily, we seldom find our way there without being beaten to it by suffering.

I cannot see this war, then, simply and purely as a struggle between the "Forces of Good" and the "Forces of Evil." If I could simplify it into a phrase at all, it would seem truer to say that the "Forces of the Past" are fighting against the "Forces of the Future." The tragedy is, to the honest spectator, that there is so much that is good in the "Forces of the Past," and so much that is evil in the "Forces of the Future."

To make this statement is not to say that "might makes right," or that it is Germany's "turn to win," or to give any such literal and facile explanations. It is not to claim that the things we dislike in Naziism *are* the forces of the future. But it is to say that somehow the leaders in Germany, Italy and Russia have discovered how to use new social and economic forces; very often they have used them badly, but nevertheless, they have recognized and used them. They have sensed the changes and they have exploited them. They have felt the wave of the future and they have leapt upon it. The evils we deplore in these systems are not in themselves the future; they are scum on the wave of the future.

If one looks back at history, one can see that it has happened before. Consider the leaders of the French Revolution, the Dantons and the Robespierres. No one today defends the atrocities of the French Revolution; but few seriously question the fundamental necessity or "rightness" of the movement. Yet had we been living then, I am sure the majority of us would have been profoundly shocked—so shocked that we would not have been able to see beyond our emotions to the necessity that lay beneath.

The forces of evil are sweeping out the forces of good, is the tenor of Burke's denunciation of the Revolution. What hope is there for the world, he pleads, in the face of such "frauds, impostures, violences, rapines, murders, confiscations . . . and every description of tyranny and cruelty"? And as I read his beautiful words now, in defense of the falling aristocratic rule of life, I, myself, am moved to his point of view, even as we are all of us moved today by equally stirring pleas in the columns of our magazines and daily newspapers. . . .

For who does not feel like this today, at least emotionally? Who does not feel, the world I love is going down, and all the things in it that I cherish? No matter how the arguments may sound to one's mind, there remains the plain fact, in one's heart, that most of us prefer the old world of England, France, and the United States to the new world of Fascist Europe. I feel this way myself. I may be completely prejudiced and conditioned by the life I have led. I have lived in both France and England, as well as America; and it is their way of thinking, living, speaking, and acting that I prefer; their codes and their laws, I respect. They were not perfect, perhaps, but they made possible a mode of life I shall look back to the rest of my days with nostalgia.

What I question is the confident assumption that this way of life—in which I include our own here in the United States—will still be there after the war is over, even if Great Britain wins; or that it would have continued for long, unchanged, had there been no war. A world in which there were widespread depressions, millions of unemployed, and drifting populations was not going to continue indefinitely. A world in which young people, willing to work, could not afford a home and family, in which the race declined in hardiness, in which one found on every side dissatisfaction, maladjustment and moral decay—that world was ripe for change. That it had to die in violence is the catastrophe; that it had to die in misery, terror and chaos; that it had to fall, dragging down with it much that was good and beautiful and right, spilling the blood, wasting the lives, warping the spirit of many who were needed for the reconstruction of the new world; that it had to die in war, which carries in its train those very miseries it seeks to escape.

I always hoped war could be avoided, or that an early peace would still save some part of a world I loved—that the good of a dying civilization could be bequeathed in comparative tranquility to the new one; as, in nature, a flower dies, but the plant puts forth a new bud from the old stem. All chance for peaceful transition passes more irretrievably with each day that the war continues. The old world we loved is going, and I doubt very much that what immediately follows—if every nation blazes in the same conflagration—will be appreciably better, even in the "Democracies," than what we have witnessed in Germany lately. In other words, I do not believe the things we condemn in Germany are innately German; but rather that they are born of war, revolution, defeat, frustration and suffering. They are evils which may come to every nation under the same conditions—conditions that are increasing in likelihood for the majority of the world with each day this war is prolonged.

What, then, is your conclusion to this discussion? may be justly asked of me. Do you urge a defeatist acceptance of the inevitable? Do you want us to concur in the violent forms (you say you oppose) of the revolution that is now going on in Europe? Should we advocate the overthrow of fundamental principles underlying our way of life? Should we go against our hearts, our faiths, our beliefs—all we love—and encourage the things we hate, in order to follow a will-o'-the-wisp, fatalistic and planetary conception that "All is for the best in the best of possible worlds"?

No, I cannot pledge my personal allegiance to those systems I disapprove of, or those barbarisms I oppose from the bottom of my heart, even if they *are* on the wave of the future. Nor do I propose the surrender of our basic beliefs. But I do feel that it is futile to get into a hopeless "crusade" to "save" civilization. . . . If we do not *better* our civilization, our way of life, and our democracy, there will be no use trying to "save" them by fighting; they will crumble away under the very feet of our armies.

It seems to me that our task, instead of crusading against an inevitable "revolution," or change, in Europe, is to work toward a peaceful "revolution" here, or, rather, a reformation—to reform at home rather than crusade abroad. Our "revolution" will not take the form of a German, an Italian or a Russian revolution. Our answer to the world's problems is not their answer. It will not be the answer France is trying desperately to work out at this moment—and I have such faith in the French that I feel convinced that their ultimate contribution to the future will be even more beautiful than their contribution to the past. It will not be the answer that England will eventually find—though one cannot doubt that the great qualities of the English will be needed and will help to build the new world after this war is over.

Our answer should not and will not be the answer of any European nation. It should be a solution peculiarly and saltily our own. It should be as American as the white steeples of New England or the skyscrapers of New York; as American as a boy's slang, as backyard life in small towns, as baseball and blue jeans. As American as our red-brick schools, standing like staunch citadels along our country roads; as white clapboard houses with green blinds; as unhedged gardens and open fields as our strato-liners and our stream-lined trains; as our air-beacons, necklacing a continent at night, with their golden beams. . . . As our country and our people and our climate, our answer must be purely and wholly American.

To desire a purely American solution is not to advocate strict "Isolationism." In national as in personal life, strict "Isolation-ism" seems to me a miserable ideal. But in both levels of living, most of us feel that our *first* duty—not our only duty, but our first duty—is to our own family and nation. Only by following this precept can we effectively give to the outsider. In national as in personal life one can give only out of strength, never out of weakness.

You may answer to my hypothesis that it is all very well to argue theoretically in a vacuum, but we have a practical world to deal with. If your nation is invaded you cannot go about with your head in the stars and survey your world as if from a planet. What good would a planetary view like yours have done France during the march on Paris; or what good would it do England under a rain of fire?

This is a just riposte and I agree with you. It would, of course, do no good at all, once war had begun. One cannot afford to be planetary when one is in the midst of battle. If I had been a French wife, waiting for word of my husband at the front; or if I were an English mother, shunting my children into a bomb-proof cellar—if I could think at all about such subjects as a new world, reformation, revolution, etc. (which is most unlikely)—I would say impatiently, angrily even, "Yes, yes, a new world—the wave of the future—reform of abuses—certainly; but *first* we must win this war; *first* we must save our husbands, our children, our homes. *Then,* we can stop to think about such things."

If one were in the war, one could not do otherwise. But we are *not* in the war here in America, and if we cannot take a planetary view of the world's troubles, who can? A planetary point of view is necessary at times. . . . The belligerents of this war can hardly help feeling hate, horror, shock, and anger. We, ourselves, cannot help feeling shock and horror; but at the same time we, in America, are in a unique position to judge the tragedies clearly. Surely our task is not voluntarily to surrender this point of vantage by climbing down into the maelstrom of war, where we can only add to the chaos; but rather to see as clearly as possible how to prevent such tragedies from happening here, and how best to assuage the sufferings caused by them abroad.

But if we are not now in the war, we *will* be, cry all the alarmists. Can't you see we will be invaded as surely as Belgium, Holland, and France? They, like you, didn't want war either. They like you, had their heads in the stars. Can't you see that the Maginot Line was our first line of defense, that the British fleet is all that now stands between us and foreign invasion? Can't you see that the ocean is no longer a barrier, that we are unprepared, etc., etc.?

The gigantic specter of fear is growing daily before us, whipped up by such arguments, speeches, denunciations and threats; and fanned by the terrible tales of war and suffering that come to us like parching winds each morning from the pages of our newspapers. There is more fear here today than in the countries which lived under the shadow of war for years in Europe. I know, because I was there. There is even more panic now, in some places in America, than in the nations that were actually under fire. . . .

We have only to contrast the constant gossip of many of us here in America with the accounts of life in England under siege. When one reads of the sense of exhilarated calm steadying each person in his daily round in a nation under hourly attacks; when one reads in a letter the words "safety doesn't exist, but who minds about safety?"—one is stung to admiration for such superb gallantry. But at the same time one feels, deep inside, a kind of sickness, near to shame, for the appearance America presents to the rest of the world.

Perhaps fear is a good thing, you say? Perhaps their lack of fear led them into danger and our possession of it will make us better prepared for our ordeals? Perhaps, but it is difficult to see that fear and panic have helped the cause of a single country in Europe. In fact, where they have appeared, they have only detracted from the strength of a nation, and they can only detract from ours.

I do not believe one should turn one's eyes or one's mind away from possible dangers. There is always possibility of danger, especially to a nation which is unprepared; and, in spite of our potential strength, we are at this moment unprepared both materially and spiritually. The people who argue that the Allies are our first line of defense cite many indisputable facts. These facts cannot be pooh-poohed or brushed aside. Their arguments are excellent. They should be faced, and faced squarely. But they should not be allowed to loom so large that they block our view completely. They should not be built up so close to our eyes that we cannot see around or behind them.

One can quite logically line up navies, armies and forts like a boy's game of tin soldiers, cancel this side against that, and say we are outnumbered. This maneuver is very convincing on paper, but it seems to me to omit all the intangibles. It is true, perfectly true; but not the whole truth. It is not the whole truth, because if this war has taught us anything, it is that we cannot put our faith in material defenses *alone*. An impregnable Maginot Line, a matchless army, an invincible navy—of what avail are these in themselves? Germany's success has not been due alone to her superb equipment. She has won as much from the national spirit incited in her people as from her mechanical strength. I am not now supporting the means by which this spirit was generated nor the direction in which it is turned; but, whether or not one likes it, one cannot deny its existence. It is the same spirit that the French military leaders tried to rouse at the eleventh hour in France. It is the same spirit Churchill inspired in England with his magnificent speeches: "I have nothing to offer but blood, toil, tears and sweat." Without this spirit of courage, self-sacrifice, and determination, it is doubtful whether any people can win a war—or avoid one.

I do not believe we need to be defended against a mechanized German army invading our shores, as much as against the type of decay, weakness, and blindness into which all the "Democracies" have fallen since the last war—have fallen into, perhaps, from a surfeit of success. We are in danger—yes, not so much from bombing planes as from those very conditions which brought on trouble in Europe, and will inevitably bring on trouble here if we do not face them. Shall we turn our backs on these weaknesses, these troubles, these mistakes of our own while we try to wipe out other mistakes abroad? . . .

There is no fighting the wave of the future, any more than as a child you could fight against the gigantic roller that loomed up ahead of you suddenly. You learned then it was hopeless to stand against it or, even worse, to run away. All you could do was to dive into it or leap with it. Otherwise, it would surely overwhelm you and pound you into the sand.

Man has never conquered the underlying forces of nature. But he has learned to understand these forces, to move erect among them, and to use them for his own ends. . . . He cannot successfully defy nature, but he is able to follow, influence, and speed her course. And in doing so, he has learned to halt disease, to lessen suffering, and to increase his capacities for health and the appreciation of life.

Before he learned to use these natural forces, he was hopelessly at their mercy. He had to bow blindly before them or be swept along in their path. Today, is it not conceivable that he must again learn to use forces growing in the world—human forces this time; that he must learn not to resist the inevitable push of progress, but to make his life conform to it?

Before this war started, there were scattered elements trying to direct the course of progress in Europe. There were moderate forces working toward the future. There were idealists who wished to correct life peacefully, within the existing pattern, without completely destroying it in the process of improvement. There were farsighted men who wanted reform, but wanted it in their own way and in their own time. These men and these forces are now overrun by a bigger and more violent force which, one may well argue, was unnecessary. That the efforts of these pioneers should apparently be wasted is one of the great calamities of our age. They were a leaven of the future in the lump of the past. The tragedy is that there were not enough of them or—for many and infinitely complicated reasons—they were unable to bring about changes of sufficient expanse or with sufficient speed or wisdom to forestall the coming violence.

We in America, however, might be able to succed where they failed. With our isolated geographical position, our potential strength, and our particular gifts of temperament, it seems to me that we might be able to meet the new order without the violence we abhor—if only we could open our eyes to our present failings and admit our problems.

It is true that many of the things we love are going down. It is true there are dangerous and difficult times ahead. What do we intend to do about it? That is the problem facing all of us at this moment. No one is wise enough to give a concrete answer or a complete solution, but we may well question our directions, our motives, and our fears. We may ask ourselves whether we must jeopardize the reforms already started here in our own country by plunging into the turmoil abroad; whether the efforts of our present pioneers also shall be wasted. Or might not a course be found which took advantage of, rather than opposed, the great forces pushing in the world?

The wave of the future is coming and there is no fighting it. What is our course to be? Shall we leave our own troubles and crusade abroad? Are we afraid, not only of German bombers but also of change, of responsibility, of growing up? Are we afraid of paying the price of peace? For peace has a price as well as war. The price of peace is to be a strong nation, not only physically but also morally and spiritually. It is to build up not only a static strength, but a strength of growth, reform, and change. For only in growth, reform, and change, paradoxically enough, is true security to be found.

The United States has a heritage of reform. Its early settlers were inspired reformers. Its nation was built not on a long struggle between nobles and kings for the possession of land. It was built not on the slow accumulation of tribal customs. It was built on ideals, prayers, and the dream of making a better world. Not only is this genius for progress in our tradition and in our veins, but we have been blessed with rare leaders in our history—practical visionaries who were not implacable fanatics or tyrants as so many leaders of the old world; but men of intelligence, tolerance, and spiritual beliefs.

Because of this tradition and this heritage, many of us have hoped that in America, if nowhere else in the world, it should be possible to meet the wave of the future in comparative harmony and peace. It should be possible to change an old life to a new without such terrible bloodshed as we see today in the process in Europe. . . .

We, unhappily, are living in the hiatus between two dreams. We have waked from one and not yet started the other. We still have our eyes, our minds, our hearts, on the dream that is dying—How beautiful it was, tinting the whole sky crimson as it fades into the west! But there is another on its way in the gray dawn. Is it not, perhaps, America's mission to find "the dream that is coming to birth"?

It is a tremendous challenge—this challenge to bring a dream to birth in a warlike world; to work out in moderation what the rest of the world is fighting out in bloodshed, intolerance, and hate. The task before us may mean sacrifice of selfish interests; it may mean giving up part of the ease of living and the high material standards we have been noted for. But it might also mean a heightening of more important standards that are not material. It might mean a gain in spirit, in vigor, and in self-reliance, for which no price could be too high. The prospect of applying to reform at home the same spirit those nations abroad are applying to war, should not discourage us. We have faced as difficult ordeals before in our history. We should go out to meet such a test of our system, our beliefs, and our faiths, rejoicing "as a strong man to run a race."

Reform, however, should be more than a test of our beliefs. It should be a reaffirmation of them, an extension of them to wider fields and deeper recesses. It need not mean abandoning our fundamental principles, but rather a re-examination of them to determine whether we are following the dead letter or the living spirit which they embody. It should not mean forsaking the beacons which have led us in the past, but a rekindling of them. It should be essentially a life-giving process. In other words, it seems to me that a creative act is demanded of us. And like all acts of creation it will take labor, patience, pain—and an infinite faith in the future.

10

May She Always Be Right
Henry R. Luce's *The American Century*

Against the reflective mood of Anne Morrow Lindbergh's poignant essay is posed the manfully assertive plea of Henry Luce for a militant national policy which would create an "American century." The China-born editor of the *Time-Life-Fortune* empire spoke eloquently from the heart of that most American of national traditions known as Manifest Destiny. It was America's mission to set an example for the world to emulate—an example of freedom, opportunity, and self-government, of ordered liberty, of material and moral progress. So the doctrine had run. And where other peoples would not follow, the mightiest Republic in Christendom would have to lead. This was no narrow parochial view, however grandly patriotic it may have sounded. This was a vision of a strong and righteous nation employing its resources to fulfill a Providential design for all humanity and for all time. Henry Luce's enthusiasms were rooted most particularly in the "new nationalist" aspirations of Theodore Roosevelt who, a generation earlier, had proclaimed a "big America" policy for the world through which the United States would lead not by concert but by the unilateral exertion of its moral and material strength, uncontained by pacts and alliances. Luce called for a forthright program of world leadership, eager to make decisions and willing to embrace the consequences of its actions. Like *The Wave of the Future*, Henry Luce's *The American Century* proposed no detailed policies or programs. It was more exhortation than analysis. Like Anne Morrow Lindbergh's essay, moreover, Luce's editorial aimed at rallying the American people and their leaders to a grand design in human history. Both were masters of the written word. The significance of their views transcended, therefore, that particular moment of crisis when the nation hovered between war and peace. Walter Johnson's *The Battle Against Isolation* (Chicago: University of Chicago Press, 1944)

Henry R. Luce, *The American Century* (New York: Farrar and Rinehart, Inc., 1941). Originally published by *Life,* February 17, 1941. Reprinted through the courtesy of Henry R. Luce, *Life* Magazine, copyright 1941 by Time, Inc.

165]

provides good background reading for this selection; so, too, does the study of American policy in these years by William L. Langer and S. Everett Gleason, *The Challenge to Isolation, 1937-1940* (New York: Harper & Brothers, 1952). In studying the Luce editorial note (1) the arguments he musters to attack what is to him the sophistry of the "all aid to the Allies short of war" policy; (2) the reasons he puts forward for considering that America had a real and an ideological investment in an Allied victory; (3) the argument supporting his contention that the American dream had validity for human beings everywhere; and (4) the implications of his call for "the first great American century" for that other American commitment to the self-determination of nations.

W E AMERICANS ARE UNHAPPY, WE ARE NOT HAPPY about America. We are not happy about ourselves in relation to America. We are nervous—or gloomy—or apathetic.

As we look out at the rest of the world we are confused; we don't know what to do. "Aid to Britain short of war" is typical of halfway hopes and halfway measures.

As we look toward the future—our own future and the future of other nations—we are filled with foreboding. The future doesn't seem to hold anything for us except conflict, disruption, war.

There is a striking contrast between our state of mind and that of the British people. On September 3, 1939, the first day of the war in England, Winston Churchill had this to say: "Outside the storms of war may blow and the land may be lashed with the fury of its gales, but in our hearts this Sunday morning there is Peace."

Since Mr. Churchill spoke those words the German Luftwaffe has made havoc of British cities, driven the population underground, frightened children from their sleep, and imposed upon everyone a nervous strain as great as any that people have ever endured. . . .

Yet close observers agree that when Mr. Churchill spoke of peace in the hearts of the British people he was not indulging in idle oratory. The British people are profoundly calm. There seems to be a complete absence of nervousness. It seems as if all the neuroses of modern life had vanished from England. . . .

The British are calm in their spirit not because they have nothing to worry about but because they are fighting for their lives. They have made that decision. And they have no further choice. All their mistakes of the past 20 years, all the stupidities and failures that they have shared with the rest of the democratic world, are now of the past. They can forget them because they are faced with a supreme task—defending, yard by yard, their island home.

With us it is different. We do not have to face any attack tomorrow or the next day. Yet we are faced with something almost as difficult. We are faced with great decisions.

* * *

We know how lucky we are compared to all the rest of mankind. At least two-thirds of us are just plain rich compared to all the rest of the human family—rich in food, rich in clothes, rich in entertainment and amusement, rich in leisure, rich.

And yet we also know that the sickness of the world is also our sickness. We, too, have miserably failed to solve the problems of our epoch. And nowhere in the world have man's failures been so little excusable as in the United States of America. Nowhere has the contrast been so great between the reasonable hopes of our age and the actual facts of failure and frustration. . . . Naturally, we have no peace.

But, even beyond this necessity for living with our own misdeeds, there is another reason why there is no peace in our hearts. It is that we have not been honest with ourselves.

In this whole matter of War and Peace especially, we have been at various times and in various ways false to ourselves, false to each other, false to the facts of history and false to the future.

In this self-deceit our political leaders of all shades of opinion are deeply implicated. Yet we cannot shove the blame off on them. If our leaders have deceived us it is mainly because we ourselves have insisted on being deceived. Their deceitfulness has resulted from our own moral and intellectual confusion. In this confusion, our educators and churchmen and scientists are deeply implicated.

Journalists, too, of course, are implicated. But if Americans are confused it is not for lack of accurate and pertinent information. The American people are by far the best informed people in the history of the world.

The trouble is not with the facts. The trouble is that clear and honest inferences have not been drawn from the facts. The day-to-day present is clear. The issues of tomorrow are befogged.

There is one fundamental issue which faces America as it faces no other nation. It is an issue peculiar to America and peculiar to America in the 20th Century—now. It is deeper even than the immediate issue of War. If America meets it correctly, then, despite hosts of dangers and difficulties, we can look forward and move forward to a future worthy of men, with peace in our hearts.

If we dodge the issue, we shall flounder for ten or 20 or 30 bitter years in a chartless and meaningless series of disasters.

The purpose of this article is to state that issue, and its solution, as candidly and as completely as possible. But first of all let us be completely candid about where we are and how we got there.

America Is in the War . . . But are we in it?]

Where are we? We are *in* the war. All this talk about whether this or that might or might not get us into the war is wasted effort. We are, for a fact, *in* the war.

If there's one place we Americans did not want to be, it was *in* the war. We didn't want much to be in any kind of war but, if there was one kind of war we most of all didn't want to be in, it was a European war. Yet, we're in a war, as vicious and bad a war as ever struck this planet, and, along with being worldwide, a European war.

Of course, we are not technically at war, we are not painfully at war, and we may never have to experience the full hell that war can be. Nevertheless the simple statement stands: we are *in* the war. The irony is that Hitler knows it—and most Americans don't. It may or may not be an advantage to continue diplomatic relations with Germany. But the fact that a German embassy still flourishes in Washington beautifully illustrates the whole mass of deceits and self-deceits in which we have been living.

Perhaps the best way to show ourselves that we are in the war is to consider how we can get out of it. Practically, there's only one way to get out of it and that is by a German victory over England. If England should surrender soon, Germany and America would not start fighting the next day. So we would be out of the war. For a while. Except that Japan might then attack in the South Seas and the Philippines. We could abandon the Philippines, abandon Australia and New Zealand, withdraw to Hawaii. And wait. We would be out of the war.

We say we don't want to be in the war. We also say we want England to win. We want Hitler stopped—more than we want to stay out of the war. So, at the moment, we're in.

We Got in Via Defense . . . But what are we defending?]

Now that we are in this war, how did we get in? We got in on the basis of defense. Even that very word, defense, has been full of deceit and self-deceit.

To the average American the plain meaning of the word defense is defense of American territory. Is our national policy today limited to the defense of the American homeland by whatever means may seem wise? It is not. We are *not* in a war to defend American territory. We are in a war to defend and even to promote, encourage and incite so-called democratic principles throughout the world. The average American begins to realize now that that's the kind of war he's in. And he's half-way for it. But he wonders how he ever got there, since a year ago he had not the slightest intention of getting into any such thing. Well, he can see now how he got there. He got there via "defense."

Behind the doubts in the American mind there were and are two different picture-patterns. One of them stressing the appalling consequences of the fall of England leads us to a war of intervention. As a plain matter of the defense of American territory is that picture necessarily true? It is not *necessarily* true. For the other picture is roughly this: while it would be much better for us if Hitler were severely checked, nevertheless regardless of what happens in Europe it would be entirely possible for us to organize a defense of the northern part of the Western Hemisphere so that this country could not be successfully attacked. You are familiar with that picture. Is it true or false? No man is qualified to state categorically that it is false. If the entire rest of the world came under the organized domination of evil tyrants, it is quite possible to imagine that this country could make itself such a tough nut to crack that not all the tyrants in the world would care to come against us. . . . No man can say that that picture of America as an impregnable armed camp is false. No man can honestly say that as a pure matter of defense —defense of our homeland—it is necessary to get into or be in this war.

The question before us then is not *primarily* one of necessity and survival. It is a question of choice and calculation. The true questions are: Do we *want* to be in this war? Do we *prefer* to be in it? And, if so, for what?

We Object to Being in it . . . Our fears have a special cause]

We are in this war. We can see how we got into it in terms of defense. Now why do we object so strongly to being in it?

There are lots of reasons. First, there is the profound and almost universal aversion to all war—to killing and being killed. But the reason which needs closest inspection, since it is one peculiar to this war and never felt about any previous war, is the fear that if we get into this war, it will be the end of our constitutional democracy. We are all acquainted with the fearful forecast—that some form of dictatorship is required to fight a modern war, that we will certainly go bankrupt, that in the process of war and its aftermath our economy will be largely socialized, that the politicians now in office will seize complete power and never yield it up, and that what with the whole trend toward collectivism, we shall end up in such a total national socialism that any faint semblances of our constitutional American democracy will be totally unrecognizable.

We start into this war with huge Government debt, a vast bureaucracy and a whole generation of young people trained to look to the Government as the source of all life. The Party in power is the one which for long years has been most sympathetic to all manner of socialist doctrines and collectivist trends. The President of the United States has continually reached for more and more power, and he owes his continuation in office today largely to the coming of the war. Thus, the fear that the United States will be driven to a national socialism, as a result of cataclysmic circumstances and contrary to the free will of the American people, is an entirely justifiable fear.

But We Will Win It . . .
The big question is how]

So there's the mess—to date. Much more could be said in amplification, in qualification, and in argument. But, however elaborately they might be stated, the sum of the facts about our present position brings us to this point—that the paramount question of this immediate moment is not whether we get into war but how do we win it?

If we are in a war, then it is no little advantage to be aware of the fact. And once we admit to ourselves we are in a war, there is no shadow of doubt that we Americans will be determined to win it—cost what it may in life or treasure. . . .

What Are We Fighting For? . . .
And why we need to know]

Having now, with candor, examined our position, it is time to consider, to better purpose than would have been possible before, the larger issue which confronts us. Stated most simply, and in general terms, that issue is: What are we fighting for? . . .

This questioning reflects our truest instincts as Americans. But more than that. Our urgent desire to give this war its proper name has a desperate practical importance. If we know what we are fighting for, then we can drive confidently toward a victorious conclusion and, what's more, have at least an even chance of establishing a workable Peace.

Furthermore—and this is an extraordinary and profoundly historical fact which deserves to be examined in detail—America and only America can effectively state the war aims of this war.

Almost every expert will agree that Britain cannot win complete victory—cannot even, in the common saying, "stop Hitler" —without American help. Therefore, even if Britain should from time to time announce war aims, the American people are continually in the position of effectively approving or not approving those aims. On the contrary, if America were to announce war aims, Great Britain would almost certainly accept them. And the entire world including Adolf Hitler would accept them as the gauge of this battle.

Americans have a feeling that in any collaboration with Great Britain we are somehow playing Britain's game and not our own. Whatever sense there may have been in this notion in the past, today it is an ignorant and foolish conception of the situation. In any sort of partnership with the British Empire, Great Britain is perfectly willing that the United States of America should assume the role of senior partner. This has been true for a long time. Among serious Englishmen, the chief complaint against America (and incidentally their best alibi for themselves) has really amounted to this—that America has refused to rise to the opportunities of leadership in the world. . . .

The big, important point to be made here is simply that the complete opportunity of leadership is *ours*. Like most great creative opportunities, it is an opportunity enveloped in stupendous difficulties and dangers. If we don't want it, if we refuse to take it, the responsibility of refusal is also ours, and ours alone.

Admittedly, the future of the world cannot be settled all in one piece. It is stupid to try to blueprint the future as you blue-print an engine or as you draw up a constitution for a sorority. But if our trouble is that we don't know what we are fighting for, then it's up to us to figure it out. Don't expect some other country to tell us. Stop this Nazi propaganda about fighting somebody else's war. We fight no wars except our wars. "Arsenal of Democracy?" We may prove to be that. But today we must be the arsenal of America and of the friends and allies of America.

Friends and allies of America? Who are they, and for what? This is for us to tell them.

Dong Dang or Democracy...
But whose Dong Dang, whose Democracy?]

But how can we tell them? And how can we tell ourselves for what purposes we seek allies and for what purposes we fight? Are we going to fight for dear old Danzig or dear old Dong Dang? Are we going to decide the boundaries of Uritania? Or, if we cannot state war aims in terms of vastly distant geography, shall we use some big words like Democracy and Freedom and Justice? Yes, we can use the big words. The President has al-ready used them. And perhaps we had better get used to using them again. Maybe they do mean something—about the future as well as the past.

Some amongst us are likely to be dying for them—on the fields and in the skies of battle. Either that, or the words themselves and what they mean die with us—in our beds.

But is there nothing between the absurd sound of distant cities and the brassy trumpeting of majestic words? And if so, whose Dong Dang and whose Democracy? Is there not some-thing a little more practically satisfying that we can get our teeth into? Is there no sort of understandable program? A pro-gram which would be clearly good for America, which would make sense for America—and which at the same time might have the blessing of the Goddess of Democracy and even help some-how to fix up this bothersome matter of Dong Dang?

Is there none such? There is. And so we now come squarely and closely face to face with the issue which Americans hate most to face. It is that old, old issue with those old, old battered labels—the issue of Isolationism versus Internationalism.

We detest both words. We spit them at each other with the fury of hissing geese. We duck and dodge them.

Let us face that issue squarely now. If we face it squarely now—and if in facing it we take full and fearless account of the realities of our age—then we shall open the way, not necessarily to peace in our daily lives but to peace in our hearts.

Life is made up of joy and sorrow, of satisfaction and difficulties. In this time of trouble, we speak of troubles. There are many troubles. There are troubles in the field of philosophy, in faith and morals. There are troubles of home and family, of personal life. All are interrelated but we speak here especially of the troubles of national policy.

In the field of national policy, the fundamental trouble with America has been, and is, that whereas their nation became in the 20th Century the most powerful and the most vital nation in the world, nevertheless Americans were unable to accommodate themselves spiritually and practically to the fact. Hence they have failed to play their part as a world power—a failure which has had disastrous consequences for themselves and for all mankind. And the cure is this: to accept wholeheartedly our duty and our opportunity as the most powerful and vital nation in the world and in consequence to exert upon the world the full impact of our influence, for such purposes as we see fit and by such means as we see fit.

* * *

"For such purposes as we see fit" leaves entirely open the question of what our purposes may be or how we may appropriately achieve them. Emphatically our only alternative to isolationism is not to undertake to police the whole world nor to impose democratic institutions on all mankind including the Dalai Lama and the good shepherds of Tibet.

America cannot be responsible for the good behavior of the entire world. But America is responsible, to herself as well as to history, for the world-environment in which she lives. Nothing can so vitally affect America's environment as America's own influence upon it, and therefore if America's environment is unfavorable to the growth of American life, then America has nobody to blame so deeply as she must blame herself.

In its failure to grasp this relationship between America and America's environment lies the moral and practical bankruptcy of any and all forms of isolationism. It is most unfortunate that this virus of isolationist sterility has so deeply infected an influential section of the Republican Party. For until the Republican Party can develop a vital philosophy and program for America's initiative and activity as a world power, it will continue to cut itself off from any useful participation in this hour of history. And its participation is deeply needed for the shaping of the future of America and of the world.

* * *

But politically speaking, it is an equally serious fact that for seven years Franklin Roosevelt was, for all practical purposes, a complete isolationist. He was more of an isolationist than Herbert Hoover or Calvin Coolidge. The fact that Franklin Roosevelt has recently emerged as an emergency world leader should not obscure the fact that for seven years his policies ran absolutely counter to any possibility of effective American leadership in international co-operation. There is of course a justification which can be made for the President's first two terms. It can be said, with reason, that great social reforms were necessary in order to bring democracy up-to-date in the greatest of democracies. But the fact is that Franklin Roosevelt failed to make American democracy work successfully on a narrow, materialistic and nationalistic basis. And under Franklin Roosevelt we ourselves have failed to make democracy work successfully. Our only chance now to make it work is in terms of a vital international economy and in terms of an international moral order.

This objective is Franklin Roosevelt's great opportunity to justify his first two terms and to go down in history as the greatest rather than the last of American Presidents. Our job is to help in every way we can, for our sakes and our children's sakes, to ensure that Franklin Roosevelt shall be justly hailed as America's greatest President.

Without our help he cannot be our greatest President. With our help he can and will be. Under him and with his leadership we can make isolationism as dead an issue as slavery, and we can make a truly *American* internationalism something as natural to us in our time as the airplane or the radio.

In 1919 we had a golden opportunity, an opportunity unprecedented in all history, to assume the leadership of the world —a golden opportunity handed to us on the proverbial silver platter. We did not understand that opportunity. Wilson mishandled it. We rejected it. The opportunity persisted. We bungled it in the 1920's and in the confusions of the 1930's we killed it.

To lead the world would never have been an easy task. To revive the hope of that lost opportunity makes the task now infinitely harder than it would have been before. Nevertheless, with the help of all of us, Roosevelt must succeed where Wilson failed.

The 20th Century Is the American Century...
Some facts about our time]

Consider the 20th Century. It is ours not only in the sense that we happen to live in it but ours also because it is America's first century as a dominant power in the world. So far, this century of ours has been a profound and tragic disappointment. No other century has been so big with promise for human progress and happiness. And in no one century have so many men and women and children suffered such pain and anguish and bitter death.

It is a baffling and difficult and paradoxical century. No doubt all centuries were paradoxical to those who had to cope with them. But, like everything else, our paradoxes today are bigger and better than ever. Yes, better as well as bigger—inherently better. We have poverty and starvation—but only in the midst of plenty. We have the biggest wars in the midst of the most widespread, the deepest and the most articulate hatred of war in all history. We have tyrannies and dictatorships—but only when democratic idealism, once regarded as the dubious eccentricity of a colonial nation, is the faith of a huge majority of the people of the world.

And ours is also a revolutionary century. The paradoxes make it inevitably revolutionary. Revolutionary, of course, in science and in industry. And also revolutionary, as a corollary in politics and the structure of society. But to say that a revolution is in progress is not to say that the men with either the craziest ideas or the angriest ideas or the most plausible ideas are going to come out on top. The Revolution of 1776 was won and established by men most of whom appear to have been both gentlemen and men of common sense.

Clearly a revolutionary epoch signifies great changes, great adjustments. And this is only one reason why it is really so foolish for people to worry about our "constitutional democracy" without worrying or, better, thinking hard about the world revolution. For only as we go out to meet and solve for our time the problems of the world revolution, can we know how to reestablish our constitutional democracy for another 50 or 100 years.

This 20th Century is baffling, difficult, paradoxical, revolutionary. But by now, at the cost of much pain and many hopes deferred, we know a good deal about it. And we ought to accommodate our outlook to this knowledge so dearly bought. For example, any true conception of our world of the 20th Century must surely include a vivid awareness of at least these four propositions.

First: our world of 2,000,000,000 human beings is for the first time in history one world, fundamentally indivisible. Second: modern man hates war and feels intuitively that, in its present scale and frequency, it may even be fatal to his species. Third: our world, again for the first time in human history, is capable of producing all the material needs of the entire human family. Fourth: the world of the 20th Century, if it is to come to life in any nobility of health and vigor, must be to a significant degree an American Century.

As to the first and second: in postulating the indivisibility of the contemporary world, one does not necessarily imagine that anything like a world state—a parliament of men—must be brought about in this century. Nor need we assume that war can be abolished. All that it is necessary to feel—and to feel deeply—is that terrific forces of magnetic attraction and repulsion will operate as between every large group of human beings on this planet. Large sections of the human family may be effectively organized into opposition to each other. Tyrannies may require a large amount of living space. But Freedom requires and will require far greater living space than Tyranny. Peace cannot endure unless it prevails over a very large part of the world. Justice will come near to losing all meaning in the minds of men unless Justice can have approximately the same fundamental meanings in many lands and among many peoples.

As to the third point—the promise of adequate production for all mankind, the "more abundant life"—be it noted that this is characteristically an American promise. It is a promise easily made, here and elsewhere, by demagogues and proponents of all manner of slick schemes and "planned economies." What we must insist on is that the abundant life is predicated on Freedom —on the Freedom which has created its possibility—on a vision of Freedom under law. Without Freedom, there will be no abundant life. With Freedom, there can be.

And finally there is the belief—shared let us remember by most men living—that the 20th Century must be to a significant degree an American Century. This knowledge calls us to action now.

America's Vision of Our World . . .
How it shall be created]

What can we say and foresee about an American Century? It is meaningless merely to say that we reject isolationism and accept the logic of internationalism. What internationalism? Rome had a great internationalism. So had the Vatican and Genghis Khan and the Ottoman Turks and the Chinese Emperors and 19th Century England. After the first World War, Lenin had one in mind. Today Hitler seems to have one in mind —one which appeals strongly to some American isolationists whose opinion of Europe is so low that they would gladly hand it over to anyone who would guarantee to destroy it forever. But what internationalism have we Americans to offer?

Ours cannot come out of the vision of any one man. It must be the product of the imaginations of many men. It must be a sharing with all peoples of our Bill of Rights, our Declaration of Independence, our Constitution, our magnificent industrial products, our technical skills. It must be an internationalism of the people, by the people and for the people.

In general, the issues which the American people champion revolve around their determination to make the society of men safe for the freedom, growth and increasing satisfaction of all individual men. Beside that resolve, the sneers, groans, catcalls, teeth-grinding, hisses and roars of the Nazi Propaganda Ministry are of small moment.

Once we cease to distract ourselves with lifeless arguments about isolationism, we shall be amazed to discover that there is already an immense American internationalism. American jazz, Hollywood movies, American slang, American machines and patented products, are in fact the only things that every community in the world, from Zanzibar to Hamburg, recognizes in common. Blindly, unintentionally, accidentally and really in spite of ourselves, we are already a world power in all the trivial ways —in very human ways. But there is a great deal more than that. America is already the intellectual, scientific and artistic capital of the world. Americans—Midwestern Americans—are today the least provincial people in the world. They have traveled the most and they know more about the world than the people of any other country. America's worldwide experience in commerce is also far greater than most of us realize.

Most important of all, we have that indefinable, unmistakable sign of leadership: prestige. And unlike the prestige of Rome or Genghis Khan or 19th Century England, American prestige throughout the world is faith in the good intentions as well as in the ultimate intelligence and ultimate strength of the whole

American people. We have lost some of that prestige in the last
few years. But most of it is still there. . . .

✳   ✳   ✳

As America enters dynamically upon the world scene, we
need most of all to seek and to bring forth a vision of America
as a world power which is authentically American and which
can inspire us to live and work and fight with vigor and enthusiasm. And as we come now to the great test, it may yet turn out
that in all our trials and tribulations of spirit during the first
part of this century we as a people have been painfully appre-
hending the meaning of our time and now in this moment of
testing there may come clear at last the vision which will guide
us to the authentic creation of the 20th Century—our Century.

✳   ✳   ✳

Consider four areas of life and thought in which we may seek
to realize such a vision:

First, the economic. It is for America and for America alone
to determine whether a system of free economic enterprise—an
economic order compatible with freedom and progress—shall or
shall not prevail in this century. We know perfectly well that
there is not the slightest chance of anything faintly resembling
a free economic system prevailing in this country if it prevails
nowhere else. What then does America have to decide? Some
few decisions are quite simple. For example: we have to decide
whether or not we shall have for ourselves and our friends freedom of the seas—the right to go with our ships and our ocean-
going airplanes where we wish, when we wish and as we wish.
The vision of America as the principal guarantor of the freedom
of the seas, the vision of America as the dynamic leader of world
trade, has within it the possibilities of such enormous human
progress as to stagger the imagination. Let us not be staggered
by it. Let us rise to its tremendous possibilities. Our thinking
of world trade today is on ridiculously small terms. For example,
we think of Asia as being worth only a few hundred millions a
year to us. Actually, in the decades to come Asia will be worth
to us exactly zero—or else it will be worth to us four, five, ten

billions of dollars a year. And the latter are the terms we must think in, or else confess a pitiful impotence.

Closely akin to the purely economic area and yet quite different from it, there is the picture of an America which will send out through the world its technical and artistic skills. Engineers, scientists, doctors, movie men, makers of entertainment, developers of airlines, builders of roads, teachers, educators. Throughout the world, these skills, this training, this leadership is needed and will be eagerly welcomed, if only we have the imagination to see it and the sincerity and good will to create the world of the 20th Century.

But now there is a third thing which our vision must immediately be concerned with. We must undertake now to be the Good Samaritan of the entire world. It is the manifest duty of this country to undertake to feed all the people of the world who as a result of this worldwide collapse of civilization are hungry and destitute—all of them, that is, whom we can from time to time reach consistently with a very tough attitude toward all hostile governments. For every dollar we spend on armaments, we should spend at least a dime in a gigantic effort to feed the word—and all the world should know that we have dedicated ourselves to this task. Every farmer in America should be encouraged to produce all the crops he can, and all that we cannot eat—and perhaps some of us could eat less—should forthwith be dispatched to the four quarters of the globe as a free gift, administered by a humanitarian army of Americans, to every man, woman and child on this earth who is really hungry.

But all this is not enough. All this will fail and none of it will happen unless our vision of America as a world power includes a passionate devotion to great American ideals. We have some things in this country which are infinitely precious and especially American—a love of freedom, a feeling for the equality of opportunity, a tradition of self-reliance and independence and also of co-operation. In addition to ideals and notions which are especially American, we are the inheritors of all the great principles of Western civilization—above all Justice, the love of Truth, the ideal of Charity. The other day Herbert Hoover said that America was fast becoming the sanctuary of the ideals of civilization. For the moment it may be enough to be the sanctuary of these ideals. But not for long. It now becomes our time to be the powerhouse from which the ideals spread throughout the world and do their mysterious work of lifting the life of mankind from the level of the beasts to what the Psalmist called a little lower than the angels.

America is the dynamic center of ever-widening spheres of enterprise, America as the training center of the skillful servants of mankind, America as the Good Samaritan, really believing again that it is more blessed to give than to receive, and America as the powerhouse of the ideals of Freedom and Justice—out of these elements surely can be fashioned a vision of the 20th Century to which we can and will devote ourselves in joy and gladness and vigor and enthusiasm.

Other nations can survive simply because they have endured so long—sometimes with more and sometimes with less significance. But this nation, conceived in adventure and dedicated to the progress of man—this nation cannot truly endure unless there courses strongly through its veins from Maine to California the blood of purpose and enterprise and high resolve.

Throughout the 17th Century and the 18th Century and the 19th Century, this continent teemed with manifold projects and magnificent purposes. Above them all and weaving them all together into the most exciting flag of all the world and of all history was the triumphal purpose of freedom.

It is in this spirit that all of us are called, each to his own measure of capacity, and each in the widest horizon of his vision, to create the first great American Century.

11

Building the Arsenal of Democracy

Franklin D. Roosevelt's Fireside Chat
December 29, 1940

Franklin D. Roosevelt, whose responsibility as Chief Executive was to form and execute a foreign policy consistent with the nation's historical traditions and legitimate interests, could not afford to engage in philosophical disquisitions. His was the infinitely more difficult (and practical) task of administration. At a time when, on the one hand, the longing for noninvolvement in the world's struggles was still widespread and, on the other, an ever-larger group of American leaders urged an interventionist policy before time ran out on the democracies, Roosevelt had to strike a balance between opposing views. In time it proved to be not only an embarrassing but an impossible task. Probably from the beginning of war, Roosevelt had committed himself (if not yet the nation) to an Allied victory, for in his opinion the nation's security, to say nothing of its political and ideological concerns, depended finally upon the defeat of Germany and Japan. The means to this end had to be shaped, however, by specific events and circumstances. The fall of France, the assault upon Denmark, Norway, and the Lowlands, and the desperate battle of Britain stepped up the tendency of his policies toward involvement in the European war. In late December, 1940, the President took the issue to the people in a fireside chat.

Sound accounts of the Roosevelt foreign policy toward the European and the Asian conflicts may be found in William L. Langer and S. Everett Gleason, *The Undeclared War, 1940-1941* (New York: Harper & Brothers, 1953), and in Herbert Feis, *The Road to Pearl Harbor* (Princeton University Press, 1950). In reading this address, note (1) what the President hoped to accomplish by keeping open

Franklin D. Roosevelt, "Fireside Chat, December 29, 1940," in Samuel I. Rosenman (ed.), *The Public Papers and Addresses of Franklin D. Roosevelt,* Vol. 9 (New York: The Macmillan Company, 1941), pp. 633-644. Reprinted through the courtesy of the trustees of the Franklin D. Roosevelt trust and of Samuel I. Rosenman.

the seas; (2) why he thought it essential that Britain survive the German attack; (3) the implications of this stated view that the policy he proposed was directed not at war but at keeping war far from American shores; and (4) his rationale for making the United States "the great arsenal for democracy."

MY FRIENDS:

This is not a fireside chat on war. It is a talk on national security; because the nub of the whole purpose of your President is to keep you now, and your children later, and your grandchildren much later, out of a last-ditch war for the preservation of American independence and all the things that American independence means to you and to me and to ours.

Tonight, in the presence of a world crisis, my mind goes back eight years to a night in the midst of a domestic crisis. It was a time when the wheels of American industry were grinding to a full stop, when the whole banking system of our country had ceased to function.

I well remember that while I sat in my study in the White House, preparing to talk with the people of the United States, I had before my eyes the picture of all those Americans with whom I was talking. I saw the workmen in the mills, the mines, the factories; the girl behind the counter; the small shopkeeper; the farmer doing his spring plowing; the widows and the old men wondering about their life's savings.

I tried to convey to the great mass of American people what the banking crisis meant to them in their daily lives.

Tonight, I want to do the same thing, with the same people, in this new crisis which faces America.

We met the issue of 1933 with courage and realism.

We face this new crisis—this new threat to the security of our nation—with the same courage and realism.

Never before since Jamestown and Plymouth Rock has our American civilization been in such danger as now.

For, on September 27, 1940, by an agreement signed in Berlin, three powerful nations, two in Europe and one in Asia, joined themselves together in the threat that if the United States of

America interfered with or blocked the expansion program of these three nations—a program aimed at world control—they would unite in ultimate action against the United States.

The Nazi masters of Germany have made it clear that they intend not only to dominate all life and thought in their own country, but also to enslave the whole of Europe, and then to use the resources of Europe to dominate the rest of the world.

It was only three weeks ago their leader stated this: "There are two worlds that stand opposed to each other." And then in defiant reply to his opponents, he said this: "Others are correct when they say: With this world we cannot ever reconcile ourselves. . . . I can beat any other power in the world." So said the leader of the Nazis.

In other words, the Axis not merely admits but *proclaims* that there can be no ultimate peace between their philosophy of government and our philosophy of government.

In view of the nature of this undeniable threat, it can be asserted, properly and categorically, that the United States has no right or reason to encourage talk of peace, until the day shall come when there is a clear intention on the part of the aggressor nations to abandon all thought of dominating or conquering the world.

At this moment, the forces of the states that are leagued against all people who live in freedom, are being held away from our shores. The Germans and the Italians are being blocked on the other side of the Atlantic by the British, and by the Greeks, and by thousands of soldiers and sailors who were able to escape from subjugated countries. In Asia, the Japanese are being engaged by the Chinese nation in another great defense.

In the Pacific Ocean is our fleet.

Some of our people like to believe that wars in Europe and in Asia are of no concern to us. But it is a matter of most vital concern to us that European and Asiatic war-makers should not gain control of the oceans which lead to this hemisphere.

One hundred and seventeen years ago the Monroe Doctrine was conceived by our Government as a measure of defense in the face of a threat against this hemisphere by an alliance in

Continental Europe. Thereafter, we stood on guard in the Atlantic, with the British as neighbors. There was no treaty. There was no "unwritten agreement."

And yet, there was the feeling, proven correct by history, that we as neighbors could settle any disputes in peaceful fashion. The fact is that during the whole of this time the Western Hemisphere has remained free from aggression from Europe or from Asia.

Does anyone seriously believe that we need to fear attack anywhere in the Americas while a free Britain remains our most powerful naval neighbor in the Atlantic? Does anyone seriously believe, on the other hand, that we could rest easy if the Axis powers were our neighbors there?

If Great Britain goes down, the Axis powers will control the continents of Europe, Asia, Africa, Australasia, and the high seas —and they will be in a position to bring enormous military and naval resources against this hemisphere. It is no exaggeration to say that all of us, in all the Americas, would be living at the point of a gun—a gun loaded with explosive bullets, economic as well as military.

We should enter upon a new and terrible era in which the whole world, our hemisphere included, would be run by threats of brute force. To survive in such a world, we would have to convert ourselves permanently into a militaristic power on the basis of war economy.

Some of us like to believe that even if Great Britain falls, we are still safe, because of the broad expanse of the Atlantic and of the Pacific.

But the width of those oceans is not what it was in the days of clipper ships. At one point between Africa and Brazil the distance is less than from Washington to Denver, Colorado—five hours for the latest type of bomber. And at the North end of the Pacific Ocean America and Asia almost touch each other.

Even today we have planes that could fly from the British Isles to New England and back again without refueling. And remember that the range of the modern bomber is ever being increased.

During the past week many people in all parts of the nation

have told me what they wanted me to say tonight. Almost all of them expressed a courageous desire to hear the plain truth about the gravity of the situation. One telegram, however, expressed the attitude of the small minority who want to see no evil and hear no evil, though they know in their hearts that evil exists. That telegram begged me not to tell again of the ease with which our American cities could be bombed by any hostile power which had gained bases in this Western Hemisphere. The gist of that telegram was: "Please, Mr. President, don't frighten us by telling us the facts."

Frankly and definitely there is danger ahead—danger against which we must prepare. But we well know that we cannot escape danger, or the fear of danger, by crawling into bed and pulling the covers over our heads.

Some nations of Europe were bound by solemn non-intervention pacts with Germany. Other nations were assured by Germany that they need *never* fear invasion. Non-intervention pact or not, the fact remains that they *were* attacked, overrun and thrown into the modern form of slavery at an hour's notice, or even without any notice at all. As an exiled leader of one of these nations said to me the other day—"The notice was a minus quantity. It was given to my Government two hours after German troops had poured into my country in a hundred places."

The fate of these nations tells us what it means to live at the point of a Nazi gun.

The Nazis have justified such actions by various pious frauds. One of these frauds is the claim that they are occupying a nation for the purpose of "restoring order." Another is that they are occupying or controlling a nation on the excuse that they are "protecting it" against the aggression of somebody else.

For example, Germany has said that she was occupying Belgium to save the Belgians from the British. Would she then hesitate to say to any Southern American country, "We are occupying you to protect you from aggression by the United States"?

Belgium today is being used as an invasion base against Britain, now fighting for its life. Any South American country, in Nazi hands, would always constitute a jumping-off place for

German attack on any one of the other Republics of this hemisphere.

Analyze for yourselves the future of two other places even nearer to Germany if the Nazis won. Could Ireland hold out? Would Irish freedom be permitted as an amazing pet exception in an unfree world? Or the Islands of the Azores which still fly the flag of Portugal after five centuries? You and I think of Hawaii as an outpost of defense in the Pacific. And yet, the Azores are closer to our shores in the Atlantic than Hawaii is on the other side.

There are those who say that the Axis powers would never have any desire to attack the Western Hemisphere. That is the same dangerous form of wishful thinking which has destroyed the powers of resistance of so many conquered peoples. The plain facts are that the Nazis have proclaimed, time and again, that all other races are their inferiors and therefore subject to their orders. And most important of all, the vast resources and wealth of this American Hemisphere constitute the most tempting loot in all the round world.

Let us no longer blind ourselves to the undeniable fact that the evil forces which have crushed and undermined and corrupted so many others are already within our own gates. Your Government knows much about them and every day is ferreting them out.

Their secret emissaries are active in our own and in neighboring countries. They seek to stir up suspicion and dissension to cause internal strife. They try to turn capital against labor, and vice versa. They try to reawaken long slumbering racial and religious enmities which should have no place in this country. They are active in every group that promotes intolerance. They exploit for their own ends our natural abhorrence of war. These trouble-breeders have but one purpose. It is to divide our people into hostile groups and to destroy our unity and shatter our will to defend ourselves.

There are also American citizens, many of them in high places, who, unwittingly in most cases, are aiding and abetting the work of these agents. I do not charge these American citizens with being foreign agents. But I do charge them with doing exactly the kind of work that the dictators want done in the United States.

These people not only believe that we can save our own skins by shutting our eyes to the fate of other nations. Some of them go much further than that. They say that we can and should become the friends and even the partners of the Axis powers. Some of them even suggest that we should imitate the methods of the dictatorships. Americans never can and never will do that.

The experience of the past two years has proven beyond doubt that no nation can appease the Nazis. No man can tame a tiger into a kitten by stroking it. There can be no appeasement with ruthlessness. There can be no reasoning with an incendiary bomb. We know now that a nation can have peace with the Nazis only at the price of total surrender.

Even the people of Italy have been forced to become accomplices of the Nazis; but at this moment they do not know how soon they will be embraced to death by their allies.

The American appeasers ignore the warning to be found in the fate of Austria, Czechoslovakia, Poland, Norway, Belgium, the Netherlands, Denmark, and France. They tell you that the Axis powers are going to win anyway; that all this bloodshed in the world could be saved; that the United States might just as well throw its influence into the scale of a dictated peace, and get the best out of it that we can.

They call it a "negotiated peace." Nonsense! Is it a negotiated peace if a gang of outlaws surrounds your community and on threat of extermination makes you pay tribute to save your own skins?

Such a dictated peace would be no peace at all. It would be only another armistice, leading to the most gigantic armament race and the most devastating trade wars in all history. And in these contests the Americas would offer the only real resistance to the Axis powers.

With all their vaunted efficiency, with all their parade of pious purpose in this war, there are still in their background the concentration camp and the servants of God in chains.

The history of recent years proves that shootings and chains and concentration camps are not simply the transient tools but the very altars of modern dictatorships. They may talk of a "new order" in the world, but what they have in mind is only a revival of the oldest and the worst tyranny. In that there is no liberty, no religion, no hope.

The proposed "new order" is the very opposite of a United States of Europe or a United States of Asia. It is not a Government based upon the consent of the governed. It is not a union of ordinary, self-respecting men and women to protect themselves and their freedom and their dignity from oppression. It is an unholy alliance of power and pelf to dominate and enslave the human race.

The British people and their allies today are conducting an active war against this unholy alliance. Our own future security is greatly dependent on the outcome of that fight. Our ability to "keep out of war" is going to be affected by that outcome.

Thinking in terms of today and tomorrow, I make the direct statement to the American people that there is far less chance of the United States getting into war, if we do all we can now to support the nations defending themselves against attack by the Axis than if we acquiesce in their defeat, submit tamely to an Axis victory, and wait our turn to be the object of attack in another war later on.

If we are to be completely honest with ourselves, we must admit that there is risk in any course we may take. But I deeply believe that the great majority of our people agree that the course that I advocate involves the least risk now and the greatest hope for world peace in the future.

The people of Europe who are defending themselves do not ask us to do their fighting. They ask us for the implements of war, the planes, the tanks, the guns, the freighters which will enable them to fight for their liberty and for our security. Emphatically we must get these weapons to them in sufficient volume and quickly enough, so that we and our children will be saved the agony and suffering of war which others have had to endure.

Let not the defeatists tell us that it is too late. It will never be earlier. Tomorrow will be later than today.

Certain facts are self-evident.

In a military sense Great Britain and the British Empire are today the spearhead of resistance to world conquest. They are putting up a fight which will live forever in the story of human gallantry.

There is no demand for sending an American Expeditionary Force outside our own borders. There is no intention by any member of your Government to send such a force. You can, therefore, nail any talk about sending armies to Europe as deliberate untruth.

Our national policy is not directed toward war. Its sole purpose is to keep war away from our country and our people.

Democracy's fight against world conquest is being greatly aided, and must be more greatly aided, by the rearmament of the United States and by sending every ounce and every ton of munitions and supplies that we can possibly spare to help the defenders who are in the front lines. It is no more unneutral for us to do that than it is for Sweden, Russia and other nations near Germany, to send steel and ore and oil and other war materials into Germany every day in the week.

We are planning our own defense with the utmost urgency; and in its vast scale we must integrate the war needs of Britain and the other free nations which are resisting aggression.

This is not a matter of sentiment or of controversial personal opinion. It is a matter of realistic, practical military policy, based on the advice of our military experts who are in close touch with existing warfare. These military and naval experts and the members of the Congress and the Administration have a single-minded purpose—the defense of the United States.

This nation is making a great effort to produce everything that is necessary in this emergency—and with all possible speed. This great effort requires great sacrifice.

I would ask no one to defend a democracy which in turn would not defend everyone in the nation against want and privation. The strength of this nation shall not be diluted by the failure of the Government to protect the economic well-being of its citizens.

If our capacity to produce is limited by machines, it must ever be remembered that these machines are operated by the skill and the stamina of the workers. As the Government is determined to protect the rights of the workers, so the nation has a right to expect that the men who man the machines will discharge their full responsibilities to the urgent needs of defense.

The worker possesses the same human dignity and is entitled to the same security of position as the engineer or the manager or the owner. For the workers provide the human power that turns out the destroyers, the airplanes and the tanks.

The nation expects our defense industries to continue operation without interruption by strikes or lock-outs. It expects and insists that management and workers will reconcile their differences by voluntary or legal means, to continue to produce the supplies that are so sorely needed.

And on the economic side of our great defense program, we are, as you know, bending every effort to maintain stability of prices and with that the stability of the cost of living.

Nine days ago I announced the setting up of a more effective organization to direct our gigantic efforts to increase the production of munitions. The appropriation of vast sums of money and a well-coordinated executive direction of our defense efforts are not in themselves enough. Guns, planes, ships and many other things have to be built in the factories and arsenals of America. They have to be produced by workers and managers and engineers with the aid of machines which in turn have to be built by hundreds of thousands of workers throughout the land.

In this great work there has been splendid cooperation between the Government and industry and labor; and I am very thankful.

American industrial genius, unmatched throughout the world in the solution of production problems, has been called upon to bring its resources and its talents into action. Manufacturers of watches, farm implements, linotypes, cash registers, automobiles, sewing machines, lawn mowers and locomotives are now making fuses, bomb packing crates, telescope mounts, shells, pistols and tanks.

But all our present efforts are not enough. We must have more ships, more guns, more planes—more of everything. This can only be accomplished if we discard the notion of "business as usual." This job cannot be done merely by superimposing on the existing productive facilities the added requirements of the nation for defense.

Our defense efforts must not be blocked by those who fear the future consequences of surplus plant capacity. The possible consequences of failure of our defense efforts now are much more to be feared.

After the present needs of our defenses are past, a proper handling of the country's peace-time needs will require all the new productive capacity—if not more.

No pessimistic policy about the future of America shall delay the immediate expansion of those industries essential to defense. We need them.

I want to make it clear that it is the purpose of the nation to build now with all possible speed every machine, every arsenal, every factory that we need to manufacture our defense material. We have the men—the skill—the wealth—and above all, the will.

I am confident that if and when production of consumer or luxury goods in certain industries requires the use of machines and raw materials that are essential for defense purposes, then such production must yield, and will gladly yield, to our primary and compelling purpose.

I appeal to the owners of plants—to the managers—to the workers—to our own Government employees—to put every ounce of effort into producing these munitions swiftly and without stint. With this appeal I give you the pledge that all of us who are officers of your Government will devote ourselves to the same whole-hearted extent to the great task that lies ahead.

As planes and ships and guns and shells are produced, your Government, with its defense experts, can then determine how best to use them to defend this hemisphere. The decision as to how much shall be sent abroad and how much shall remain at home must be made on the basis of our over-all military necessities.

We must be the great arsenal of democracy. For us this is an emergency as serious as war itself. We must apply ourselves to our task with the same resolution, the same sense of urgency, the same spirit of patriotism and sacrifice as we would show were we at war.

We have furnished the British great material support and we will furnish far more in the future.

There will be no "bottlenecks" in our determination to aid Great Britain. No dictator, no combination of dictators, will weaken that determination by threats of how they will construe that determination.

The British have received invaluable military support from the heroic Greek army, and from the forces of all the governments in exile. Their strength is growing. It is the strength of men and women who value their freedom more highly than they value their lives.

I believe that the Axis powers are not going to win this war. I base that belief on the latest and best information.

We have no excuse for defeatism. We have every good reason for hope—hope for peace, hope for the defense of our civilization and for the building of a better civilization in the future.

I have the profound conviction that the American people are now determined to put forth a mightier effort than they have ever yet made to increase our production of all the implements of defense, to meet the threat to our democratic faith.

As President of the United States I call for that national effort. I call for it in the name of this nation which we love and honor and which we are privileged and proud to serve. I call upon our people with absolute confidence that our common cause will greatly succeed.

12

The War through the Eyes of the Common Soldier
Ernie Pyle's *Brave Men*

The war, once joined, engaged the total energies and resources of the nation. It was a grim task, a task that challenged the courage, imagination, and ingenuity of a people which had always prided itself on its capacity to get the job done, whatever the odds. No war was ever better reported. The demands of wartime secrecy kept many good stories out of the press, but human interest could be exploited without fear of springing security leaks. Of the legion of correspondents who reported the war through the eyes of the common soldier, Ernie Pyle, the G.I.'s own favorite, was one of the very best. There was a ring of unpretentious honesty in all he wrote. False heroics and sentimentality had no more place in his columns than they did in the lives of the soldiers, sailors, and marines whose stories he chronicled. To be cited in one of his reports was better than to win medals and awards. He personalized the war to those millions who stayed at home and wondered what it was really like for those whom they knew and loved who stood guard in remote and exotic places in scattered theaters of war throughout the world. Anyone who had seen first hand the events of which he wrote, anyone who at home had read a fully candid letter from some "dog-face" overseas knew that Ernie Pyle wrote the crude, unvarnished truth of this war. A good social and military history of the war is Fletcher Pratt, *War for the World* (New Haven: Yale University Press, 1950); W. P. Hall's *Iron out of Calvary* (New York: D. Appleton-Century Company, 1946) is another good account. As for Ernie Pyle, daily he courted death. For years he was spared; but one spring day on Okinawa, half-way around the world, a few months before the war ended, his luck ran out. He joined in death his friends and comrades whose exploits he had not celebrated but merely set down. This is the way it was. In reading these selections, note (1) the ways in which the common soldiers themselves reacted to the hunger, filth, discomforts, frustra-

Ernie Pyle, "The Fabulous Infantry," and "A Last Word," from *Brave Men* (New York: Henry Holt and Company, Inc., 1944) pp. 124-136, 318-320. Reprinted through the courtesy of Holt, Rinehart and Winston, Inc.

tions, the little ironies and joys, the agonies, and the "hurry-up-and-wait" of war; (2) the significance of the lack of idealism in interpreting the meaning of the war; and (3) the reasons for Ernie Pyle's immense popularity both on the home front and on the part of the men whose stories he narrated.

The Fabulous Infantry]

KNOWING MY WEAKNESS FOR THE FOOT SOLDIER, YOU won't be surprised to learn that my next port of call was an infantry company of the Thirty-fourth Division. The Thirty-fourth was the oldest division on that side of the Atlantic. It had been away from home two full years.

Two years is a long time overseas, even if a division did nothing but travel around and work hard. But when in addition those two years meant campaign after bitter campaign a division became wise and worn and old, like a much-read book, or a house that wears its aging stone stoutly, ignoring the patchwork of new concrete that holds it together. . . .

A lot of people have morale confused with the desire to fight. I don't know of one soldier out of ten thousand who wants to fight. They certainly didn't in that company. The old-timers were sick to death of battle, and the new replacements were scared to death of it. And yet the company went on into battle, and it was a proud company.

When I joined the outfit it was during one of those lulls that sometimes come in war. The company was still "in the lines," but not actually fighting. They had taken a town a few days before, and since then had been merely waiting for the next attack. These intervals gave the soldiers time to restore their gear and recuperate their spirits. Usually such intervals came weeks apart.

The regiment was bivouacked over an area a mile or more square, with the men in foxholes under olive trees, and the company, battalion, and regimental command posts set up in farmhouses. It was the first time our company command post had been inside walls since they hit Italy five months before. . . .

Of the nearly two hundred men who came overseas in my company, only eight were left. Those eight men had everything a military man would want in a soldier. They had all been in the Army nearly three years—away from America two years. They had served in Northern Ireland, Scotland, England, Algeria, Tunisia and Italy. They had been at it so long they had become more soldier than civilian.

Their life consisted wholly and solely of war, for they were and always had been front-line infantrymen. They survived because the fates were kind to them, certainly—but also because they had become hard and immensely wise in animal-like ways of self-preservation. None of them liked war. They all wanted to go home, but they had been at it so long they knew how to take care of themselves and how to lead others. Around a little group like them every company was built.

I wouldn't go so far as to say those boys hadn't changed since they left America. Of course they changed—they had to. And yet when I sat and talked with them they seemed just like ordinary human beings back home. . . .

Some of the remarks the men made in fun were pathetically revealing. There was the thing Sergeant Jack Pierson said one day in battle.

Jack was a wonderful guy, almost a Sergeant Quirt, except that he was good-looking, smart and friendly. But he was tough. As the other men said, "Jack is really a rough man. He would be rough even back home." He had been in the Commandos with Tag Allumbaugh.

He came from Sidney, Iowa, and was older than most of the others. For many years he ran a pile driver, doing construction work along the Missouri and Mississippi rivers. He called himself a river rat. The boys called him a "one-man army." He had been wounded once.

Jack was married and had three children. He had a girl nine, a boy seven, and then he had Junior. Junior was going on two and Jack had never seen him. Jack pretty much doted on Junior, and everybody in the company knew about Junior and how badly Jack wanted to see him.

One day in battle they were having it tough. There were rifle fire, mortars, and hand grenades all around, and soldiers on both sides getting knocked off like flies. Tag Allumbaugh was lying within shouting distance of where Jack was pinned down, and he yelled over, "How you doin', Jack?"

And then this man who was hard in peacetime, and was hard in war, called back a resigned answer that expressed in a general way every combat soldier's pathetic reason for wanting to live and hating to die.

He called back—and he wasn't joking, "It don't look like I'm gonna get to see Junior." (But he did. He survived, and went back to America in rotation, so I guess he saw Junior after all— and how he deserved to!). . . .

Sometimes a person says the silliest things without being able to account for them. For example, one night our command post made a night move of about five miles. I went in a jeep, perched high on top of a lot of bedrolls.

The night was pure-black and the road was vicious. We were in low gear all the time, and even that was too fast. Many times we completely lost the trail, and would wander off and bump into trees or fall into deep ditches.

It was one of those sudden nose dives that undid me. We were far off the trail, but didn't know it. Suddenly the front end of the jeep dropped about three feet and everything stopped right there. That is, everything but me.

I went sailing right over the driver's shoulder, hit the steering wheel, and slid out onto the hood. And as I flew past the driver I said, "Excuse me." . . .

At an Army chow line near a village or close to farms, there were usually a few solemn and patient children with tin buckets —waiting to get what was left over.

One soldier said to me, "I just can't bear to eat when they stand and look at me like they do. Lots of times I've filled my mess kit and just walked over and dumped it in their buckets and gone back to my foxhole. I wasn't hungry."

Lieutenant Sheehy was tremendously proud of the outfit. He told me, "Every man in the company deserves the Silver Star."

We were walking around the bivouac where the men of the

company were sitting on the edges of their foxholes, talking or cleaning their gear.

"Let's go over there," he said. "I want to introduce you to my personal hero."

I figured that the lieutenant's own "personal hero," out of a whole company of men who deserved the Silver Star, must be a real soldier indeed.

And this is how I was first introduced to Sergeant Frank ("Buck") Eversole, one of the old-timers. He shook hands sort of timidly and said, "Pleased to meet you," and then didn't say any more. I could tell by his eyes, and by his slow, courteous speech when he did talk, that he was a Westerner. Conversation with him was rather hard, but I didn't mind his reticence, for I know how Westerners like to size people up first. The sergeant wore a brown stocking cap on the back of his head. His eyes were the piercing kind. I noticed his hands too— they were outdoor hands, strong and rough.

Later in the afternoon I came past his foxhole again, and we sat and talked a little while alone. We didn't talk about the war, but mainly about our West, and just sat and made figures on the ground with sticks as we talked. We got started that way, and in the days that followed I came to know him well. He was to me, and to all those with whom he served, one of the great men of the war.

Buck was a cowboy before the war. He was born in the little town of Missouri Valley, Iowa, and his mother still lived there. But Buck went west on his own before he was sixteen, and worked as a ranch hand. He was twenty-eight years old, and unmarried. He worked a long time around Twin Falls, Idaho, and then later down in Nevada. Like so many cowboys, he made the rodeos in season. He was never a star or anything. Usually he just rode the broncs out of the chute, for pay—$7.50 a ride. Once he did win a fine saddle. He rode at Cheyenne and the other big rodeos. . . .

Buck Eversole had the Purple Heart and two Silver Stars for bravery. He was cool and deliberate and very effective in battle. His commanders depended more on him than on any other man. He had been wounded once, and had had countless narrow escapes. A person instinctively felt safer when he was around. He was not helpless like most of us. He was practical. He could improvise, patch things, fix things.

His grammar was the unschooled grammar of the plains and the soil. He used profanity, but never violently. Even in the familiarity of his own group his voice was always low. It was impossible to conceive of his doing anything dishonest. He was such a confirmed soldier by then he always said "sir" to any stranger.

After the war Buck wanted to go back west to the land he loved. He wanted to get a little place and feed a few head of cattle, and be independent. "I don't want to be just a ranch hand no more," he said. "It's all right and I like it all right, but it's a rough life and it don't get you nowhere. When you get a little older you kinda like a place of your own."

Buck Eversole had no hatred for Germans, although he had killed many of them. He killed because he was trying to keep alive himself. The years rolled over him and the war became his only world, and battle his only profession. He armored himself with a philosophy of accepting whatever might happen.

"I'm mighty sick of it all," he said quietly, "but there ain't no use to complain. I just figure it this way, that I've been given a job to do and I've got to do it. And if I don't live through it, there's nothing I can do about it."

His job was platoon sergeant. That means he had charge of about forty front-line fighting men. He had been at the front for more than a year. War was old to him and he had become almost the master of it, a senior partner in the institution of death.

The personnel of his platoon had turned over many times as battle whittled down the old ones and the replacement system brought up the new ones. Only a handful were veterans.

"It gets so it kinda gets you, seein' these new kids come up," Buck told me one night in his slow, barely audible Western voice, so full of honesty and sincerity. "Some of them have just got fuzz on their faces, and don't know what it's all about, and they're scared to death. No matter what, some of them are bound to get killed."

We talked about some of the other old-time noncoms who could take battle themselves, but had gradually grown morose under the responsibility of leading green boys to their slaughter. Buck spoke of one sergeant especially, a brave and hardened man, who went to his captain and asked to be reduced to a private in the lines.

"I know it ain't my fault that they get killed," Buck finally said, "and I do the best I can for them. But I've got so I feel like it's me killin' 'em instead of a German. I've got so I feel like a murderer. I hate to look at them when the new ones come in."

Buck himself had been fortunate. His one wound was a bullet through the arm. His own skill and wisdom had saved him many times, but luck had saved him countless other times.

One night Buck and an officer took refuge from shelling in a two-room Italian stone house. As they sat there, a shell came through the wall of the far room, crossed the room and buried itself in the middle wall, with its nose pointing upward. It didn't go off. . . .

The ties that grow between men who live savagely together, relentlessly communing with Death, are ties of great strength. There is a sense of fidelity to each other in a little corps of men who have endured so long, and whose hope in the end can be so small.

One afternoon Buck's turn came to go back to rest camp for five days. He knew the company was due to attack that night. Buck went to Sheehy and said, "Lieutenant, I don't think I better go. I'll stay if you need me."

The lieutenant said, "Of course I need you, Buck, I always need you. But it's your turn and I want you to go. In fact, you're ordered to go."

The truck taking the few boys away to rest camp left just at dusk. It was drizzling and the valleys were swathed in a dismal mist. Artillery of both sides flashed and rumbled around the horizon. The encroaching darkness was heavy and foreboding.

Buck came to the little group of old-timers in the company

with whom I was standing. You'd have thought he was leaving forever. He shook hands all around. "Well, good luck to you all." And then he added, "I'll be back in just five days." He was a man stalling off his departure. Another round of good-byes, and he slowly started away. But he stopped and said good-bye all around again, and again he repeated, "Well, good luck to you all."

I walked with him toward the truck in the dusk. He kept his eyes on the ground, and I think he might have cried if he had known how, and he said to me very quietly, "This is the first battle I've ever missed that this battalion has been in. Even when I was in the hospital with my arm, they were in bivouac. This will be the first one I've ever missed. I sure do hope they have good luck." And then, "I feel like a deserter."

He climbed in, and the truck dissolved into the blackness. I went back and lay down on the ground among my other friends, waiting for the night orders to march. I lay there in the darkness thinking—terribly touched by the great simple devotion of that soldier who was a cowboy—thinking of the millions of people far away at home who would remain forever unaware of the powerful fraternalism in this ghastly brotherhood of war.

A Last Word]

THIS FINAL CHAPTER IS BEING WRITTEN IN THE LATter part of August, 1944; it is being written under an apple tree in a lovely green orchard in the interior of France. It could well be that the European war will be over and done with by the time you read this book. Or it might not. But the end is inevitable, and it cannot be put off for long. The German is beaten and he knows it.

It will seem old when, at some given hour, the shooting stops and everything suddenly changes again. It will be odd to drive down an unknown road without the little knot of fear in your stomach; odd not to listen with animal-like alertness for the meaning of every distant sound; odd to have your spirit released from the perpetual weight that is compounded of fear and death and dirt and noise and anguish.

The end of the war will be a gigantic relief, but it cannot be a matter of hilarity for most of us. Somehow it would seem sacrilegious to sing and dance when the great day comes—there are so many who can never sing and dance again. The war in France has not been easy by any manner of means. True, it has gone better than most of us had hoped. And our casualties have been fewer than our military leaders had been willing to accept. But do not let anyone lead you to believe that they have been low. Many, many thousands of Americans have come to join the ones who already have slept in France for a quarter of a century.

For some of us the war has already gone on too long. Our feelings have been wrung and drained; they cringe from the effort of coming alive again. Even the approach of the end seems to have brought little inner elation. It has brought only a tired sense of relief.

I do not pretend that my own feeling is the spirit of our armies. If it were, we probably would not have had the power to win. Most men are stronger. Our soldiers still can hate, or glorify, or be glad, with true emotion. For them death has a pang, and victory a sweet scent. But for me war has become a flat, black depression without highlights, a revulsion of the mind and an exhaustion of the spirit.

The war in France has been especially vicious because it was one of the last stands for the enemy. We have won because of many things. We have won partly because the enemy was weakened from our other battles. The war in France is our grand finale, but the victory here is the result of all the other victories that went before. It is the result of Russia, and the western desert, and the bombings, and the blocking of the sea. It is the result of Tunisia and Sicily and Italy; we must never forget or belittle those campaigns.

We have won because we have had magnificent top leadership, at home and in our Allies and with ourselves overseas. Surely America made its two perfect choices in General Eisenhower and General Bradley. They are great men—to me doubly great because they are direct and kind.

We won because we were audacious. One could not help but be moved by the colossus of our invasion. It was a bold and mighty thing, one of the epics of all history. In the emergency of war our nation's powers are unbelievable. The strength we have spread around the world is appalling even to those who make up the individual cells of that strength. I am sure that in the past two years I have heard soldiers say a thousand times, "If only we could have created all this energy for something good." But we rise above our normal powers only in times of destruction.

We have won this war because our men are brave, and because of many other things—because of Russia, and England, and the passage of time, and the gift of nature's materials. We did not win it because destiny created us better than all other peoples. I hope that in victory we are more grateful than we are proud. I hope we can rejoice in victory—but humbly. The dead men would not want us to gloat.

The end of one war is a great fetter broken from around our lives. But there is still another to be broken. The Pacific war may yet be long and bloody. Nobody can foresee, but it would be disastrous to approach it with easy hopes. Our next few months at home will be torn beween the new spiritual freedom of half peace and the old grinding blur of half war. It will be a confusing period for us.

Thousands of our men will soon be returning to you. They have been gone a long time and they have seen and done and felt things you cannot know. They will be changed. They will have to learn how to adjust themselves to peace. Last night we had a violent electrical storm around our countryside. The storm was half over before we realized that the flashes and the crashings around us were not artillery but plain old-fashioned thunder and lightning. It will be odd to hear only thunder again. You must remember that such little things as that are in our souls, and will take time.

And all of us together will have to learn how to reassemble our broken world into a pattern so firm and so fair that another great war cannot soon be possible. To tell the simple truth, most of us over in France don't pretend to know the right answer.

Submersion in war does not necessarily qualify a man to be the master of the peace. All we can do is fumble and try once more —try out of the memory of our anguish—and be as tolerant with each other as we can.

13

Equality for the Negro in a Democratic Society
Gunnar Myrdal's
"America Again at the Crossroads"

The second great war, a war for democracy no less than the first, began to focus the nation's attention upon its greatest dilemma—that a people formally dedicated to human liberty, equality of opportunity, and brotherhood denied the enjoyment of those ideals to citizens of colored skin. When Gunnar Myrdal, distinguished Swedish sociologist, and his American associates began their investigations into the problems of race in contemporary American society, therefore, they were driven not only to analyze the position of the Negro in American society and his changing status but also to criticize the whole American democratic society—its ideals, its dynamics, its tensions, its dilemmas. What was finally at stake, then, was not the plight of the colored American, however important that surely was; what finally mattered was America itself. On the eve of war, in the summer of 1941, Franklin D. Roosevelt had been persuaded, by a threatened march of Negroes on Washington, to extend government protection for fair employment in defense industries without regard to race, color, and creed. But in the armed services Americans were segregated by color; and the pattern of Jim Crow continued generally to prevail throughout the nation.

Two accounts of the changing status of the American Negro during these years are Henry Lee Moon's *Balance of Power: The Negro Vote* (Garden City, N. Y.: Doubleday, 1948), and Herbert Garfinkel, *When Negroes March* (New York: Free Press of Glencoe, 1959). The reader will wish to note (1) the comparison and contrast of conditions for the Negro American in the North and South; (2) the internal dynamics working toward larger opportunity during the war years; (3) evidence of the persisting contradiction between avowed

Gunnar Myrdal, "America Again at the Crossroads," in *An American Dilemma: The Negro Problem and Modern Democracy* (New York: Harper & Brothers, 1944), pp. 997-1024. Reprinted through the courtesy of Harper & Row, Publishers.

ideal and practice; (4) the impact of the revolutionary desires of
colored peoples throughout the world for self-determination upon the
civil rights movement within the United States; (5) the expectations
that Myrdal and his associates entertained for the future of race relations in America and in the world; and (6) the validity of these expectations in light of developments in race relations since 1944, and in
light of the Negro Revolution and the Civil Rights Act of 1964.

1. The Negro Problem and the War]

THE THREE GREAT WARS OF THIS COUNTRY HAVE BEEN
fought for the ideals of liberty and equality to which
the nation was pledged. As a consequence of all of them, the American Negro made great strides toward freedom and opportunity.
The Revolutionary War started a development which ultimately
ended slavery in all Northern states, made new import of slaves
illegal and nearly accomplished abolition even in the South—
though there the tide soon turned in a reaction toward fortification
of the plantation system and of Negro slavery. The Civil War gave
the Negro Emancipation and Reconstruction in the South—
though it was soon followed by Restoration of white supremacy.
The First World War provided the Negro his first real opportunity as a worker in Northern industry, started the Great Migration out of the South, and began the "New Negro" movement—
though the end of the War saw numerous race riots and the
beginning of a serious decline in employment opportunities.
After the advances on all three occasions there were reactions,
but not as much ground was lost as had been won. Even taking
the subsequent reactions into account, each of the three great
wars in the history of America helped the Negro take a permanent step forward.

Now America is again in a life-and-death struggle for liberty
and equality, and the American Negro is again watching for
signs of what war and victory will mean in terms of opportunity
and rights for him in his native land. To the white American,
too, the Negro problem has taken on a significance greater than
it has ever had since the Civil War. This War is crucial for the

future of the Negro, and the Negro problem is crucial in the War. There is bound to be a redefinition of the Negro's status in America as a result of this War.

The exact nature of this structural change in American society cannot yet be foreseen. History is not the result of a predetermined Fate. Nothing is irredeemable until it is past. The outcome will depend upon decisions and actions yet to be taken by whites and Negroes. What we can know definitely, however, are the trends as they developed up to the War and the changes so far during the War. On the basis of this knowledge, we can discern the gamut of possibilities for the future. If, in addition, we have some insight into the temper and inclination of the people who are both the actors and the spectators of the drama being staged, we can estimate which are the most probable developments.

2. Social Trends]

Looking back over the ground we have mapped in our inquiry, we can make two general observations. One is the following: *What we usually call "social trends" have their main significance for the Negro's status because of what is in white people's minds.* It is true, for instance, that the decreasing relative demand for unskilled work, compared with skilled and semi-skilled work, and the change of much dirty and heavy labor to clean and easy labor, have dangerous implications for the Negro's employment opportunities. But if these technological and economic trends have disastrous effects on the Negro, the cause of this is the persistency with which white people want to keep him out of skilled and pleasant work. It is also true that the trend toward mass unemployment in America tends to turn Negro labor into a relief burden. But, again, the concentration of unemployment upon the Negro people is explainable only as the direct and indirect effects of discrimination. . . .

The second observation is this: *The important changes in the Negro problem do not consist of, or have close relations with, "social trends" in the narrower meaning of the term but are made up of changes in people's beliefs and valuations.* We started by stating the hypothesis that the Negro problem has its existence in the American's mind. There the decisive struggle goes on. It is there that the changes occur. Our investigation has amply confirmed our basic assumption, as an abbreviated summary of some of our main findings regarding recent trends will demonstrate.

In the field of *"social"* relations we traced a slow but visible decrease of discrimination in the South during recent decades up until the outbreak of the present War. The racial etiquette was gradually loosening. White people were beginning to take cognizance of distinctions in education and class within the Negro community and becoming prepared to treat Negroes somewhat differently according to their individual worth. The "no social equality" theory was not quite so rigid as in earlier generations. The entire Jim Crow apparatus was maintained, but its motivation was no longer so self-evident. Southern liberals were demanding with increasing courage and determination that the doctrine "separate, but equal" should be followed out in its "equality" aspect as well as in its "separateness" aspect— that segregation should not be utilized as a means of discrimination.

The separation of the two groups in the South was, meanwhile, becoming more and more perfected as the frequency of personal master-servant relations was decreasing and as the segregated Negro institutions and Negro professions were being built up. There even seemed to be a growing mental isolation between whites and Negroes. Behind this potentially most dangerous development was not only the exclusionist policy of the whites, but also the sullen dissatisfaction and bitter race pride of the Negroes themselves. They were "withdrawing" themselves as a reaction to the segregation and discrimination enforced by the whites.

In the North the sudden influx of Southern Negroes during the Great Migration caused a temporary rise in social discrimination. Since, in spite of this, there was much less of it in the North than in the South, the migration meant a decrease of social segregation and discrimination for the Negro people as a whole. It also seemed that, despite the sharp temporary rise on account of the migration, the trend in the North, too, was toward decreasing race prejudice.

In the administration of *justice* there was a definite improvement in the South, even if Negroes in that region are still far from enjoying equality before the law. There was a slow rise in the quality of the police and the courts. Lynching, peonage, and other conspicuous aberrations of justice were becoming stamped out. This development was spurred by the increasing interest and interference in the judicial order of the region, shown by the federal courts and other federal agencies, and also by the state governments. The activity of such private organizations as the N.A.A.C.P. and the Interracial Commission were also of paramount importance for this development. More fundamentally the prestige of law was rising in the South and people were becoming more law-abiding. These changes were related to a general rise in education of the Southerners and to their fuller participation in the larger American culture.

In the North the Negro continued to enjoy full equality before the law. There was some strain in the North during the Great Migration, sometimes mounting to race riots during which the arm of the law was not always just and impartial. But on the whole the judicial order of the region was upheld, and equality in justice was not a major problem.

In the *political* sphere, the South continued to disfranchise the Negro, contrary to the clear precept of the American Creed and the Constitution. The masses of whites were also kept from political participation. Real issues were kept out of politics and there was a great amount of corruption. But these things proved increasingly difficult to keep up. Economic and ideological changes, related to the region's rapid industrialization, urbanization, and labor unionization, stepped up by the Great Depression and the New Deal, caused political splits in the Southern Democratic party machines. The splits usually remained latent, but here and there, now and then, they forced themselves into the open. The "Solid South" seemed definitely endangered. The poll tax was under fierce attack in all Southern states, and some had already abolished it.

Meanwhile such things as the rise of the price level since the

'nineties and the improved educational level of Southern Negroes made the statutory devices to keep Negroes from the
polls—by property and literacy requirements as well as by the
poll tax—less and less effective. Negro disfranchisement came
increasingly to depend upon extra-legal and illegal sanctions.
We viewed this situation as extremely unstable for several reasons: the legal culture of the South was rising; there were no
more loopholes left for legalizing Negro disfranchisement; the
Solid South was showing signs of breaking up; the liberal forces
in the North were getting increasingly exasperated with the
South; and the Supreme Court was starting to enforce the Constitution as it applied to voting in the South. Southern liberals
were standing up, not only against the poll tax, but often also
against the one-party system and the exclusion of Negro voters
from the primaries. Even conservative Southerners were occasionally found to hold the opinion that sometime in the future
the Negro was going to vote in the South. While the Negro was
almost as effectively disfranchised in the South in the years before the outbreak of the present War as he has ever been, our
judgment, when taking all these changes into account, thus was
that his political position was potentially much stronger and
that his gradual enfranchisement was bound to come.

In the North the Negro enjoyed uninfringed his right to vote,
and the steadily continuing migration to the North meant that
the Negro vote was growing.

In the enjoyment of *public services* the Negro was discriminated against severely in the South in blunt repudiation of the
Constitution and the state laws. But even in this sphere we saw
a slow improvement of his status as a result of the rising legal
culture of the region; the pressures from the Negroes, from
public opinion in the North, from the federal courts and administration as well as from the white Southerners' own better
conscience. It was becoming somewhat less unusual that a play-
ground or even a little park was arranged for Negroes in some
cities. The Negro schools were greatly improved even if they
usually still remained inferior. Without question the New Deal
was of tremendous importance for the Negro in respect to the
share he received of public services. It is true that the Washing-

ton administration did not dare and, in any case, did not succeed in stamping out discrimination in relief, agricultural policies, or anything else in the South, but it definitely decreased it. It also brought a new kind of public servant to the South, educated and zealous officials who were not primarily interested in "keeping the Negro in his place" but in encouraging and advancing him. This introduced a new and wholesome type of public contact for the Negro people in the South, and Negroes got a feeling that public authority could be other than arbitrary and suppressive.

In the North public services were, on the whole, granted to Negroes as to other citizens in similar circumstances.

While in all these spheres the trends at the outbreak of the present War were definitely in the direction of a rise in the status of the Negro in America, the same cannot be said about those relating to his occupational status. In Southern agriculture the Negro's plight had been becoming continually worse and showed no prospects for a brighter future. His low place on the occupational ladder usually as a plantation tenant—the increase of Negro landownership had stopped 40 years earlier—his dependence on cotton, his lack of education, and the intense race prejudice in the blighted rural regions of the South made him the main sufferer of the boll weevil, of Southern over-population and "white infiltration," of mechanization and, during the 'thirties, of the collapsing world market and the contractionist national agricultural policy. Yet there were no wholehearted attempts on a mass scale, either by the federal government or by any other agency, to re-educate rural Southern Negroes to take up new occupations in other areas. America was under the spell of economic defeatism so far as a belief in continued rapid industrialization was concerned, and there was no hope of placing the dislocated Negro sharecropper in the industrial cities.

Some rural Negroes moved to Northern and Southern cities, increasing unemployment there. Monopoly of jobs by the whites increased during the Great Depression, and Negroes did not find any new employment openings. Various national policies, such as the Wages and Hours Law, instituted to stamp out sweatshop conditions, could not avoid hurting the employment opportunities of Negroes since they were marginal workers. . . . Negro unemployment mounted in all cities, particularly in the North, and the Negro workers increasingly became a relief burden. The whole country, and particularly the North, was much more generous toward the Negro in doling out relief to him than in allowing him to work and earn his bread by his own labor.

Meanwhile, the new unions in the mass production industries gave Negro workers hope by organizing them together with whites in fields in which Negroes were already working. But, with few exceptions, they did not open up new industries for Negro employment during the 'thirties, neither did they pave the way for Negroes to rise by promotion from the level of unskilled workers to that of the semi-skilled and skilled. Negro business did not flourish either, and the small gains made in a few professions were quantitatively insignificant. There is no question but that the development in the economic sphere was grave. But as discrimination was slowly decreasing in all other spheres, as there were good prospects that national politics would remain liberal and progressive, as Negro defense organization and the Negro advisors in the federal administration were hammering on the inequalities, and as the new unions were pledged to nondiscrimination, there seemed to be good prospects that even the threatening trends respecting the Negro's economic status could have been turned, if the country had got out of the long stagnation in a normal way and had entered a new era of continued industrialization. . . .

3. The Decay of the Caste Theory]

The problem of what would have occurred if there had been no war is now purely academic. The Second World War is bound to change all trends. But before we analyze the implications of the War for the Negro problem, we need to take a still broader perspective and ask: what has happened to white opinions on the Negro problem in the span of three generations since Emancipation?

In the South three generations ago white people had for their defense a consistent and respectable theory, endorsed by the church and by all sciences, printed in learned books and periodicals, and expounded by the South's great statesmen in the Capitol at Washington. The Negro's subordinate status was a principle integrated into a whole philosophy of society and of human life. The Negro was a completely different species of mankind: undeveloped, "child-like," amoral, and much less endowed with intellectual capacities than the white man; he was meant by the Creator to be a servant forever; if kept in his "place" he was useful or at least tolerable, and there he was also happy; "social equality" was unthinkable as it implied intermarriage which would destroy the white race and Anglo-Saxon civilization. Much of this theory—which acquired an elaborate structure to satisfy the specific needs to justify discrimination in various spheres of life—remained through Reconstruction, and it was again hailed in the Restoration of white supremacy. Indeed, much of it remained until a couple of decades ago. But now it is almost destroyed for upper class and educated people. Its maintenance among lower class and uneducated people meets increasing difficulties. *The gradual destruction of the popular theory behind race prejudice is the most important of all social trends in the field of interracial relations.*

It is significant that today even the white man who defends discrimination frequently describes his motive as "prejudice" and says that it is "irrational." The popular beliefs rationalizing caste in America are no longer intellectually respectable. They can no longer, therefore, be found in current books, newspapers or public speeches. They live a surreptitious life in thoughts and private remarks. There we have had to hunt them when studying the matter in this inquiry. When they were thus drawn out into the open they looked shabby and ashamed of themselves. Everybody who has acquired a higher education knows that they are wrong. Most white people with a little education also have a hunch that they are wrong. There is today a queer feeling of *credo quia absurdum* hovering over the whole complex of popular beliefs sustaining racial discrimination. This makes the prejudiced white man nearly as pathetic as his Negro victim.

The white man is thus in the process of losing confidence in the theory which gave reason and meaning to his way of life. And since he has not changed his life much, he is in a dilemma. This change is probably irreversible and cumulative. It is backed by the American Creed. The trend of psychology, education, anthropology, and social science is toward environmentalism in the explanation of group differences, which means that the racial beliefs which defended caste are being torn away. It also means, by implication, that the white majority group in power is accused of being the cause of the Negro's deficiencies and unhappiness. Authority and respectability are no longer supporting the popular beliefs. The beliefs are no longer nourished from above. Instead they are increasingly fought. There is a considerable time-lag between what is thought in the higher and in the lower social classes. But as time passes the lower social strata also will change their beliefs. These ideas are spread by the advance of education.

All of this is important. People want to be rational, and they want to feel that they are good and righteous. They want to have the society they live in, and their behavior in this society, explained and justified to their conscience. And now their theory is being torn to pieces; its expression is becoming recognized as a mark of ignorance.

On the other side of the caste gulf the development leads to increased bitterness. To the Negro the white man's trouble with his conscience cannot but seem to be insincerity or something worse. The Negro protest is rising, spurred by the improvement in education. The Negro group is being permeated by the democratic and equalitarian values of the American culture. Since at the same time there has been increasing separation between the two groups, Negroes are beginning to form a self-conscious "nation within the nation," defining ever more clearly their fundamental grievances against white America.

America can never more regard its Negroes as a patient, submissive minority. Negroes will continually become less well "accommodated." They will organize for defense and offense. They will be more and more vociferous. They will watch their opportunities ever more keenly. They will have a powerful tool in the caste struggle against white America: the glorious American ideals of democracy, liberty, and equality to which America is pledged not only by its political Constitution but also by the sincere devotion of its citizens. The Negroes are a minority, and they are poor and suppressed, but they have the advantage that they can fight wholeheartedly. The whites have all the power, but they are split in their moral personality. Their better selves are with the insurgents. The Negroes do not need any other allies.

This moral process had proceeded far when the Second World War broke out.

4. Negroes in the War Crisis]

This War is an ideological war fought in defense of democracy. The totalitarian dictatorships in the enemy countries had even made the ideological issue much sharper in this War than it was in the First World War. Moreover, in this War the principle of democracy had to be applied more explicitly to race. Fascism and nazism are based on a racial superiority dogma—not unlike the old hackneyed American caste theory—and they came to power by means of racial persecution and oppression. In fighting fascism and nazism, America had to stand before the whole world in favor of racial tolerance and cooperation and of racial equality. It had to denounce German racialism as a reversion to barbarism. It had to proclaim universal brotherhood and the inalienable human freedoms. The fact that the Japanese utilize anti-white feelings in Asia and elsewhere made it even more necessary to stress the racial equality principle. . . .

For the Negroes this new War carried unpleasant reminiscences of the earlier one. The situation looked bitterly ironical. This time, too, the Negro had to fight desperately to get the right to fight for his country. In the armed forces Negroes were discriminated against in the usual ways and to almost the same extent. Mobs had attacked Negro soldiers and war workers, and a Southern senator had requested the Army to keep Negro soldiers out of the South. Negroes also had to fight to get into the war industries and had only partial success. In the First World

War they actually made considerable advances in industrial employment, and the Great Migration was a welcome consequence. But this time the nation was well stocked with unemployed whites at the beginning of the defense boom. A technological development had also intervened, decreasing the industrial demand for unskilled labor—the type of jobs for which Negroes are least unwelcome. . . .

Under the threat of a Negro march on Washington, skillfully staged by A. Philip Randolph, the President made a solemn proclamation against discrimination in the defense industries and government agencies and appointed a committee, having both Negro and white members, to see that it was observed. Other branches of the Administration made declarations and issued orders against discrimination: some of these statements were apparently sincere in their intention, some were face-saving moves, and most had their locus somewhere in the wide range between. The Republican National Committee resolved that racial discriminations are "wrongs under the Constitution" and pledged the opposition party to work to correct them. The national labor unions also lined up for nondiscrimination. The Negroes heard and read the kindly promises. They again noted the public acceptance of their own reading of the Constitution and the American Creed. But they knew the grim reality.

In the twenty years between the two World Wars the general level of education of the American Negroes had become considerably higher, and so had their capacity for democracy. The Negro press had become better equipped, and it reached farther. The Negro organizations had grown in strength. The national Negro leaders had become firmer, and they were more resentful. This time they were not willing cheerfully to postpone their complaints until the War was over. The elderly Du Bois renounced with bitterness the credulous advice he once gave his people in the First World War to "close ranks." In this new War the Negro leaders advertised freely—and sometimes provocatively—the danger of a low morale among Negroes.

In this War there was a "colored" nation on the other side—Japan. And that nation started out by beating the white Anglo-Saxons on their own ground. The smoldering revolt in India against British rule had significance for the American Negroes, and so had other "color" incidents in the world conflict: the wavering sympathies of several native populations in the Dutch and British possessions in the Pacific, the mistrust against Great Britain among the Arab peoples, the first abandonment of Ethiopia, and the ambiguity of the plans for the colonial chessboard of Africa. Even unsophisticated Negroes began to see vaguely a color scheme in world events, although their thoughts are usually not yet organized in a definite pattern. In a "letter to the editor" by a Negro, which crept into a liberal white paper in the Upper South, the concluding sentences read:

The Negro races on earth are very suspicious of the white man's good intentions. This is very likely to be the last war that the white man will be able to lead humanity to wage for plausible platitudes.

And this low-toned threat from a single Southern Negro became occasionally more shrill in the North: all colored people should be united in their interests against the whites, and the aim should not be "national unity" but a real color war which would definitely end white imperialism and exploitation.

Regarding the Negro press and hearing all the reports from observers who have been out among common Negroes in the South and the North convince me that there is much sullen skepticism, and even cynicism, and vague, tired, angry dissatisfaction among American Negroes today. The general bitterness is reflected in the stories that are circulating in the Negro communities: A young Negro, about to be inducted into the Army, said, "Just carve on my tombstone, 'Here lies a black man killed fighting a yellow man for the protection of a white man.'" Another Negro boy expressed the same feeling when he said he was going to get his eyes slanted so that the next time a white man shoved him around he could fight back. Their caste status being what it is in America, Negroes would, indeed, not be ordinary human beings if such dissatisfaction and bitterness were not their reaction to all the morale talk about democracy, the four freedoms, the American way of life, all the violent denunciations of Nazi race hatred and the lack of freedom under totalitarian rule. We should also remember, however, that even

if Negroes are still mainly excluded from work in the manufacturing industries and from employment offering much future
prospect, the war boom has created a lot of secondary employment for Negroes, too. There is more money in circulation and
some trickles down to the Negroes. With a little money in his
pocket even the poor Negro day laborer or domestic worker
feels that he can afford to stiffen himself. Many white house-
wives notice strange thoughts and behavior on the part of their
Negro servants these days.

The loyalty of the American Negro in war and peace is, however, proverbial. The only thing Negroes ask for is to be accepted as Americans. The American Constitution is even dearer
to them than to their white compatriots. They are more unre-
servedly anti-fascist. Few American Negroes want the Axis
powers to win the War. But this is not much of an issue to Negroes, as they, about as much as white Americans, are convinced
of the invincibility of their country. Negroes have never doubted
the strength and resourcefulness of the whites. Even more, they
know that America offers more possibility of democracy, even
for themselves, than do the Axis nations. In one of the most
thoughtful statements on the question of Negro loyalties since
the beginning of the war crisis, Ralph Bunche says:

There should be no illusion about the nature of this struggle. . . .
The fight now is not to save democracy, for that which does not exist
cannot be saved. But the fight is to maintain those conditions under
which people may continue to strive for realization of the democratic
ideals. This is the inexorable logic of the nation's position as dictated
by the world anti-democratic revolution and Hitler's projected new
world order. . . .

A white commentator complained some months ago that the
Negro press is something of a fifth column. He received the
unanimous and angry answer in all Negro papers that this is
exactly contrary to the truth. Negroes are standing only for the
democratic principles, to defend which America is waging war.
They are dissatisfied because these principles are ignored in
America itself. They are just the opposite of war dodgers and
traitors; they pray to have the right to fight and die for their

country and to work in the war industries, but they are excluded. They can, with new reason, point to the inconsistency between American ideals and practices, as does one of their wisest editors, Elmer A. Carter: ". . . this strange and curious picture, this spectacle of America at war to preserve the ideal of government by free men, yet clinging to the social vestiges of the slave system." This ideological attack is so clear-cut and simple and so obviously to the point that it appeals even to the least educated Negro. The cause of the American Negro has supreme logical strength. And the Negro is better prepared than ever before in his history to fight for it.

5. The War and the Whites]

This simple logic is, of course, apparent to white Americans, too. And the whites were on the way, even before the War, to lose their caste theory and their complacency in the face of obvious abuses of the American Creed. They are also stirred up by the War and the great cause of human liberties at sake. In the North the question can be publicly approached in only one spirit, that of the American Creed. . . .

The titular leader of the Republican party, Wendell Willkie, speaking in July, 1942, at the annual conference of the N.A.A.C.P. in Los Angeles, California, had this to say:

Today it is becoming increasingly apparent to thoughtful Americans that we cannot fight the forces and ideas of imperialism abroad and maintain a form of imperialism at home. The war has done this to our thinking. . . . So we are finding under the pressures of this present conflict that long-standing barriers and prejudices are breaking down. The defense of our democracy aginst the forces that threaten it from without has made some of its failures to function at home glaringly apparent. Our very proclamations of what we are fighting for have rendered our own inequities self-evident. When we talk of freedom and opportunity for all nations the mocking paradoxes in our own society become so clear they can no longer be ignored.

The world conflict and America's exposed position as the defender of the democratic faith is thus accelerating an ideological process which was well under way. In this dramatic stage of the American caste struggle a strategic fact of utmost importance is this, that the entire caste order is extra-legal if not actually illegal and unconstitutional. The legal order of the land does not sanction caste but, on the contrary, is framed to guarantee equality and to suppress caste. The only important exceptions are the Jim Crow laws in the Southern states. But even they are written upon the fiction of equality, although, if equality were enforced, they would not only lose in efficacy as means of expressing caste subordination, but also become tremendously burdensome economically for society and, consequently, the whites would be robbed of one of their main interests in upholding them.

The whites are aware of the tremendous social costs of keeping up the present irrational and illegal caste system. Among other things, this anomaly is one of the main factors keeping the respect for law and order and the administration of laws at such a low level in America. The whites investigate these irrationalities and the consequent social wastage; they build scientific systems to explain their social causation, in fact, they know all about it and deplore it. They have the political power to make caste legal and orderly, whether with Negro consent or without it. But practically never will whites be heard making such proposals, and still less will they seriously discuss and plan for such a change. They cannot afford to compromise the American Creed.

Caste may exist, but it cannot be recognized. Instead, the stamp of public disapproval is set upon it, and this undermines still more the caste theory by which the whites have to try to explain and justify their behavior. And *the Negroes are awarded the law as a weapon in the caste struggle.* Here we see in high relief how the Negroes in their fight for equality have their allies in the white man's own conscience. The white man can humiliate the Negro; he can thwart his ambitions; he can starve him; he can press him down into vice and crime; he can occasionally beat him and even kill him; but he does not have the moral stamina to make the Negro's subjugation legal and approved by society. Against that stands not only the Constitution and the laws which could be changed, but also the American Creed which is firmly rooted in the Americans' hearts.

6. The North Moves Toward Equality]

In the North the Creed was strong enough long before the War to secure for the Negro practically unabridged civic equality in all his relations with public authority, whether it was in voting, before the courts, in the school system or as a relief recipient. But he is discriminated against ruthlessly in private relations, as when looking for a job or seeking a home to live in. The white Northerner, in his private dealings with people to whom he does not feel akin, has dangerous traditions derived from the exploitation of new immigrants. But even in those non-public spheres, and particularly in the problem of breadwinning, the white Northerner is becoming prepared, as a citizen, to give the Negro his just opportunity. But apparently, as a private individual, he is less prepared to feel that he himself is the man to give the Negro a better chance: in his own occupation, trade union, office or workshop, in his own residential neighborhood or in his church. The social paradox in the North is exactly this, that almost everybody is against discrimination in general but, at the same time, almost everybody practices discrimination in his own personal affairs.

It is the cumulation of all these personal discriminations which creates the color bar in the North and for the Negro causes unusually severe unemployment, crowded housing conditions, crime and vice. About this social process the ordinary white Northerner keeps sublimely ignorant and unconcerned. This aloofness is, of course, partly opportunistic but it can be fought by education. When now, in the war emergency, the Negro is increasingly given sympathetic publicity by newspapers, periodicals, and the radio, and by administrators and public personalities of all kinds, one result is that the white Northerner is gradually waking up and seeing what he is doing to the Negro and is seeing also the consequences of his democratic Creed for his relations with Negroes. We have become convinced in the course of this inquiry that the North is getting prepared for a fundamental redefinition of the Negro's status in America. The North will accept it if the change is pushed by courageous leadership. And the North has much more power than the South. The white South is itself a minority and a national problem.

Also working in favor of the Negro is another trend, namely, the concentration of responsibility. Particularly in the crucial economic sphere this trend is rapid. Labor relations are coming increasingly to be planned and regulated by broad union policies and by national legislation and administration. The War will force this change forward step by step. After the War, in the great crisis of demobilization and liquidation, mass unemployment will be a main problem. Large-scale public intervention will be a necessity. In this endeavor no national administration will dare to allow unemployment to be too much concentrated upon the Negro.

The average white Northerner will probably agree with a policy which holds open employment opportunities for Negroes, because, as we said, he is against economic discrimination as a general proposition. There is also—together with all opportunistic ignorance and unconcernedness—a bit of rational defense for the distance he preserves between his political and his private opinion. In the individual shop where he works or the residential section where he lives, he sees the danger in admitting a few Negroes, since this will bring an avalanche of Negroes on his shop or his neighborhood. This danger is, of course, due to the fact of the Negro's general exclusion. It is part of the vicious circle holding the Negro down.

If government policy prevents general discrimination, however, there will be no avalanche of Negroes on any one white employer or group of employers. The Negroes, who comprise less than 10 per cent of the population must be given their chance in private enterprise or be supported by public funds. "Buck-passing" is no longer possible when the problem comes to be viewed nationally. . . .

These are the reasons why we foresee that the trend of unionization, social legislation, and national planning will tend to break down economic discrimination, the only type of discrimination which is both important and strong in the North. Other types of discrimination will then tend to decrease according to the law of cumulative causation which has been frequently referred to in this book.

7. Tension in the South]

The situation in the South is different. Unlike the white Northerner, who is most inclined to give the Negro equality in public relations and least inclined to do so in private relations, the white Southerner does not differentiate between public and private relations—the former as well as the latter have significance for prestige and social equality. Moreover, he is traditionally and consistently opposed to Negro equality for its own sake, which the Northerner is not. He may be privately indulgent much more than the white Northerner, but he is not as willing to give the Negro equal treatment by public authority. This is one of the romantic principles behind the legal inequity in the South. But the Southerner is a good American, too, and the region has been becoming rapidly "Americanized" during the last generation.

The ordinary conservative white Southerner has, therefore, a deeper split in his moral personality than does the white Northerner. The War is stirring up the conflict in his soul. The air is filled with reminders of the great cause of democracy and the equality of peoples, which is the main issue in the War America is waging against nazism, fascism, and Japanese imperialism. His "own Negroes" are making some money, reading the Negro press and getting restless. The N.A.A.C.P. and other protest organizations are fighting ever more daringly in his own cities. In his newspapers he reads how the national leaders, from the President down, come out with blunt denunciations of racial discrimination. He is finding that Northern leaders are increasingly getting interested in the poll tax, the white primary, Negro disfranchisement, injustices against Negroes, and other peculiar institutions of the South which he guards behind the doctrine of "states' rights."

What is he supposed to do? Give up Jim Crow and so perhaps allow a Negro to marry his daughters; build good schools for Negroes, though the schools are not too good for his own children; punish white invaders of Negro rights, though they otherwise may be perfectly good and upright citizens; relinquish white supremacy? Is he supposed to retreat from all "Southern traditions"? He sees "outside aggression" wherever he turns.

This is an old story and a phase of a mental cycle through which the unfortunate South has often passed before. The fact that this time the white Southerner's caste theory is weaker than ever and does not inspire much of his own intellectual confidence makes his dilemma worse. His emotions on the color issue are less stable also because his personal ties to the Negro group have been decreasing, and racial isolation has been intensified during the last generation. He "knows the Negro" less well than did his father and grandfather, though he continues to pretend that he knows him well, because to "know the Negro" is also a Southern tradition. Having fewer personal contacts with Negroes he is likely to exaggerate the signs of opposition from the Negroes, for he feels that the Negroes have good reason to develop opposition. . . .

An important element in the situation is that the Southern Negroes, if they are attacked, are more prepared to fight this time than they have ever been before. . . .

The situation is grave, and the years to come will provide a serious test of the political resourcefulness of white public authorities and of other white and Negro leaders. But regardless of what happens, we do not believe that this is a turn for the worse in race relations in the South. Even if there are going to be serious clashes and even if their short-run effects will be devastating to the Negroes involved and, perhaps, to Negroes in the whole region, we believe that the long-run effect of the present opinion crisis in the South, because it is a catharsis for the whites, will be a change toward increased equality for the Negro. When we make this judgment, we recall a remark once made in a conversation by a prominent and conservative Negro social scientist in the South. He stated as his considered opinion that tensions are not necessarily bad and that under certain conditions even race riots may have wholesome effects in the long run. He continued in about the following way: "They stir up people's conscience. People will have to think matters over. They prevent things from becoming settled. If the race situation should ever become fixed, if the Negro were really accommodated, then, and only then, would I despair about a continued great improvement for Negroes. As long as there is friction and fighting, there is hope." . . .

The national compromise has lasted for two generations; it may now be approaching its end, at least relatively. Ten years from now this period in the history of interracial relations in America may come to look as a temporary *interregnum*. The compromise was not a stable power equilibrium. Signs of its end have been frequent during the 'thirties: a whole set of Supreme Court decisions, the New Deal in the South, the increasing activity of federal agencies to stamp out peonage, the agitation for a federal lynching law and for an abolition of the poll tax by Congress, the repeal of the two-thirds majority rule for the nomination of the Democratic candidate for the Presidency, and so on.

The Negro problem is becoming national in scope in a different sense than was meant when white Southerners expressed a belief that the Negro migration to the North would give the North more of a share in the trouble of having Negroes as neighbors and that then the North would understand the racial philosophy of the South better. The Negro vote and the labor vote in the North also have considerable weight in checking Southern conservatism and have increasing power to do so. But aside from all that, national planning cannot leave out the South or humor too much its irrationality. As a matter of fact the South, particularly its agriculture and its population pressure, will continue to remain one of the main national worries.

Because of this development, spurred by the war crisis and the coming peace crisis, it seems justifiable to predict a growing tension between the two regions, one which will not be restricted to the Negro issue. There is not going to be a civil war, of course. The South is this time relatively much weaker in all respects. The North will probably not become more considerate

if the interracial tension in the South gets out of hand and results in bloody clashes. As recourse to civil war is out of the
question and as things thus have to be settled by political means,
the fact becomes of importance that the white South is not united
against a redefinition of the Negro's status. The South has been,
and is, changing rapidly, and Southern liberalism has been coming to be a force though it was practically nowhere in political
power and today is fearfully timid on the Negro issue. Even
the ordinary conservative white Southerner has a deeply split
personality. In the short run this can be suppressed, and the
tension can lead to violent reactions. But in the long run it
means that the conservative white Southerner himself can be
won over to equalitarian reforms in line with the American
Creed.

8. International Aspects]

What has actually happened within the last few years is not
only that the Negro problem has become national in scope after
having been mainly a Southern worry. It has also acquired
tremendous international implications, and this is another and
decisive reason why the white North is prevented from com-
promising with the white South regarding the Negro. The situation is actually such that any and all concessions to Negro rights
in this phase of the history of the world will repay the nation
many times, while any and all injustices inflicted upon him will
be extremely costly. This is not yet seen clearly by most Americans, but it will become increasingly apparent as the War goes
on. . . .

But this is a minor part of the international implications. The
American Negro is thoroughly American in his culture and
whole outlook on the world. He is also loyal to America, and
there is no danger that he will betray it. This is at least certain
in the short-range view, which covers this War and the coming
peace. How the Negro would react if he were left dissatisfied
and if later a new war were to be fought more definitely along
color lines is more difficult to predict.

The main international implication is, instead, that America, for its international prestige, power, and future security, needs to demonstrate to the world that American Negroes can be satisfactorily integrated into its democracy. In a sense, this War marks the end of American isolation. America has had security behind the two protecting oceans. . . . Statesmen will have to take cognizance of the changed geopolitical situation of the nation and carry out important adaptations of the American way of life to new necessities. A main adaptation is bound to be a redefinition of the Negro's status in American democracy. . . .

Perhaps the War can this time be won even without the colored people's confidence. But the absence of their full cooperation, and still more their obstructive activities, will be tremendously costly in time, men and materials. Caste is becoming an expensive luxury of white men.

It seems more definitely certain that it will be impossible to make and preserve a good peace without having built up the fullest trust and good-will among the colored peoples. They will be strong after the War, and they are bound to become even stronger as time passes. . . . Many of the Western nations, including America and all those other peoples on the highest level of industrial civilization, will probably start to shrink in population numbers within a few decades. The colored nations, on the other hand, are just entering the first stage where expansion is likely to be pushed by an increasingly improved control over death, and it is unlikely that the increase in birth control will keep pace with the improvement of the control over death. The whites will, therefore, from now on become a progressively smaller portion of the total world population. If we except the Russian peoples, who are still rapidly increasing, the rapid change in proportion stands out still more dramatically.

Another broad trend is almost as certain, namely, that the "backward" countries, where most colored people live, are going to become somewhat industrialized. The examples of Japan and, more recently, of Russia and China give support to the view that in the future we shall see many backward countries industrialized at a tremendously more rapid rate than were the pioneer Western countries, who had to find out everything for themselves. The same examples illustrate also how such backward nations can advantageously use the newly created industrial apparatus for producing war materials, and they illustrate, too, how they can fight with them.

Particularly as Russia cannot be reckoned on to adhere to white supremacy, it is evident from these facts—though nobody in our countries seems to take it seriously—that within a short period the shrinking minority of white people in our Western lands will either have to succumb or to find ways of living on peaceful terms with colored people. If white people, for their own preservation, attempt to reach a state in which they will be tolerated by their colored neighbors, equality will be the most they will be strong enough to demand.

History is never irredeemable, and there is still time to come to good terms with colored peoples. Their race pride and race prejudice is still mostly a defensive mental device, a secondary reaction built up to meet the humiliations of white supremacy. This is apparent in the case of the American Negro. It probably holds true even for other colored people who have not yet had a taste of power. . . . It should be apparent that the time to come to an understanding on the basis of equality is rapidly running out. When colored nations have once acquired power but still sense the scorn of white superiority and racial discrimination, they are likely to become indoctrinated by a race prejudice much more akin to that of the whites—a race prejudice which can be satisfied only by the whites' humiliation and subjugation.

9. Making the Peace]

Americans in general are concerned with the task of making a constructive peace after the War. It is commonly understood that this task is fraught with immense and unprecedented difficulties and, particularly, that the flagrant mismanagement of international affairs by the great democracies in the period between the two World Wars, the devastation caused by the Second World War, the breaking up of the state structures of Europe, and the approaching liquidation of colonial imperialism in the Far East have created a psychological state in mankind which, aside from all physical and economic deficiencies, raises almost insurmountable obstacles for the peacemakers. . . .

Americans also recognize that America has to take world leadership. The coming difficult decades will be America's turn in the endless sequence of main actors of the world stage. America then will have the major responsibility for the manner in which humanity approaches the long era during which the white peoples will have to adjust to shrinkage while the colored are bound to expand in numbers, in level of industrial civilization and in political power. For perhaps several decades, the whites will still hold the lead, and America will be the most powerful white nation.

America goes to this task with the best of intentions. Declarations of inalienable human rights for people all over the world are now emanating from America. Wilson's fourteen points were a rehearsal; Roosevelt's four freedoms are more general and more focused on the rights of the individual. The national leaders proclaim that the coming peace will open an age of human liberty and equality everywhere. This was so in the First World War, too. This time something must be done to give reality to the glittering generalities, because otherwise the world will become entirely demoralized. It will probably be impossible to excite people with empty promises a third time. It is commonly agreed, and taken as proved by the coming of this War, that peace cannot be preserved if the development of a democratic life in every nation is not internationally guaranteed and the possibility of oppression is not checked. It is anticipated that international agencies will be created to sanction such a development. . . .

Behind her two protecting oceans America has until now lived an exuberant and carefee life without having to bother much about its international reputation. Probably no other modern people has cared less about what impression it makes on other nations. The ordinary American might have been interested to know, but has not bothered much about, the fact that lynchings and race riots are headlines in Bombay; that Huey Long and Father Coughlin, the wave of organized crime during and after Prohibition, the fiscal bankruptcy of Chicago some years ago, the corrupt political machines in Philadelphia, the Dayton trial of Darwinism, provided stories for the Sunday papers in Oslo; that many men and women in democratic countries around the entire world have had their first and decisive impression of American public life from the defense of Sacco and Vanzetti and the Scottsboro boys. Friends of America abroad have tried to make the picture of American life more balanced and more accurate by fixing public attention on the numerous good sides, on American accomplishments, on all the good intentions and on the favorable trends. . . .

The loss of American isolation makes all this most serious. America has now joined the world and is tremendously dependent upon the support and good-will of other countries. Its rise to leadership brings this to a climax. None is watched so suspiciously as the one who is rising. None has so little license, none needs all his virtue so much as the leader. And America, for its own security, cannot retreat from leadership.

There is, of course, another possible solution besides good-will, and that is power. In some quarters in America the observer finds exaggerated notions about the power which America's financial strength after the War will allow her. . . .

Military power, however, can be substituted for good-will. But America does not have the will or stamina for real imperialism. The farmer, the laborer, the merchant, the intellectual, in one word, the common man who ultimately makes political decisions is against suppression abroad. In the international field the Southerner is not unlike his Northern compatriot. All American adventures in imperialism give abundant proofs of half-heartedness and show again the power over the Americans of the American Creed. If America does not go fascist, American militarism will not be an adequate substitute for good-will.

The treatment of the Negro is America's greatest and most conspicuous scandal. It is tremendously publicized, and democratic America will continue to publicize it itself. For the colored peoples all over the world, whose rising influence is axiomatic, this scandal is salt in their wounds. In all white nations which, because of the accident of ethnic homogeneity or for other causes, have not been inculcated with race prejudice, the color of the victim does not provide any excuse for white solidarity. That this is so in Russia is well known and advertised. It holds true also in many other white nations.

10. America's Opportunity]

But these consequences of the present course of America's and the world's history should not be recorded only in terms of compelling forces. The bright side is that the conquering of color caste in America is America's own innermost desire. This nation early laid down as the moral basis for its existence the principles of equality and liberty. However much Americans have dodged this conviction, they have refused to adjust their laws to their own license. Today, more than ever, they refuse to discuss systematizing their caste order to mutual advantage, apparently because they most seriously mean that caste is wrong and should not be given recognition. They stand warmheartedly against oppression in all the world. . . .

America feels itself to be humanity in miniature. When in this crucial time the international leadership passes to America, the great reason for hope is that this country has a national experience of uniting racial and cultural diversities and a national theory, if not a consistent practice, of freedom and equality for all. What America is constantly reaching for is democracy at home and abroad. The main trend in its history is the gradual realization of the American Creed.

In this sense the Negro problem is not only America's greatest failure but also America's incomparably great opportunity for the future. If America should follow its own deepest convictions, its well-being at home would be increased directly. At the same time America's prestige and power abroad would rise immensely. The century-old dream of American patriots, that America should give to the entire world its own freedoms and its own faith, would come true. America can demonstrate that justice, equality and cooperation are possible between white and colored people.

In the present phase of history this is what the world needs to believe. Mankind is sick of fear and disbelief, of pessimism and cynicism. It needs the youthful moralistic optimism of America. But empty declarations only deepen cynicism. Deeds are called for. If America in actual practice could show the world a progressive trend by which the Negro became finally integrated into modern democracy, all mankind would be given faith again—it would have reason to believe that peace, progress and order are feasible. And America would have a spiritual power many times stronger than all her financial and military resources—the power of the trust and support of all good people on earth. *America is free to choose whether the Negro shall remain her liability or become her opportunity.* . . .

We have given the reasons why we believe that the *interregnum* during which the forces balanced each other fairly well, is now at an end. The equilibrium, contrary to common belief, was unstable and temporary. As American Negroes became educated and culturally assimilated, but still found themselves excluded, they grew bitter. Meanwhile the whites were in the process of losing their caste theory. The international upheavals connected with the two World Wars and the world depression brought these developments to a crisis. American isolation was lost. Technical developments brought all nations to be close neighbors even though they were not trained to live together.

We are now in a deeply unbalanced world situation. Many human relations will be readjusted in the present world revolution, and among them race relations are bound to change considerably. As always in a revolutionary situation when society's moorings are temporarily loosened, there is, on the one hand, an opportunity to direct the changes into organized reforms and, on the other hand, a corresponding risk involved in letting the changes remain uncontrolled and lead into disorganization. To do nothing is to accept defeat.

From the point of view of social science, this means, among other things, that social engineering will increasingly be demanded. Many things that for a long period have been predominantly a matter of individual adjustment will become more and more determined by political decision and public regulation. We are entering an era where fact-finding and scientific theories of causal relations will be seen as instrumental in planning controlled social change. The peace will bring nothing but problems, one mounting upon another, and consequently, new urgent tasks for social engineering. The American social scientist, because of the New Deal and the War, is already acquiring familiarity with planning and practical action. He will never again be given the opportunity to build up so "disinterested" a social science. . . .

The rationalism and moralism which is the driving force behind social study, whether we admit it or not, is the faith that institutions can be improved and strengthened and that people are good enough to live a happier life. With all we know today, there should be the possibility to build a nation and a world where people's great propensities for sympathy and cooperation would not be so thwarted.

To find the practical formulas for this never-ending reconstruction of society is the supreme task of social science. The world catastrophe places tremendous difficulties in our way and may shake our confidence to the depths. Yet we have today in social science a greater trust in the improvability of man and society than we have ever had since the Enlightenment.

14

National Planning and Responsibility in Science
Vannevar Bush's *Science the Endless Frontier*

Science—pure and applied—had always played a major role in shaping events in the Western world in the modern era; in the twentieth century the impact of the accelerating development of science and technology was of surpassing and incalculable weight. The institutionalization of scientific research—by business, university, and government—together with the growing proliferation of specialization within the disciplines devoted to the analysis and manipulation of the natural universe advanced at an exponential rate. The more man learned the larger became the circumference of what lay beyond—unknown. Science moved, as Vannevar Bush observed, into an "endless frontier." Nothing would ever be the same, everything was ever different—because of science. The goods man consumed, the age to which they lived, the ideas they held, their modes of worship, the means of their destruction—all were transformed by science. Science, directed by Mars, gave man the means of his defense and the instruments of his obliteration—radar, the rocket, the atomic bomb. Vannevar Bush, distinguished research scientist and science administrator from the Massachusetts Institute of Technology, had played a major role in directing the Manhattan Project, whose ultimate experiments were conducted over Hiroshima and Nagasaki. At war's end, anxious to turn the force of science to the ends of human progress and peace, Dr. Bush sketched in broad outline the policies he felt were essential in the postwar world if these humane ends were to be served.

The role of science in government is touched upon, in different ways, in William L. Laurence, *Men and Atoms* (New York: Simon and Schuster, 1959), and in Fletcher Knebel and Charles W. Bailey, II, *No High Ground* (New York: Harper & Row, 1960). In reading this matter-of-fact summary of the relationship of government and science, note (1) the historical precedents for government sponsorship and protection of scientific development; (2) the areas in which

Vannevar Bush, *Science the Endless Frontier: A Report to the President* (Washington, D. C.: U. S. Government Printing Office, 1945), pp. 4-21.

science relates to the total well-being of society; (3) the implied invitation for scientists to play a role of larger responsibility in public affairs; and (4) the practical measures proposed to harness science to social welfare through government.

Introduction]

Scientific Progress Is Essential]

W<small>E ALL KNOW HOW MUCH THE NEW DRUG,</small> penicillin, has meant to our grievously wounded men on the grim battlefronts of this war—the countless lives it has saved—the incalculable suffering which its use has prevented. Science and the great practical genius of this nation made this achievement possible.

Some of us know the vital role which radar has played in bringing the United Nations to victory over Nazi Germany and in driving the Japanese steadily back from their island bastions. Again it was painstaking scientific research over many years that made radar possible.

What we often forget are the millions of pay envelopes on a peacetime Saturday night which are filled because new products and new industries have provided jobs for countless Americans. Science made that possible, too.

In 1939 millions of people were employed in industries which did not even exist at the close of the last war—radio, air conditioning, rayon and other synthetic fibers, and plastics are examples of the products of these industries. But these things do not mark the end of progress—they are but the beginning if we make full use of our scientific resources. New manufacturing industries can be started and many older industries greatly strengthened and expanded if we continue to study nature's laws and apply new knowledge to practical purposes.

Great advances in agriculture are also based upon scientific research. Plants which are more resistant to disease and are adapted to short growing seasons, the prevention and cure of livestock diseases, the control of our insect enemies, better fertilizers, and improved agricultural practices, all stem from painstaking scientific research.

Advances in science when put to practical use mean more jobs, higher wages, shorter hours, more abundant crops, more leisure for recreation, for study, for learning how to live without the deadening drudgery which has been the burden of the common man for ages past. Advances in science will also bring higher standards of living, will lead to the prevention or cure of diseases, will promote conservation of our limited national resources, and will assure means of defense against aggression. But to achieve these objectives—to secure a high level of employment, to maintain a position of world leadership—the flow of new scientific knowledge must be both continuous and substantial.

Our population increased from 75 million to 130 million between 1900 and 1940. In some countries comparable increases have been accompanied by famine. In this country the increase has been accompanied by more abundant food supply, better living, more leisure, longer life, and better health. This is, largely, the product of three factors—the free play of initiative of a vigorous people under democracy, the heritage of great natural wealth, and the advance of science and its application.

Science, by itself, provides no panacea for individual, social, and economic ills. It can be effective in the national welfare only as a member of a team, whether the conditions be peace or war. But without scientific progress no amount of achievement in other directions can insure our health, prosperity, and security as a nation in the modern world.

Science Is a Proper Concern of Government]
It has been basic United States policy that Government should foster the opening of new frontiers. It opened the seas to clipper ships and furnished land for pioneers. Although these frontiers have more or less disappeared, the frontier of science remains. It is in keeping with the American tradition—one which has made the United States great—that new frontiers shall be made accessible for development by all American citizens.

Moreover, since health, well-being, and security are proper

concerns of Government, scientific progress is, and must be, of vital interest to Government. Without scientific progress the national health would deteriorate without scientific progress we could not hope for improvement in our standard of living or for an increased number of jobs for our citizens; and without scientific progress we could not have maintained our liberties against tyranny.

Government Relations to Science—Past and Future]

From early days the Government has taken an active interest in scientific matters. During the nineteenth century the Coast and Geodetic Survey, the Naval Observatory, the Department of Agriculture, and the Geological Survey were established. Through the Land Grant College Acts the Government has supported research in state institutions for more than 80 years on a gradually increasing scale. Since 1900 a large number of scientific agencies have been established within the Federal Government, until in 1939 they numbered more than 40.

Much of the scientific research done by Government agencies is intermediate in character between the two types of work commonly referred to as basic and applied research. Almost all Government scientific work has ultimate practical objectives but, in many fields of broad national concern, it commonly involves long-term investigation of a fundamental nature. Generally speaking, the scientific agencies of Government are not so concerned with immediate practical objectives as are the laboratories of industry nor, on the other hand, are they as free to explore any natural phenomena without regard to possible economic applications as are the educational and private research institutions. Government scientific agencies have splendid records of achievement, but they are limited in function.

We have no national policy for science. The Government has only begun to utilize science in the nation's welfare. There is no body within the Government charged with formulating or executing a national science policy. There are no standing committees of the Congress devoted to this important subject. Science has been in the wings. It should be brought to the center of the stage—for in it lies much of our hope for the future.

There are areas of science in which the public interest is acute but which are likely to be cultivated inadequately if left without more support than will come from private sources. These areas—such as research on military problems, agriculture, housing, public health, certain medical research, and research involving expensive capital facilities beyond the capacity of private institutions—should be advanced by active Government support. To date, with the exception of the intensive war research conducted by the Office of Scientific Research and Development, such support has been meager and intermittent.

For reasons presented in this report we are entering a period when science needs and deserves increased support from public funds.

Freedom of Inquiry Must Be Preserved]

The publicly and privately supported colleges, universities, and research institutes are the centers of basic research. They are the wellsprings of knowledge and understanding. As long as they are vigorous and healthy and their scientists are free to pursue the truth wherever it may lead, there will be a flow of new scientific knowledge to those who can apply it to practical problems in Government, in industry, or elsewhere.

Many of the lessons learned in the war-time application of science under Government can be profitably applied in peace. The Government is peculiarly fitted to perform certain functions, such as the coordination and support of broad programs on problems of great national importance. But we must proceed with caution in carrying over the methods which work in wartime to the very different conditions of peace. We must remove the rigid controls which we have had to impose, and recover freedom of inquiry and that healthy competitive scientific spirit so necessary for expansion of the frontiers of scientific knowledge.

Scientific progress on a broad front results from the free play of free intellects, working on subjects of their own choice, in the manner dictated by their curiosity for exploration of the unknown. Freedom of inquiry must be preserved under any plan for Government support of science. . . .

The War Against Disease]

In War]

The death rate for all diseases in the Army, including the overseas forces, has been reduced from 14.1 per thousand in the last war to 0.6 per thousand in this war.

Such ravaging diseases as yellow fever, dysentery, typhus, tetanus, pneumonia, and meningitis have been all but conquered by penicillin and the sulfa drugs, the insecticide DDT, better vaccines, and improved hygienic measures. Malaria has been controlled. There has been dramatic progress in surgery.

The striking advances in medicine during the war have been possible only because we had a large backlog of scientific data accumulated through basic research in many scientific fields in the years before the war.

In Peace]

In the last 40 years life expectancy in the United States has increased from 49 to 65 years largely as a consequence of the reduction in the death rates of infants and children; in the last 20 years the death rate from the diseases of childhood has been reduced 87 percent.

Diabetes has been brought under control by insulin, pernicious anemia by liver extracts; and the once widespread deficiency diseases have been much reduced, even in the lowest income groups, by accessory food factors and improvement of diet. Notable advances have been made in the early diagnosis of cancer, and in the surgical and radiation treatment of the disease.

These results have been achieved through a great amount of basic research in medicine and the preclinical sciences, and by the dissemination of this new scientific knowledge through the physicians and medical services and public health agencies of the country. In this cooperative endeavour the pharmaceutical industry has played an important role, especially during the war. All of the medical and public health groups share credit for these achievements; they form interdependent members of a team.

Progress in combating disease depends upon an expanding body of new scientific knowledge.

Unsolved Problems]

. . . [T]he annual deaths from one or two diseases are far in excess of the total number of American lives lost in battle during this war. A large fraction of these deaths in our civilian population cut short the useful lives of our citizens. This is our present position despite the fact that in the last three decades notable progress has been made in civilian medicine. The reduction in the death rate from diseases of childhood has shifted the emphasis to the middle and old age groups, particularly to the malignant diseases and the degenerative processes prominent in later life. Cardiovascular disease, including chronic disease of the kidneys, arteriosclerosis, and cerebral hemorrhage, now account for 45 percent of the deaths in the United States. Second are the infectious diseases, and third is cancer. Added to these are many maladies (for example, the common cold, arthritis, asthma and hay fever, peptic ulcer) which, though infrequently fatal, cause incalculable disability.

Another aspect of the changing emphasis is the increase of mental diseases. Approximately 7 million persons in the United States are mentally ill; more than one-third of the hospital beds are occupied by such persons, at a cost of $175 million a year. Each year 125,000 new mental cases are hospitalized.

Notwithstanding great progress in prolonging the span of life and in relief of suffering, much illness remains for which adequate means of prevention and cure are not yet known. While additional physicians, hospitals, and health programs are needed, their full usefulness cannot be attained unless we enlarge our knowledge of the human organism and the nature of disease. Any extension of medical facilities must be accompanied by an expanded program of medical training and research.

Broad and Basic Studies Needed]

Discoveries pertinent to medical progress have often come from remote and unexpected sources, and it is certain that this

will be true in the future. It is wholly probable that progress
in the treatment of cardiovascular disease, renal disease, cancer,
and similar refractory diseases will be made as the result of
fundamental discoveries in subjects unrelated to those diseases,
and perhaps entirely unexpected by the investigator. Further
progress requires that the entire front of medicine and the underlying sciences of chemistry, physics, anatomy, biochemistry,
physiology, pharmacology, bacteriology, pathology, parasitology,
etc., be broadly developed.

Progress in the war against disease results from discoveries
in remote and unexpected fields of medicine and the underlying
sciences.

Coordinated Attack on Special Problems]

Penicillin reached our troops in time to save countless lives
because the Government coordinated and supported the program of research and development on the drug. The development moved from the early laboratory stage to large scale
production and use in a fraction of the time it would have taken
without such leadership. The search for better anti-malarials,
which proceeded at a moderate tempo for many years, has been
accelerated enormously by Government support during the war.
Other examples can be cited in which medical progress has been
similarly advanced. In achieving these results, the Government
has provided over-all coordination and support; it has not dictated how the work should be done within any cooperating
institution.

Discovery of new therapeutic agents and methods usually results from basic studies in medicine and the underlying sciences.
The development of such materials and methods to the point at
which they become available to medical practitioners requires
teamwork involving the medical schools, the science departments of universities, Government, and the pharmaceutical industry. Government initiative, support, and coordination can be
very effective in this development phase.

Government initiative and support for the development of
newly discovered therapeutic materials and methods can reduce
the time required to bring the benefits to the public.

Action Is Necessary]

The primary place for medical research is in the medical schools and universities. In some cases coordinated direct attack on special problems may be made by teams of investigators, supplementing similar attacks carried on by the Army, Navy, Public Health Service, and other organizations. Apart from teaching, however, the primary obligation of the medical schools and universities is to continue the traditional function of such institutions, namely, to provide the individual worker with an opportunity for free, untrammeled study of nature, in the directions and by the methods suggested by his interests, curiosity, and imagination. The history of medical science teaches clearly the supreme importance of affording the prepared mind complete freedom for the exercise of initiative. It is the special province of the medical schools and universities to foster medical research in this way—a duty which cannot be shifted to government agencies, industrial organizations, or to any other institutions.

Where clinical investigations of the human body are required, the medical schools are in a unique position, because of their close relationship to teaching hospitals, to integrate such investigations with the work of the departments of preclinical science, and to impart new knowledge to physicians in training. At the same time, the teaching hospitals are especially well qualified to carry on medical research because of their close connection with the medical schools, on which they depend for staff and supervision.

Between World War I and World War II the United States overtook all other nations in medical research and assumed a position of world leadership. To a considerable extent this progress reflected the liberal financial support from university endowment income, gifts from individuals, and foundation grants in the 20's. The growth of research departments in medical schools has been very uneven, however, and in consequence most of the important work has been done in a few large schools. This should be corrected by building up the weaker institutions, especially in regions which now have no strong medical research activities.

The traditional sources of support for medical research, largely endowment income, foundation grants, and private donations, are diminishing, and there is no immediate prospect of a change in this trend. Meanwhile, research costs have steadily risen. More elaborate and expensive equipment is required, supplies are more costly, and the wages of assistants are higher. Industry is only to a limited extent a source of funds for basic medical research.

It is clear that if we are to maintain the progress in medicine which has marked the last 25 years, the Government should extend financial support to basic medical research in the medical schools and in the universities, through grants both for research and for fellowships. The amount which can be effectively spent in the first year should not exceed 5 million dollars. After a program is under way perhaps 20 million dollars a year can be spent effectively.

Science and the Public Welfare]

Relation to National Security]

In this war it has become clear beyond all doubt that scientific research is absolutely essential to national security. The bitter and dangerous battle against the U-boat was a battle of scientific techniques—and our margin of success was dangerously small. The new eyes which radar supplied to our fighting forces quickly evoked the development of scientific counter-measures which could often blind them. This again represents the ever continuing battle of techniques. The V-1 attack on London was finally defeated by three devices developed during this war and used superbly in the field. V-2 was countered only by capture of the launching sites.

The Secretaries of War and Navy recently stated in a joint letter to the National Academy of Sciences:

This war emphasizes three facts of supreme importance to national security: (1) Powerful new tactics of defense and offense are developed around new weapons created by scientific and engineering re-

search; (2) the competitive time element in developing those weapons
and tactics may be decisive; (3) war is increasingly total war, in
which the armed services must be supplemented by active participation of every element of civilian population.

To insure continued preparedness along farsighted technical
lines, the research scientists of the country must be called upon
to continue in peacetime some substantial portion of those types
of contribution to national security which they have made so
effectively during the stress of the present war. . . .

There must be more—and more adequate—military research
during peacetime. We cannot again rely on our allies to hold
off the enemy while we struggle to catch up. Further, it is clear
that only the Government can undertake military research; for
it must be carried on in secret, much of it has no commercial
value, and it is expensive. The obligation of Government to
support research on military problems is inescapable.

Modern war requires the use of the most advanced scientific
techniques. Many of the leaders in the development of radar
are scientists who before the war had been exploring the nucleus
of the atom. While there must be increased emphasis on science
in the future training of officers for both the Army and Navy,
such men cannot be expected to be specialists in scientific research. Therefore a professional partnership between the officers
in the Services and civilian scientists is needed.

The Army and Navy should continue to carry on research and
development on the improvement of current weapons. For many
years the National Advisory Committee for Aeronautics has supplemented the work of the Army and Navy by conducting basic
research on the problems of flight. There should now be permanent civilian activity to supplement the research work of the
Services in other scientific fields so as to carry on in time of
peace some part of the activities of the emergency war-time
Office of Scientific Research and Development.

Military preparedness requires a permanent independent, ci-
vilian-controlled organization, having close liaison with the
Army and Navy, but with funds directly from Congress and with
the clear power to initiate military research which will supple-

ment and strengthen that carried on directly under the control of the Army and Navy.

One of our hopes is that after the war there will be full employment, and that the production of goods and services will serve to raise our standard of living. We do not know yet how we shall reach that goal, but it is certain that it can be achieved only by releasing the full creative and productive energies of the American people.

Surely we will not get there by standing still, merely by making the same things we made before and selling them at the same or higher prices. We will not get ahead in international trade unless we offer new and more attractive and cheaper products.

Where will these new products come from? How will we find ways to make better products at lower cost? The answer is clear. There must be a stream of new scientific knowledge to turn the wheels of private and public enterprise. There must be plenty of men and women trained in science and technology for upon them depend both the creation of new knowledge and its application to practical purposes.

More and better scientific research is essential to the achievement of our goal of full emploment.

Basic research is performed without thought of practical ends. It results in general knowledge and an understanding of nature and its laws. This general knowledge provides the means of answering a large number of important practical problems, though it may not give a complete specific answer to any one of them. The function of applied research is to provide such complete answers. The scientist doing basic research may not be at all interested in the practical applications of his work, yet the further progress of industrial development would eventually stagnate if basic scientific research were long neglected.

One of the peculiarities of basic science is the variety of paths which lead to productive advance. Many of the most important discoveries have come as a result of experiments undertaken with very different purposes in mind. Statistically it is certain that important and highly useful discoveries will result from some fraction of the undertakings in basic science; but the results of any one particular investigation cannot be predicted with accuracy.

Basic research leads to new knowledge. It provides scientific capital. It creates the fund from which the practical applications of knowledge must be drawn. New products and new processes do not appear full-grown. They are founded on new principles and new conceptions, which in turn are painstakingly developed by research in the purest realms of science.

Today, it is truer than ever that basic research is the pacemaker of technological progress. In the nineteenth century, Yankee mechanical ingenuity, building largely upon the basic discoveries of European scientists, could greatly advance the technical arts. Now the situation is different.

A nation which depends upon others for its new basic scientific knowledge will be slow in its industrial progress and weak in its competitive position in world trade, regardless of its mechanical skill.

Centers of Basic Research]

Publicly and privately supported colleges and universities and the endowed research institutes must furnish both the new scientific knowledge and the trained research workers. These institutions are uniquely qualified by tradition and by their special characteristics to carry on basic research. They are charged with the responsibility of conserving the knowledge accumulated by the past, imparting that knowledge to students, and contributing new knowledge of all kinds. It is chiefly in these institutions that scientists may work in an atmosphere which is relatively free from the adverse pressure of convention, prejudice, or commercial necessity. At their best they provide the scientific worker with a strong sense of solidarity and security, as well as a substantial degree of personal intellectual freedom. All of these factors are of great importance in the development of new knowledge, since much of new knowledge is certain to arouse opposition because of its tendency to challenge current beliefs or practice.

Industry is generally inhibited by preconceived goals, by its own clearly defined standards, and by the constant pressure of commercial necessity. Satisfactory progress in basic science seldom occurs under conditions prevailing in the normal industrial laboratory. There are some notable exceptions, it is true, but even in such cases it is rarely possible to match the universities in respect to the freedom which is to important to scientific discovery.

To serve effectively as the centers of basic research these institutions must be strong and healthy. They must attract our best scientists as teachers and investigators. They must offer research opportunities and sufficient compensation to enable them to compete with industry and government for the cream of scientific talent.

During the past 25 years there has been a great increase in industrial research involving the application of scientific knowledge to a multitude of practical purposes—thus providing new products, new industries, new investment opportunities, and millions of jobs. During the same period research within Government—again largely applied research—has also been greatly expanded. In the decade from 1930 to 1940 expenditures for industrial research increased from $116,000,000 to $240,000,000 and those for scientific research in Government rose from $24,-000,000 to $69,000,000. During the same period expenditures for scientific research in the colleges and universities increased from $20,000,000 to $31,000,000, while those in the endowed research institutes declined from $5,200,000 to $4,500,000. These are the best estimates available. The figures have been taken from a variety of sources and arbitrary definitions have necessarily been applied, but it is believed that they may be accepted as indicating the following trends:

(a) Expenditures for scientific research by industry and Government—almost entirely applied research—have more than doubled between 1930 and 1940. Whereas in 1930 they were six times as large as the research expenditures of the colleges, universities, and research institutes, by 1940 they were nearly ten times as large.

(b) While expenditures for scientific research in the colleges and universities increased by one-half during this period, those for the endowed research institutes have slowly declined.

If the colleges, universities, and research institutes are to meet the rapidly increasing demands of industry and Government for new scientific knowledge, their basic research should be strengthened by use of public funds.

Research Within the Government]

Although there are some notable exceptions, most research conducted within governmental laboratories is of an applied nature. This has always been true and is likely to remain so. Hence Government, like industry, is dependent upon the colleges, universities, and research institutes to expand the basic scientific frontiers and to furnish trained scientific investigators.

Research within the Government represents an important part of our total research activity and needs to be strengthened and expanded after the war. Such expansion should be directed to fields of inquiry and service which are of public importance and are not adequately carried on by private organizations.

The most important single factor in scientific and technical work is the quality of personnel employed. The procedures currently followed within the Government for recruiting, classifying and compensating such personnel place the Government under a severe handicap in competing with industry and the universities for first-class scientific talent. Steps should be taken to reduce that handicap.

In the Government the arrangement whereby the numerous scientific agencies form parts of larger departments has both advantages and disadvantages. But the present pattern is firmly established and there is much to be said for it. There is, however, a very real need for some measure of coordination of the common scientific activities of these agencies, both as to policies and budgets, and at present no such means exist.

A permanent Science Advisory Board should be created to consult with these scientific bureaus and to advise the executive and legislative branches of Government as to the policies and budgets of Government agencies engaged in scientific research.

This board should be composed of disinterested scientists who have no connection with the affairs of any Government agency.

Industrial Research]

The simplest and most effective way in which the Government can strengthen industrial research is to support basic research and to develop scientific talent.

The benefits of basic research do not reach all industries equally or at the same speed. Some small enterprises never receive any of the benefits. It has been suggested that the benefits might be better utilized if "research clinics" for such enterprises were to be established. Businessmen would thus be able to make more use of research than they now do. This proposal is certainly worthy of further study.

One of the most important factors affecting the amount of industrial research is the income-tax law. Government action in respect to this subject will affect the rate of technical progress in industry. Uncertainties as to the attitude of the Bureau of Internal Revenue regarding the deduction of research and development expenses are a deterrent to research expenditure. These uncertainties arise from lack of clarity of the tax law as to the proper treatment of such costs.

The Internal Revenue Code should be amended to remove present uncertainties in regard to the deductibility of research and development expenditures as current charges against net income.

Research is also affected by the patent laws. They stimulate new invention and they make it possible for new industries to be built around new devices or new processes. These industries generate new jobs and new products, all of which contribute to the welfare and the strength of the country.

Yet, uncertainties in the operation of the patent laws have impaired the ability of small industries to translate new ideas into processes and products of value to the nation. These uncertainties are, in part, attributable to the difficulties and expense incident to the operation of the patent sysem as it presently exists.

These uncertainties are also attributable to the existence of certain abuses, which have appeared in the use of patents. The abuses should be corrected. They have led to extravagantly critical attacks which tend to discredit a basically sound system.

It is important that the patent system continue to serve the country in the manner intended by the Constitution, for it has been a vital element in the industrial vigor which has distinguished this nation. . . .

International Exchange of Scientific Information]

International exchange of scientific information is of growing importance. Increasing specialization of science will make it more important than ever that scientists in this country keep continually abreast of developments abroad. In addition a flow of scientific information constitutes one facet of general international accord which should be cultivated.

The Government can accomplish significant results in several ways: by aiding in the arrangement of international science congresses, in the official accrediting of American scientists to such gatherings, in the official reception of foreign scientists of standing in this country, in making possible a rapid flow of technical information, including translation service, and possibly in the provision of international fellowships. Private foundations and other groups partially fulfill some of these functions at present, but their scope is incomplete and inadequate.

The Government should take an active role in promoting the international flow of scientific information.

The Special Need for Federal Support]

We can no longer count on ravaged Europe as a source of fundamental knowledge. In the past we have devoted much of our best efforts to the application of such knowledge which has been discovered abroad. In the future we must pay increased attention to discovering this knowledge for ourselves particularly since the scientific applications of the future will be more than ever dependent upon such basic knowledge.

New impetus must be given to research in our country. Such new impetus can come promptly only from the Government. Expenditures for research in the colleges, universities, and research institutes will otherwise not be able to meet the additional demands of increased public need for research.

Further, we cannot expect industry adequately to fill the gap. Industry will fully rise to the challenge of applying new knowledge to new products. The commercial incentive can be relied upon for that. But basic research is essentially noncommercial in nature. It will not receive the attention it requires if left to industry.

For many years the Government has wisely supported research in the agricultural colleges and the benefits have been great. The time has come when such support should be extended to other fields.

In providing Government support, however, we must endeavor to preserve as far as possible the private support of research both in industry and in the colleges, universities, and research institutes. These private sources should continue to carry their share of the financial burden.

The Cost of a Program]

It is estimated that an adequate program for Federal support of basic research in the colleges, universities, and research institutes and for financing important applied research in the public interest, will cost about 10 million dollars at the outset and may rise to about 50 million dollars annually when fully underway at the end of perhaps 5 years.

Renewal of Our Scientific Talent]

Nature of the Problem]

The responsibility for the creation of new scientific knowledge rests on that small body of men and women who understand the fundamental laws of nature and are skilled in the techniques of scientific research. While there will always be the rare individual who will rise to the top without benefit of formal education and training, he is the exception and even he might make a more notable contribution if he had the benefit of the best education we have to offer. I cannot improve on President Conant's statement that:

". . . [I]n every section of the entire area where the word science may properly be applied, the limiting factor is a human one. We shall have rapid or slow advance in this direction or in that depending on the number of really first-class men who are engaged in the work in question. . . . So in the last analysis, the future of science in this country will be determined by our basic educational policy."

A Note of Warning]

It would be folly to set up a program under which research in the natural sciences and medicine was expanded at the cost of the social sciences, humanities, and other studies so essential to national well-being. This point has been well stated by the Moe Committee as follows:

"As citizens, as good citizens, we therefore think that we must have in mind while examining the question before us—the discovery and development of scientific talent—the needs of the whole national welfare. We could not suggest to you a program which would syphon into science and technology a disproportionately large share of the nation's highest abilities, without doing harm to the nation, nor, indeed, without crippling science. . . . Science cannot live by and unto itself alone. . . . The uses to which high ability in youth can be put are various and, to a large extent, are determined by social pressures and rewards. When aided by selective devices for picking out scientifically talented youth, it is clear that large sums of money for scholarships and fellowships and monetary and other rewards in disproportionate amounts might draw into science too large a percentage of the nation's high ability, with a result highly detrimental to the nation and to science. Plans for the discovery and development of scientific talent must be related to the other needs of society for high ability. . . . There is never enough ability at high levels to satisfy all the needs of the nation; we would not seek to draw into science any more of it than science's proportionate share."

The Wartime Deficit]

Among the young men and women qualified to take up scientific work, since 1940 there have been few students over 18, except some in medicine and engineering in Army and Navy programs and a few 4-F's, who have followed an integrated scientific course of studies. Neither our allies nor, so far as we know, our enemies have done anything so radical as thus to suspend almost completely their educational activities in scientific pursuits during the war period.

Two great principles have guided us in this country as we have turned our full efforts to war. First, the sound democratic principle that there should be no favored classes or special privilege in a time of peril, that all should be ready to sacrifice equally; second, the tenet that every man should serve in the capacity in which his talents and experience can best be applied for the prosecution of the war effort. In general we have held these principles well in balance.

In my opinion, however, we have drawn too heavily for non-scientific purposes upon the great natural resource which resides in our trained young scientists and engineers. For the general good of the country too many such men have gone into uniform, and their talents have not always been fully utilized. With the exception of those men engaged in war research, all physically fit students at graduate level have been taken into the armed forces. Those ready for college training in the sciences have not been permitted to enter upon that training.

There is thus an accumulating deficit of trained research personnel which will continue for many years. The deficit of science and technology students who, but for the war, would have received bachelor's degrees is about 150,000. The deficit of those holding advanced degrees—that is, young scholars trained to the point where they are capable of carrying on original work—has been estimated as amounting to about 17,000 by 1955 in chemistry, engineering, geology, mathematics, physics, psychology, and the biological sciences.

With mounting demands for scientists both for teaching and for research, we will enter the post-war period with a serious deficit in our trained scientific personnel.

Improve the Quality]

Confronted with these deficits, we are compelled to look to the use of our basic human resources and formulate a program which will assure their conservation and effective development.

The committee advising me on scientific personnel has stated the following principle which should guide our planning:

"If we were all-knowing and all-wise we might, but we think probably not, write you a plan whereby there might be selected for training, which they otherwise would not get, those who, 20 years hence, would be scientific leaders, and we might not bother about any lesser manifestations of scientific ability. But in the present state of knowledge a plan cannot be made which will select, and assist, only those young men and women who will give the top future leadership to science. To get top leadership there must be a relatively large base of high ability selected for development and then successive skimmings of the cream of ability at successive times and at higher levels. No one can select from the bottom those who will be the leaders at the top because unmeasured and unknown factors enter into scientific, or any, leadership. There are brains and character, strength and health, happiness and spiritual vitality, interest and motivation, and no one knows what else, that must needs enter into this supra-mathematical calculus.

"We think we probably would not, even if we were all-wise and all-knowing, write you a plan whereby you would be assured of scientific leadership at one stroke. We think as we think because we are not interested in setting up an elect. We think it much the best plan, in this constitutional Republic, that opportunity be held out to all kinds and conditions of men whereby they can better themselves. This is the American way; this is the way the United States has become what it is. We think it very important that circumstances be such that there be no ceiling, other than ability, itself, to intellectual ambition. We think it very important that every boy and girl shall know that, if he shows that he has what it takes, the sky is the limit. Even if it be shown subsequently that he has not what it takes to go to the top, he will go further than he would otherwise go if there had been a ceiling beyond which he always knew he could not aspire.

"By proceeding from point to point and taking stock on the way, by giving further opportunity to those who show themselves worthy of further opportunity, by giving the most oppor-

tunity to those who show themeselves continually developing
—this is the way we propose. This is the American way: a man
works for what he gets."

Remove the Barriers]

Higher education in this country is largely for those who have
the means. If those who have the means coincided entirely with
those persons who have the talent we should not be squandering
a part of our higher education on those undeserving of it, nor
neglecting great talent among those who fail to attend college
for economic reasons. There are talented individuals in every
segment of the population, but with few exceptions those without the means of buying higher education go without it. Here
is a tremendous waste of the greatest resource of a nation—the
intelligence of its citizens.

If ability, and not the circumstance of family fortune, is made
to determine who shall receive higher education in science, then
we shall be assured of constantly improving quality at every
level of scientific activity.

The Generation in Uniform Must Not Be Lost]

We have a serious deficit in scientific personnel partly because
the men who would have studied science in the colleges and
universities have been serving in the Armed Forces. Many had
begun their studies before they went to war. Others with
capacity for scientific education went to war after finishing high
school. The most immediate prospect of making up some of the
deficit in scientific personnel is by salvaging scientific talent from
the generation in uniform. For even if we should start now to
train the current crop of high school graduates, it would be
1951 before they would complete graduate studies and be prepared for effective scientific research. This fact underlines the
necessity of salvaging potential scientists in uniform.

The Armed Services should comb their records for men who,
prior to or during the war, have given evidence of talent for
science, and make prompt arrangements, consistent with current
discharge plans, for ordering those who remain in uniform as
soon as militarily possible to duty at institutions here and overseas where they can continue their scientific education. More-

over, they should see that those who study overseas have the benefit of the latest scientific developments.

A Program]

The country may be proud of the fact that 95 percent of boys and girls of fifth grade age are enrolled in school, but the drop in enrollment after the fifth grade is less satisfying. For every 1,000 students in the fifth grade, 600 are lost to education before the end of high school, and all but 72 have ceased formal education before completion of college. While we are concerned primarily with methods of selecting and educating high school graduates at the college and higher levels, we cannot be complacent about the loss of potential talent which is inherent in the present situation.

Students drop out of school, college, and graduate school, or do not get that far, for a variety of reasons: they cannot afford to go on; schools and colleges providing courses equal to their capacity are not available locally; business and industry recruit many of the most promising before they have finished the training of which they are capable. These reasons apply with particular force to science: the road is long and expensive; it extends at least 6 years beyond high school ;the percentage of science students who can obtain first-rate training in institutions near home is small.

Improvement in the teaching of science is imperative; for students of latent scientific ability are particularly vulnerable to high school teaching which fails to awaken interest or to provide adequate instruction. To enlarge the group of specially qualified men and women it is necessary to increase the number who go to college. This involves improved high school instruction, provision for helping individual talented students to finish high school (primarily the responsibility of the local communities), and opportunities for more capable, promising high school students to go to college. Anything short of this means serious waste of higher education and neglect of human resources.

To encourage and enable a larger number of young men and women of ability to take up science as a career, and in order gradually to reduce the deficit of trained scientific personnel, it is recommended that provision be made for a reasonable number of (a) undergraduate scholarships and graduate fellowships and (b) fellowships for advanced training and fundamental research. The details should be worked out with reference to the interests of the several States and of the universities and colleges; and care should be taken not to impair the freedom of the institutions and individuals concerned. . . .

The plan is, further, that all those who receive such scholarships or fellowships in science should be enrolled in a National Science Reserve and be liable to call into the service of the Government, in connection with scientific or technical work in time of war or other national emergency declared by Congress or proclaimed by the Preisdent. Thus, in addition to the general benefits to the nation by reason of the addition to its trained ranks of such a corps of scientific workers, there would be a definite benefit to the nation in having these scientific workers on call in national emergencies. The Government would be well advised to invest the money involved in this plan even if the benefits to the nation were thought of solely—which they are not—in terms of national preparedness. . . .

The Lid Must Be Lifted]

While most of the war research has involved the application of existing scientific knowledge to the problems of war, rather than basic research, there has been accumulated a vast amount of information relating to the application of science to particular problems. Much of this can be used by industry. It is also needed for teaching in the colleges and universities here and in the Armed Forces Institutes overseas. Some of this information must remain secret, but most of it should be made public as soon as there is ground for belief that the enemy will not be able to turn it against us in this war. To select that portion which should be made public, to coordinate its release, and definitely to encourage its publication, a Board composed of Army, Navy, and civilian scientific members should be promptly established.

A Program for Action]

The Government should accept new responsibilities for promoting the flow of new scientific knowledge and the development of scientific talent in our youth. These responsibilities are the proper concern of the Government, for they vitally affect our health, our jobs, and our national security. It is in keeping also with basic United States policy that the Government should foster the opening of new frontiers and this is the modern way to do it. For many years the Government has wisely supported research in the agricultural colleges and the benefits have been great. The time has come when such support should be extended to other fields.

The effective discharge of these new responsibilities will require the full attention of some over-all agency devoted to that purpose. There is not now in the permanent Governmental structure receiving its funds from Congress an agency adapted to supplementing the support of basic research in the colleges, universities, and research institutes, both in medicine and the natural sciences, adapted to supporting research on new weapons for both Services, or adapted to administering a program of science sholarships and fellowships.

Therefore I recommend that a new agency for these purposes be established. Such an agency should be composed of persons of broad interest and experience, having an understanding of the peculiarities of scientific research and scientific education. It should have stability of funds so that long-range programs may be undertaken. It should recognize that freedom of inquiry must be preserved and should leave internal control of policy, personnel, and the method and scope of research to the institutions in which it is carried on. It should be fully responsible to the President and through him to the Congress for its program.

Early action on these recommendations is imperative if this nation is to meet the challenge of science in the crucial years ahead. On the wisdom with which we bring science to bear in the war against disease, in the creation of new industries, and in the strengthening of our Armed Forces depends in large measure our future as a nation.

15

New Deal Valedictory
Franklin D. Roosevelt's
State of the Union Message
January 11, 1944

By 1944 the war was going well for the United States and its Allies; victory lay many months and many lives ahead, but at least the nation could take hope and dare to look ahead. In his annual "State of the Union" address in January, 1944, President Roosevelt took the occasion to summarize briefly the military, economic, and diplomatic progress the nation had enjoyed in the turning year just past, and to exhort the nation to accept the sacrifices that lay ahead. Mario Einaudi's *The Roosevelt Revolution* (New York: Harcourt, Brace & World, 1959) is a book which concerns itself with the impact of the Roosevelt leadership in the world as well as within the continental limits of the nation. Allan Nevins' *The New Deal and World Affairs* (New Haven: Yale University Press, 1950) and Willard Range's *Franklin D. Roosevelt's World Order* (Athens: University of Georgia Press, 1959) both essay an evaluation of the President's impact upon the course of world history. The reader will note, in studying this last selection (1) what plans the President advanced for total mobilization of labor and capital for final victory; (2) his vision of the shape of the postwar world—both at home and abroad; (3) his enunciation of a "second" or an "economic" Bill of Rights and what it comprised; and (4) upon what principles the President hoped to see a finer world built when the war was won.

Franklin D. Roosevelt, "State of the Union Message, January 11, 1944," Samuel I. Rosenman (ed.), *The Public Papers and Addresses of Franklin D. Roosevelt*, Vol. 13 (New York: The Macmillan Company, 1945), pp. 32-42. Reprinted through the courtesy of the trustees of the Franklin D. Roosevelt trust and of Samuel I. Rosenman.

To the congress of the united states:

This Nation in the past two years has become an active partner in the world's greatest war against human slavery.

We have joined with like-minded people in order to defend ourselves in a world that has been gravely threatened with gangster rule.

But I do not think that any of us Americans can be content with mere survival. Sacrifices that we and our allies are making impose upon us all a sacred obligation to see to it that out of this war we and our children will gain something better than mere survival.

We are united in determination that this war shall not be followed by another interim which leads to new disaster—that we shall not repeat the tragic errors of ostrich isolationism—that we shall not repeat the excesses of the wild twenties when this Nation went for a joyride on a roller coaster which ended in a tragic crash.

When Mr. Hull went to Moscow in October, and when I went to Cairo and Teheran in November, we knew that we were in agreement with our allies in our common determination to fight and win this war. But there were many vital questions concerning the future peace, and they were discussed in an atmosphere of complete candor and harmony.

In the last war such discussions, such meetings, did not even begin until the shooting had stopped and the delegates began to assemble at the peace table. There had been no previous opportunities for man-to-man discussions which lead to meetings of minds. The result was a peace which was not a peace.

That was a mistake which we are not repeating in this war.

And right here I want to address a word or two to some suspicious souls who are fearful that Mr. Hull or I have made "commitments" for the future which might pledge this Nation to secret treaties, or to enacting the role of Santa Claus.

To such suspicious souls—using a polite terminology—I wish to say that Mr. Churchill, and Marshal Stalin, and Generalissimo Chiang Kai-shek are all thoroughly conversant with the provisions of our Constitution. And so is Mr. Hull. And so am I.

Of course we made some commitments. We most certainly committed ourselves to very large and very specific military plans which require the use of all Allied forces to bring about the defeat of our enemies at the earliest possible time.

But there were no secret treaties or political or financial commitments.

To one supreme objective for the future, which we discussed for each nation individually, and for all the United Nations, can be summed up in one word: Security.

And that means not only physical security which provides safety from attacks by aggressors. It means also economic security, social security, moral security—in a family of nation.

In the plain down-to-earth talks that I had with the Generalissimo and Marshal Stalin and Prime Minister Churchill, it was abundantly clear that they are all most deeply interested in the resumption of peaceful progress by their own peoples—progress toward a better life. All our allies want freedom to develop their lands and resources, to build up industry, to increase education and individual opportunity, and to raise standards of living.

All our allies have learned by bitter experience that real development will not be possible if they are to be diverted from their purpose by repeated wars—or even threats of war.

China and Russia are truly united with Britain and America in recognition of this essential fact:

The best interests of each nation, large and small, demand that all freedom-loving nations shall join together in a just and durable system of peace. In the present world situation, evidenced by the actions of Germany, Italy, and Japan, unquestioned military control over disturbers of the peace is as necessary among nations as it is among citizens in a community. And an equally basic essential to peace is a decent standard of living for all individual men and women and children in all nations. Freedom from fear is eternally linked with freedom from want.

There are people who burrow through our Nation like unseeing moles, and attempt to spread the suspicion that if other nations are encouraged to raise their standards of living, our own American standard of living must of necessity be depressed.

The fact is the very contrary. It has been shown time and

again that if the standard of living of any country goes up, so does its purchasing power—and that such a rise encourages a better standard of living in neighboring countries with whom it trades. That is just plain common sense—and it is the kind of plain common sense that provided the basis for our discussions at Moscow, Cairo, and Teheran.

Returning from my journeyings, I must confess to a sense of "let-down" when I found many evidences of faulty perspectives here in Washington. The faulty perspective consists in over-emphasizing lesser problems and thereby underemphasizing the first and greatest problem.

The overwhelming majority of our people have met the demands of this war with magnificent courage and understanding. They have accepted inconveniences; they have accepted hardships; they have accepted tragic sacrifices. And they are ready and eager to make whatever further contributions are needed to win the war as quickly as possible—if only they are given the chance to know what is required of them.

However, while the majority goes on about its great work without complaint, a noisy minority maintains an uproar of demands for special favors for special groups. There are pests who swarm through the lobbies of the Congress and the cocktail bars of Washington, representing these special groups as opposed to the basic interests of the Nation as a whole. They have come to look upon the war primarily as a chance to make profits for themselves at the expense of their neighbors—profits in money or in terms of political or social preferment.

Such selfish agitation can be highly dangerous in war-time. It creates confusion. It damages morale. It hampers our national effort. It muddies the waters and therefore prolongs the war.

If we analyze American history impartially, we cannot escape the fact that in our past we have not always forgotten individual and selfish and partisan interests in time of war—we have not always been united in purpose and direction. We cannot overlook the serious dissensions and the lack of unity in our War of the Revolution, in our War of 1812, or in our War between the States, when the survival of the Union itself was at stake.

In the first World War we came closer to national unity than in any previous war. But that war lasted only a year and a half, and increasing signs of disunity began to appear during the final months of the conflict.

In this war we have been compelled to learn how interdependent upon each other are all groups and sections of the population of America.

Increased food costs, for example, will bring new demands for wage increases from all war workers, which will in turn raise all prices of all things including those things which the farmers themselves have to buy. Increased wages or prices will each in turn produce the same results. They all have a particularly disastrous result on all fixed income groups.

And I hope you will remember that all of us in this Government represent the fixed-income group just as much as we represent business owners, workers, and farmers. This group of fixed-income people includes: teachers, clergy, policemen, firemen, widows, and minors on fixed incomes, wives and dependents of our soldiers and sailors, and old-age pensioners. They and their families add up to one-quarter of our one hundred and thirty million people. They have few or no high pressure representatives at the Capitol. In a period of gross inflation they would be the worst sufferers.

If ever there was a time to subordinate individual or group selfishness to the national good, that time is now. Disunity at home—bickerings, self-seeking partisanship, stoppages of work, inflation, business as usual, politics as usual, luxury as usual— these are the influences which can undermine the morale of the brave men ready to die at the front for us here.

Those who are doing most of the complaining are not deliberately striving to sabotage the national war effort. They are laboring under the delusion that the time is past when we must make prodigious sacrifices—that the war is already won and we can begin to slacken off. But the dangerous folly of that point of view can be measured by the distance that separates our troops from their ultimate objectives in Berlin and Tokyo—and by the sum of all the perils that lie along the way.

Overconfidence and complacency are among our deadliest enemies. Last spring—after notable victories at Stalingrad and in Tunisia and against the U-boats on the high seas—overconfidence became so pronounced that war production fell off. In two months, June and July, 1943, more than a thousand airplanes that could have been made and should have been made were not made. Those who failed to make them were not on strike. They were merely saying, "The war's in the bag—so let's relax."

That attitude on the part of anyone—Government or management or labor—can lengthen this war. It can kill American boys.

Let us remember the lessons of 1918. In the summer of that year the tide turned in favor of the Allies. But this Government did not relax. In fact, our national effort was stepped up. In August 1918, the draft-age limits were broadened from 21-31 to 18-45. The President called for "force to the utmost," and his call was heeded. And in November, only three months later, Germany surrendered.

That is the way to fight and win a war—all-out—and not with half-an-eye on the battle fronts abroad and the other eye-and-a-half on personal, selfish, or political interests here at home. . . .

The Federal Government already has the basic power to draft capital and property of all kinds for war purposes on a basis of just compensation.

As you know, I have for three years hesitated to recommend a national service act. Today, however, I am convinced of its necessity. Although I believe that we and our allies can win the war without such a measure, I am certain that nothing less than total mobilization of all our resources of manpower and capital will guarantee an earlier victory, and reduce the toll of suffering and sorrow and blood.

I have received a joint recommendation for this law from the heads of the War Department, the Navy Department, and the Maritime Commission. These are the men who bear responsibility for the procurement of the necessary arms and equipment, and for the successful prosecution of the war in the field. They say:

"When the very life of the Nation is in peril the responsibility for service is common to all men and women. In such a time there can be no discrimination between the men and women who are assigned by the Government to its defense at the battle-front and the men and women assigned to producing the vital materials essential to successful military operations. A prompt enactment of a National Service Law would be merely an expression of the universality of this responsibility."

I believe the country will agree that those statements are the solemn truth.

National service is the most democratic way to wage a war. Like selective service for the armed forces, it rests on the obligation of each citizen to serve his Nation to his utmost where he is best qualified.

It does not mean reduction in wages. It does not mean loss of retirement and seniority rights and benefits. It does not mean that any substantial numbers of war workers will be disturbed in their present jobs. Let these facts be wholly clear.

Experience in other democratic Nations at war—Britain, Canada, Australia, and New Zealand—has shown that the very existence of national service makes unnecessary the widespread use of compulsory power. National service has proven to be a unifying moral force—based on an equal and comprehensive legal obligation of all people in a nation at war.

There are millions of American men and women who are not in this war at all. It is not because they do not want to be in it. But they want to know where they can best do their share. National service provides that direction. It will be a means by which every man and woman can find that inner satisfaction which comes from making the fullest possible contribution to victory.

I know that all civilian war workers will be glad to be able to say many years hence to their granchildren: "Yes, I, too, was in service in the great war. I was on duty in an airplane factory, and I helped make hundreds of fighting planes. The Government told me that in doing that I was performing my most useful work in the service of my country."

It is my conviction that the American people will welcome national service is necessary. But our soldiers and sailors know that this is not true. We are going forward on a long, rough road—and, in all journeys, the last miles are the hardest. And it is for that final effort—for the total defeat of our enemies—that we must mobilize our total resources. The national war program calls for the employment of more people in 1944 than in 1943.

It is my conviction that the American people will welcome this win-the-war measure which is based on the eternally just principle of "fair for one, fair for all."

It will give our people at home the assurance that they are standing four-square behind our soldiers and sailors. And it will give our enemies demoralizing assurance that we mean business —that we, 130,000,000 Americans, are on the march to Rome, Berlin, and Tokyo.

I hope that the Congress will recognize that, although this is a political year, national service is an issue which transcends politics. Great power must be used for great purposes.

As to the machinery for this measure, the Congress itself should determine its nature—but it should be wholly non-partisan in its make-up.

Our armed forces are valiantly fulfilling their responsibilities to our country and our people. Now the Congress faces the responsibility for taking those measures which are essential to national security in this the most decisive phase of the Nation's greatest war.

Several alleged reasons have prevented the enactment of legislation which would preserve for our soldiers and sailors and marines the fundamental prerogative of citizenship—the right to vote. No amount of legalistic argument can becloud this issue in the eyes of these ten million American citizens. Surely the signers of the Constitution did not intend a document which, even in wartime, would be construed to take away the franchise of any of those who are fighting to preserve the Constitution itself.

Our soldiers and sailors and marines know that the overwhelming majority of them will be deprived of the opportunity to vote, if the voting machinery is left exclusively to the States under existing State laws—and that there is no likelihood of these laws being changed in time to enable them to vote at the next election. The Army and Navy have reported that it will be impossible effectively to administer forty-eight different soldier-voting laws. It is the duty of the Congress to remove this unjustifiable discrimination against the men and women in our armed forces—and to do it as quickly as possible.

It is our duty now to begin to lay the plans and determine the strategy for the winning of a lasting peace and the establishment of an American standard of living higher than ever before known. We cannot be content, no matter how high that general standard of living may be, if some fraction of our people— whether it be one-third or one-fifth or one-tenth—is ill-fed, ill-clothed, ill-housed, and insecure.

This Republic had its beginning, and grew to its present strength, under the protection of certain inalienable political rights—among them the right of free speech, free press, free worship, trial by jury, freedom from unreasonable searches and seizures. They were our rights to life and liberty.

As our Nation has grown in size and stature, however—as our industrial economy expanded—these political rights proved inadequate to assure us equality in the pursuit of happiness.

We have come to a clear realization of the fact that true individual freedom cannot exist without economic security and independence. "Necessitous men are not free men." People who are hungry and out of a job are the stuff of which dictatorships are made.

In our day these economic truths have been accepted as self-evident. We have accepted, so to speak, a second Bill of Rights under which a new basis of security and prosperity can be established for all—regardless of station, race, or creed.

Among these are:

The right to a useful and remunerative job in the industries or shops or farms or mines of the Nation;

The right to earn enough to provide adequate food and clothing and recreation;

The right of every farmer to raise and sell his products at a return which will give him and his family a decent living;

The right of every businessman, large and small, to trade in an atmosphere of freedom from unfair competition and domination by monopolies at home or abroad;

The right of every family to a decent home;

The right to adequate medical care and the opportunity to achieve and enjoy good health;

The right to adequate protection from the economic fears of old age, sickness, accident, and unemployment;

The right to a good education.

All of these rights spell security. And after this war is won, we must be prepared to move forward, in the implementation of these rights, to new goals of human happiness and well-being.

America's own rightful place in the world depends in large part upon how fully these and similar rights have been carried into practice for our citizens. For unless there is security here at home there cannot be lasting peace in the world.

One of the great American industrialists of our day—a man who has rendered yeoman service to his country in this crisis—recently emphasized the grave dangers of rightist reaction in this Nation. All clear-thinking businessmen share his concern. Indeed, if such reaction should develop—if history were to repeat itself and we were to return to the so-called normalcy of the 1920's—then it is certain that, even though we shall have conquered our enemies on the battlefields abroad, we shall have yielded to the spirit of fascism here at home.

I ask the Congress to explore the means for implementing this economic bill of rights—for it is definitely the responsibility of the Congress so to do. Many of these problems are already before committees of the Congress in the form of proposed legislation. I shall from time to time communicate with the Congress with respect to these and further proposals. In the event that no adequate program of progress is evolved, I am certain that the Nation will be conscious of the fact.

Our fighting men abroad—and their families at home—expect such a program and have the right to insist upon it. It is to their demands that this Government should pay heed rather than to the whining demands of selfish pressure groups who seek to feather their nests while young Americans are dying.

The foreign policy that we have been following—the policy

that guided us at Moscow, Cairo, and Teheran—is based on the common-sense principle which was best expressed by Benjamin Franklin on July 4, 1776: "We must all hang together, or assuredly we shall all hang separately."

I have often said that there are no two fronts for America in this war. There is only one front. There is one line of unity which extends from the hearts of the people at home to the men of our attacking forces in our farthest outposts. When we speak of our total effort, we speak of the factory and the field and the mine as well as of the battleground—we speak of the soldier and the civilian, the citizen and his Government.

Each and every one of us has a solemn obligation under God to serve this Nation in its most critical hour—to keep this Nation great—to make this Nation greater in a better world.